THE BOOK OF LENNON

THE BOOK OF LENNON

Bill Harry

A *Delilah* BOOK
DISTRIBUTED BY THE PUTNAM PUBLISHING GROUP
N E W • Y O R K

A Delilah Book
Delilah Communications, Ltd.
118 East 25th Street
New York, N.Y. 10010

ISBN: 0—933328—91—5
Library of Congress Catalog Card Number: 83:46122

Manufactured in the United States of America

First published in the United States of America
   by Delilah Communications, Ltd. in 1984.
Originally published in Great Britain by Aurum Press Limited in 1984.

Designed by Neil H. Clitheroe

CONTENTS

Introduction

John Lennon was assassinated twice —
the first time by his murderer, the second
by a series of books, ghost-written by
friends and acquaintances, which have
attempted to tear his reputation to
shreds.

It comes as no surprise to most people
that John was at times hot-headed,
abrasive, trusting, naive, ungrateful,
aggressive, loving, absent-minded,
grumpy, ungrateful, appreciative,
randy, depressed, ecstatic, kind and
cruel. It is no surprise because he was a
human being, subject to the same
strains and pressures as all of us.

There were as many different John
Lennon's as there are rungs on a ladder.
Different people saw specific aspects of
his personality. People who had never
met him formed their own impressions
from what they had read and thus
created a John of their own. Some
people held him in awe, some hated
him, others loved him, many were
frightened by him and even more envied
him.

If he had lived, the 'kiss-and-tell'
books might never have been written. In
death he became vulnerable, as Brian
Epstein became vulnerable, neither of
them being able to protect themselves
from the writers who sought the more
sensational, salacious incidents in their
lives, composing works from a mixture
of facts, speculation, half-truths, imagination, rumour and bias.

A few weeks after John's death I was
approached by a publisher who asked
me to write a book about John. I refused

because I felt that to do so at that time would be like capitalizing on the tragedy. Yet I could not escape the fact that the people I met in the daily course of my life were thirsty for information about him. There had already been a spate of biographies, so I decided to assemble various facts, building them into a mini-encyclopedia which would present the information and afford readers the opportunity of arriving at their own conclusion as to whether he was saint or sinner, hellspawn or hero.

Just how many hours I spent with John is difficult to assess. The times we were at the art college, drinking in Ye Cracke, talking throughout the night at students' flats; the years I spent writing about him in *Mersey Beat*, the gigs ranging from art school dances and coffee bars to theatre tours; the meetings in pubs and clubs from the late 'fifties to the mid-'sixties; the visits to Apple, the get-togethers at clubs such as the Speakeasy and Bag O'Nails. Certainly, I must have spent hundreds of hours with him . . . and he remained a mystery. I knew he had a stroke of genius, that he was a poet, a musician, a talented artist. I was also aware that some people considered him bullying, uncouth and dangerous. There was certainly a cruel side to his nature — but there was also a generous one.

He was as perplexed about himself as we all were. He was no chameleon, changing his character on a whim. His character was complex. He realized that and spent many years attempting to dis-cover who he really was, to understand his own nature, to seek after some basic truths. He sought understanding through meditation and mysticism, through LSD, through primal therapy, the I Ching, the Tarot. John was a seeker, his philosopher's stone was the transcendence of consciousness. He sought universal truths, some of which are found in his works.

Why, then, are they trying to crucify him?

I feel it is simply because a great deal of money can be made from books which sensationalize the more vulnerable aspects of a celebrity. The vast fortune made by a particular book which dwelt on the sad and tragic private life of Elvis must have sent the former friends and aides of many stars to their typewriters with visions of dollars pouring from the keyboards. They were right.

You will not find details of Lennon's assassin here. He sought a form of immortality by his act, but why should such a worthless person find a place in this book? Friends, relatives, rivals . . . yes, these you'll find. You will also find details of John's songs, books, films — the legacy he left us. In the final analysis I find that I prefer to remind people of the positive side of John's life. When you consider it, only part of him is gone. The songs remain and they each contain some essence of a unique person during his brief sojourn on this earth.

BILL HARRY
January 1984

To Les, Sheila, Mark and Simon Chadwick

My appreciation to the many people who have aided me in this project: Kathy Gardner, Brian Southall, David Hughes, Tony Wadsworth and Brian Munns of EMI Records, London; Shirley Stone of Polydor Records, London; Liz and Jim Hughes of Cavern Mecca; Clive Epstein; Jonathan Hague; Charles Lennon; Eddie Porter; Marsha Ewing of Instant Karma; all at Beatles Unlimited; Charles F. Rosenay of Good Day Sunshine; Bill and Leslie King of Beatlefan; The British Film Institute; the late Millie Sutcliffe; Bob Eaton; Jacques Volcouve; Billy J. Kramer; Roger Akehurst of Beatles Now; and Johnny Hamp.

THE BOOK OF LENNON

Four fab little eskimos on stage at the Hammersmith Palais.

Love is . . . wearing dark glasses together.

John's skiffle group The Quarrymen go smiling on.

People

Tariq Ali Prominent Pakistani-born political intellectual who settled in England and was a major force in the anti-establishment movement of the late 'sixties, when he advocated direct political action by the people. A campaigner who led several anti-Vietnam war marches, he was the first person to interview John in depth about his political opinions, which were published in Ali's newspaper, The *Red Mole*. Soon after the interview, John wrote 'Power To The People' and said that his political awareness was sparked off by Tariq Ali's influence. Ali set up house in Hornsey, London and continued to be politically active.

Les Anthony Former Welsh guardsman whom John hired as a chauffeur-cum-bodyguard during his early days in Weybridge.

David Arnold Chaplain to Liverpool Polytechnic. He was one of the speakers at the special memorial service for John in Liverpool Town Centre on 14 December 1980. He asked, 'Which do you think is the most powerful, a bullet or a song? I tell you that a song is, because a bullet can kill one man, but a song can bring a thousand people to life.'

Fred Astaire Legendary movie song

Smile, lads, I hear Busby Berkeley's in the audience!

and dance man who made a guest appearance on John's *Imagine* film. He was also one of the characters on the *Sergeant Pepper* sleeve.

Lauren Bacall Widow of Humphrey Bogart and a leading star. Lauren was living in the Dakota Building close to the apartments which John and Yoko bought.

It had been no secret that the two women disliked each other. In 1983 a feud was sparked off when Lauren's son, Sam Robards, came to visit his mother. As he got out of the lift he was confronted by two armed men who manhandled him. They were Yoko's bodyguards.

Another incident occurred on Yoko's 50th birthday, when fans gathered on the pavement outside the Dakota with a special cake for Yoko. Lauren told the security guards to clear them away as she was expecting guests. Yoko, hearing of this, sent for candles and the waiting throng broke into song, singing Beatles hits as the dinner-party guests struggled to get past them.

Arthur Ballard A Liverpool-born artist who attended the Liverpool College of Art and then spent most of the time until his retirement in 1981 teaching at the college.

At one time he displayed a great potential and was part of what almost seemed to be a Liverpool renaissance in art in the 'fifties. There was some controversy in 1956 when one of his abstract works was hung upside down in the Walker Art Gallery, but it resulted in several sales for him.

In 1957 he left for Paris for a short time to paint and study, and in 1958 had an exhibition at the New Shakespeare Gallery in Liverpool. His work was exhibited in the John Moore exhibitions at the Walker Art Gallery in 1959 and 1961. He also had a metal relief, one of his best works, fitted on the door to Johnson's TV shop in Lord Street.

Commenting about Arthur in his book *Art In A City*, art critic John Willett wrote, 'He has great faith in Liverpool's individuality, which he thinks will assert itself in art sooner or later: we'll see something "better than The Beatles". He's proud of the efforts he's made to support individualists in the college, e.g. precisely, Lennon of The Beatles, whom the graphic design department were reluctant to accept. "The boy was no good as an artist", he claims, "and an intolerable, rebellious nuisance. But he had character."

Arthur was particularly struck by the talent of Stuart Sutcliffe and used to visit Stuart in his Percy Street flat, close to the college, as Stu was reluctant to attend the lessons at the college. It was through his belief in Stu's talent that Arthur championed John, who was a student continually on the verge of being expelled, due to his raucous behaviour and unsatisfactory work. Arthur also used to meet students in the local pub Ye Cracke in Rice Street.

He did prevent John from being expelled at one point but was unsuccessful in obtaining a place for him in the graphic design department.

On his retirement, Arthur moved to London to be near his sister and began regularly meeting other Liverpool expatriates in a Chelsea pub on Friday nights.

Donald Ballou Manager of radio station in Ogdensberg in New York State. In 1966 following the *Datebook* magazine article which misquoted John's interview with Maureen Cleave, he was one of the many radio executives to ban Beatle records. He said, 'I have personally read the article and do not appreciate my child listening to any group that would condemn Christianity. Neither would I allow my audience to listen to such a group.'

Brigitte Bardot French film star known as the sex kitten, a dream figure for growing lads in the late 'fifties and early 'sixties. She was John Lennon's favourite film actress and Cynthia used to model herself on Bardot to please John.

When The Beatles first flew to Paris in 1964, they mentioned that they'd all like to meet Bardot. The French branch of their record company sent a large box of chocolates to them at their suite at the George V Hotel with a note stating, 'Unfortunately, Brigitte Bardot is detained in Brazil, let's hope that these sweets will make up for her.'

Klaus Baruck German hairdresser who gave John a short back and sides at the Inn On The Heath hotel near Celle in Hanover, West Germany in September 1966 for the film *How I Won The War*.

Don Beatty When a schoolboy, Don was responsible for first switching John onto Elvis Presley and thus indirectly steering John's steps towards a life in music. In 1956 both Don and John were in form 4C of Quarry Bank Grammar School. Don was interested in records and showed John a copy of the *New Musical Express* and directed his attention to the chart position of 'Heartbreak Hotel'. John commented 'Don said it was great, but I thought it sounded a bit

phoney. I'd never heard it. We never listened to pop music in our house. Then one night I heard it on Radio Luxembourg. That was it. Nothing really affected me until Elvis.'

Lord Beeching Former head of British Rail who became a controversial figure throughout the British Isles in the 'sixties for his plans for ruthlessly pruning the rail network in an attempt to make it more cost-effective.

On discovering that Apple needed skilled financial management, John approached Lord Beeching and spoke to him about administering Apple. Beeching turned down the job and gave him the advice that The Beatles should stick to making music and forget about becoming business entrepreneurs.

Chuck Berry Legendary American rock and roll star, born in St Louis, Missouri in 1931, who was one of The Beatles' seminal influences. They were impressed by the vitality of the songs he wrote, and recorded his 'Rock & Roll

Music' for their *Beatles For Sale* album and 'Roll Over Beethoven' for their *With The Beatles* LP. His 'I'm Talkin About You' and 'Little Queenie' are featured on their Star Club performance in 1962, recorded by Adrian Barber and featured on several packages of a *Star Club* album. John performed two Chuck Berry titles on his *Rock And Roll* album: 'You Can't Catch Me' and 'Sweet Little Sixteen'.

In 1972 John achieved an ambition and actually performed with Chuck Berry. This occurred when John and Yoko were given a week's residency as hosts on the American TV programme *The Mike Douglas Show* with the option of selecting their own guests. John picked Chuck Berry and the two of them performed a duet on 'Johnny B. Goode' and 'Memphis'.

On John's death, Berry stated: 'I feel as if I lost a little part of myself when John died.'

Pete Best Drummer with The Beatles for two years from August 1960 until August 1962. Taciturn, good-looking Pete was one of Mona Best's sons. Mona was an enterprising woman who opened a club called The Casbah in the basement of her home, providing John, George and Paul with their first residency.

It was during their appearances at the Casbah where Pete was to appear in a group called The Blackjacks that they got to know him. On the eve of their Hamburg debut, Paul McCartney phoned Pete and asked him to join them.

When he was ousted a few years later, he was unsuccessful in his attempts to forge a career for himself in the music business. He became so depressed that he attempted suicide.

In 1980 together with London-based show business writer Patrick Doncaster he wrote a book of his reminiscences called *Beatle* which, although not published until 1984, was serialised in the *News Of The World* to coincide with The Beatles' 20th anniversary in October 1982.

Best's tale, although suffering from the slick and often cloying style of Doncaster's writing, provides an interesting viewpoint of the days when the group were living on the breadline. Best claims that on their journey to Hamburg, John indulged in shoplifting, a habit he inflicted upon Woolworth's and Marks & Spencer's in Liverpool.

Pete also relates how one night he and John decided to mug a sailor. He relates how he and John knocked the man down. John pinched his wallet but the sailor pulled out a gun.

Fortunately, it was only a gas gun. They fled, but when they reached John's room, they discovered that he'd dropped the wallet.

The dress may be fancy . . . but John was always a Rocker at heart.

Best's revelations continue in this vein with tales of John taking pills, visiting the Herbertstrasse (street of prostitutes) and, when back in Liverpool, taking photographs of partly-dressed girl fans.

Patti Boyd A young model who became known as the Smith's Crisps girl following TV commercials in Britain in 1963. She first met The Beatles when she was 20 and hired by Dick Lester to appear in *A Hard Day's Night*.

Patti was later to marry George Harrison, then Eric Clapton and was the person who first interested The Beatles in the Maharishi Mahesh Yogi.

John Blake, in his book *All You Needed Was Love*, reports an incident that occurred at the Royal Lancaster Hotel on 21 December 1968.

Paul and Jane Asher were dressed as a pearly king and queen, Maureen Starkey was a mini-skirted red indian, Ringo was a regency buck, Cynthia Lennon was clad in a lilac period dress, George Harrison wore a cavalier-type outfit and Patti appeared as a belly-dancer. Among the guests were Cilla Black as Charlie Chaplin and Lulu in a Shirley Temple-style little-girl outfit.

According to Blake, John in leather jacket and drainpipes 'had steamed up to her (Patti) ignoring George and turned on every iota of his charm to persuade her to join him between the sheets.' An embarrassing moment, particularly for Cynthia, until little Lulu with her fiery temper gave him a telling off, after which he rejoined his wife.

Peter Boyle American actor whose films include *Young Frankenstein* and *The Producers*. He and his wife Loraine Alterman were one of the few couples invited to the Lennons' apartment in the

Dakota Building during John's reclusive years.

Peter Brown Bebington-born friend of Brian Epstein who was one of a number of close associates invited by Brian to join his organization. Former manager of the record department at Lewis's department store in Liverpool, he replaced Brian at the Charlotte Street branch of Nems and was later invited to join Brian in London at Nems Enterprises.

In manner and tastes he was very similar to Brian and, following Brian's death, he became an executive at Apple. People were to refer to him as a 'Brian clone' and it was also suggested that he had ambitions of becoming The Beatles' manager, having had the experience of being Brian's personal assistant.

In his book *The Longest Cocktail Party*, Richard Di Lello describes him as 'The impeccable Signor Suave of the Apple diplomatic corps and personal assistant and social co-ordinator to The Beatles.'

Di Lello also mentioned an incident in which Peter displayed his diplomatic skills. When members of the San Francisco chapter of Hell's Angels visited Apple and attended the Apple Christmas party, a 43 pound turkey was to be served later.

One of the Hell's Angels didn't like waiting and became involved in a verbal battle with John, which could have become nasty. Peter Brown was called for. He sized up the situation immediately, tapped the Hell's Angel on the shoulder and explained the delay to him. Having received a straight answer to a straight question, the Angel seemed satisfied and what could have been a nasty confrontation between him and John was averted.

It was Peter Brown who accompanied John and Yoko to Gibraltar and acted as best man at his wedding. John mentions Peter by name on his single, 'The Ballad Of John And Yoko'.

Peter left Apple to join Robert Stigwood's Organisation (he and Allen Klein were incompatible) and moved to America where he enjoyed considerable success.

He was offered a very large advance payment to write what is known as a 'kiss-and-tell' book about his days with Brian and The Beatles. Entitled *The Love You Make: An Insider's Story Of The Beatles*, it was first published in America in January 1983 by McGraw-Hill.

The book was co-written with ex-music critic Stephen Gaines, and there are some highly controversial stories abounding in the work. Peter suggests that Yoko Ono was responsible for The Beatles' break-up and that she turned John into a heroin addict.

Señor Bueno De Mesquita A commissioner for oaths, in a ceremony on the rooftop of Apple's Savile Row offices on 22 April 1969, he officially changed John's name from John WINSTON Lennon to John ONO Lennon.

Sally Bulloch Nanny whom Cynthia Lennon intended to hire to look after Julian when he was five years old. Cynthia first heard of Sally when she was dining with John at comedian Peter Cook's home. Sally had been nanny to his two children. However, John prevented her hiring the nanny as he felt that a growing child should be cared for by its mother.

George Carpozi American journalist, author or more than 70 books. He specializes in crime reportage and show biz news and has written *The Brigitte Bardot Story*, *Marilyn Monroe: Her Own Story* and books about Cher, Bing Crosby and John Wayne. These are in addition to crime books such as *Son Of Sam: 44 Caliber Killer* and *Chicago Nurse Murders*.

He combined both his interests to pen the Manor Books paperback *John Lennon: Death Of A Dream*, rush released following John's murder.

Lewis Carroll Pen-name of Charles Lutwidge Dodgson, Victorian author of many works including *Alice's Adventures In Wonderland* and *Through The Looking Glass*. Carroll was one of the people whose work influenced John in both his humorous writing and his song lyrics.

Carroll produced a nonsense poem called 'The Hunting Of The Snark'. John's two books could be described as nonsense books. Also many people sought hidden meanings in the Alice books, just as they did with various songs written by John, such as 'I Am The Walrus'. The song was partly inspired by Carroll's 'The Walrus And The Carpenter'.

When he included the number in *Magical Mystery Tour*, John hadn't realized that of the two, the walrus was the villain because he was conscious of tricking the poor oysters into being devoured.

The carpenter isn't even mentioned in John's song. He explained later: 'I should have said "I am the Carpenter", but that wouldn't have been the same, would it?'' He also made the ambiguous statement, 'The walrus was Paul' in his song 'The Glass Onion'. Lewis Carroll was included in the series of cut-out figures on the cover of the *Sergeant Pepper* album.

Jimmy Carter American president at the time of John's death. He commented: 'John Lennon helped to create the music and spirit of our time. In the songs he composed, he leaves an extraordinary and permanent legacy. I know I speak for millions of Americans when I say I am saddened by his death and the senseless manner of it.'

Randy Clark American singer/actor who has been involved in a number of John Lennon impressions. He portrayed John in the Broadway run of *Beatlemania* and also provided vocals for the TV movie *Birth Of The Beatles* when he was a member of The Beatle soundalike group Rain, who specialized in performing Beatle numbers. For a time he was also a member of another Beatle-style group Imagine who, like Rain, also performed at Beatle conventions, but he left them to pursue a career as an actor.

Maureen Cleave Oxford-educated journalist who joined the *Evening Standard* newspaper in the early 'sixties as a staff writer, evolving into a highly respected interviewer.

It was Maureen in February 1963 who interviewed The Beatles, thus giving them their first exposure in a large circulation newspaper.

The *Evening Standard* was one of London's two evening papers.

For the next three years she became a friend of The Beatles, particularly of John. She interviewed them frequently, covering their exploits in France and America by travelling on some of their

19

jaunts abroad. She later said: 'If John hadn't liked me, I would never have dared to like him, but I had a nice pair of red boots that were considered rather *outre* at the time, and he fancied those.'

The most controversial item of all was sparked off by an interview Maureen had with John which was originally published in the *Evening Standard* in May 1966. The article covered John's life in Weybridge, his social activities, the cars he owned, details of John's possessions, the books he read and his general life style.

There were lots of fascinating little details such as the fact that he had five television sets, had his own gorilla suit which fitted him perfectly, read books such as *Curiosities Of Natural History* and described himself as a Celt: 'I'm on Boadicea's side — all those bloody blue-eyed blonds chopping people up.'

A mere few paragraphs mentioned his feelings regarding the current state of Christianity, among them the sentences: 'Christianity will go. It will vanish and shrink. I needn't argue about that; I'm right and I will be proved right. We're more popular than Jesus now; I don't know which will go first — rock and roll or Christianity. Jesus was all right but his disciples were thick and ordinary. It's them twisting it that ruins it for me.'

Americans were burned up over John's comments about Christ and Beatles records went up in flames.

The comments didn't arouse any response in Britain at the time, but when an American magazine called *Datebook* printed excerpts from the interview in July on the eve of The Beatles' American tour the opinions about Christianity appeared out of context and sparked off a storm of protest in the States.

Tommy Charles implored his listeners on the WAGY radio station in Birmingham, Alabama to burn The Beatles' records and photographs. His action was echoed throughout the Bible belt region, being taken up by more than 30 other radio stations and received support from the Ku Klux Klan.

The controversy raged on with public burnings of Beatle records, but there was also support from Church leaders and fans who regarded John's comments as legitimate opinion.

Brian Epstein decided that John would have to make a formal explanation. He held a press conference in America before their 19-day tour, and at this John commented: 'I'm sorry. I'm sorry I said it, really. I never meant it as a lousy anti-religious thing.

'I am not a practising Christian like I was brought up, but I don't have any un-Christian thoughts. I didn't mean to say that The Beatles are better than Jesus; I just used the word Beatles because it's familiar to me. I might just as well have said TV or cinema or cars are more important to people than Christ nowadays.'

Maureen Cleave in the meantime had become quite upset at the furore caused by her article and said: 'John was certainly not comparing The Beatles to Christ. He was simply observing that so weak was the state of Christianity that The Beatles were to many people better known. He was deploring rather than

approving this. Sections of the American public seem to have been given an impression of his views that is totally absurd.'

Charles J. Cohen American publicist based in Boston who was hired by John in July 1980 on a 20-week trial basis.

Ray Coleman British journalist who became editor of *Disc* in the mid-sixties and interviewed The Beatles on several occasions.

One interview with John was for a *Disc* feature called 'Treasure Chest', in which John discussed various belongings to which he was attached.

They included his first Rickenbacker guitar, two Stuart Sutcliffe pictures, the outsize boot used in the film *Help!*, books by Aldous Huxley, a record by the Singing Postman, a stone frog and four number plates displayed on his playroom wall.

In January 1969 John told Ray his feelings about the state of Apple, commenting 'Apple is losing money. If it carries on like this, we'll be broke in six months.' This was the story which inspired Allen Klein to make his attempt to take control of The Beatles affairs.

Ray left *Disc*, which later folded, to become editor of *Melody Maker*, a position he retained until the early 'eighties when he decided to become a freelance journalist and author. He immediately found success with his interviews with Yoko Ono, which he placed with several British national newspapers.

His most ambitious project to date is a two-volume work on John's life, scheduled for publication in 1984 by Sidgwick and Jackson.

Ray Connolly Merseyside writer who was a student of social anthropology at the London School of Economics. He then became a journalist writing for the *Liverpool Daily Post* before graduating to Britain's largest evening newspaper the *Evening Standard* in London.

When he joined the paper in 1967 as a columnist specializing in the rock music field, he wrote about The Beatles on numerous occasions and interviewed them regularly.

He became a *confidante* and learned many of their secrets, the biggest of which was the story of John's intention to leave The Beatles.

Ray respected John's wishes that he hold up the story. Four months later, Paul was able to make his own annoucement to the press and John regretted that he had asked Ray to keep the announcement on ice.

Ray also travelled to Toronto and stayed at Ronnie Hawkins' farm during John and Yoko's visit there. After John's period of being a househusband, Ray was one of the journalists invited to New York to interview John about his future plans.

His interview was set for 9 December 1980. On 8 December Yoko called Ray to inform him of the tragedy. In his book *John Lennon. 1940-1980* Ray has an illustration from one of the letters John sent him with a sketch of John, Yoko and Sean.

The book begins with a comment John made to him in December, 1970: 'Have you written my obituary yet? I'd love to read it when you do.' In the biography, Ray also makes the observation 'Future historians will find the understanding of the 'sixties and 'seventies widened immeasurably by focusing on the life of John Lennon.'

Ray is one of a handful of major free-lance columnists in Britain, and his writings frequently appear in publications ranging from the *Sunday Times* to the *Standard*. His books/film scripts include *That'll Be The Day* and *Stardust*, the latter winning him the Writers' Guild of Great Britain Award for the best original screenplay.

Peter Cook British humorist, satirist and TV personality who in the 'sixties was one half of a successful comedy partnership with Dudley Moore. They appeared in films including *Bedazzled* and had their own TV series *Not Only . . . But Also* on which John appeared. John and Cynthia were guests of Cook and his wife at their Hampstead dinner

John is not only an attendant but also at your convenience.

parties. The Cook/Moore duo recorded a single in which some people believed that John was involved. It was called 'LS Bumble Bee'.

Bill Corbett Driver hired by John to become the chauffeur of his recently acquired £5,000 Rolls-Royce in 1964. Corbett had originally been an employee of a car hire firm which had assigned him to drive The Beatles around in an Aston Martin.

Jonathan Cott American author and journalist who conducted the first interview with John Lennon for *Rolling Stone* magazine on 23 November 1968. Jonathan was the magazine's European correspondent and the interview which took place in London was arranged via Robert Fraser, owner of The Fraser Gallery where John was holding an exhibition.

Cott has been an associate editor of *Rolling Stone* since 1967, has penned several books and co-wrote the text for *Get Back* the lavish book issued with the original *Let It Be* album in Britain. Several of his articles about John are collected in the book *The Ballad Of John And Yoko* which he co-edited.

Anthony Cox Yoko's second husband. The couple married in Japan after Cox had attempted to console her following a suicide attempt. The marriage did not work, although their baby daughter Kyoko was born the same year as their marriage in 1963.

The couple apparently argued regularly, but soon settled down to a relationship which was more that of good friends than man and wife. It was while Tony was in France that John invited Yoko to Weybridge in May 1968

where the two became lovers for the first time.

Cox, an erstwhile filmmaker, did not seem unduly worried that his wife had found another man, although he insisted on retaining care of Kyoko. Their divorce came through via the Virgin Islands on 2 February 1969 and Tony received £6,700 as a divorce settlement.

Cox began to live with a woman called Melinda, whom he later married. For a time, they moved to Aalberg, a small village in Denmark. John and Yoko joined them in December 1969 when Kyoko was ill. It was during this trip that Cox filmed John and the five-year old Kyoko having a bath together, a film which he was to use in court during a custody hearing.

Yoko decided that she would like to have custody of Kyoko and travelled to Majorca where Tony and Kyoko were staying. John and Yoko attempted to take the little girl from the island, but Cox alerted the police and Kyoko was re-united with her father.

Cox then realized that Yoko was determined to have the child and had the money and legal muscle to achieve her ends, so he fled the island. Yoko applied to the Virgin Islands for an order giving her custody of Kyoko. Cox, however, had resurfaced in Houston, Texas and obtained a custody order in his favour.

By that time he'd changed Kyoko's name to Rosemary. John and Yoko arrived in America and insisted on having Kyoko to stay with them over Christmas. Cox refused and was jailed for three days as a result. Yoko's high-powered lawyers went into action and managed to talk the court in Houston into giving custody of the child to Yoko, but by that time Tony, Melinda and

Kyoko had fled again and neither John nor Yoko were to see them again.

Kyoko Cox Daughter of Yoko and her second husband Anthony Cox. Kyoko was born on 8 August 1963 in Japan. The trio then moved to New York for a time before uprooting themselves again and setting off for England.

When Yoko began her affair with John, Tony Cox took Kyoko to Paris for a while. When the couple's divorce became final in February 1969, Kyoko remained with her father. But Yoko had access to the child.

In May 1969 Kyoko began travelling with John and Yoko initially to their proposed 'lie-in' in the Bahamas then to Toronto, Canada for their bed-in and finally back to England where they were joined by John's son Julian for a short holiday in Scotland.

A car crash brought the vacation to an abrupt halt and Kyoko returned to her father. Later that year Tony contacted Yoko to tell her that her daughter was ill, and in December the Lennons flew to Denmark where Kyoko was living with Cox and his girl friend Melinda.

It has been suggested that Yoko had a sudden desire to have custody of Kyoko following her first miscarriage of John's child.

Over the next few years, a battle for custody began initially when John and Yoko attempted to take Kyoko away from Majorca, where she had been attending a nursery.

They were prevented from spiriting her away from the island by the Spanish authorities. They were accused of kidnapping and had to appear in court.

The court officials took Kyoko aside and asked her if she would prefer to go with her father or her mother. She opted for her father. A legal battle began in earnest, with John calling in Allen Klein, and the Lennons spent six months in the courts in Texas, New York and the Virgin Islands.

Despite the Lennons' wealth, Cox managed to flee with Kyoko to somewhere in America. John and Yoko had to admit defeat and were unable to trace them. The Lennons did not see her again.

It was because of their time spent in America in their efforts to trace Kyoko that they decided to remain in the States. Years later they reflected on their efforts to gain custody of Kyoko and admitted that they were wrong. John added that they had been 'idiots' to set private detectives and the courts on to a little girl who simply wanted to remain with her father.

Marshall Crenshaw American singer born in 1954 who portrayed John in the American road show of *Beatlemania*.

Discussing his career, he commented, 'I started playing in bands in school in the 'sixties when The Beatles came out, and when The Beatles made it in the US every little kid wanted a guitar. Most of them got them and a few of them learned to play.

'I played Lennon in *Beatlemania*, which was this terrible show in the United States; but the funny thing about it was it was a very big hit for quite a couple of years.

'It was running on Broadway for about a year and it was a touring company also, so it was really going strong after a while.

'It was a multi-media sort of show with a group of actors on stage who were supposed to look like The Beatles, and then there'd be all those films and different visual images going around from the 'sixties.

'They were trying to show how it was done in such a silly way that it made the whole thing look like a parody of itself. I did it because I was sick of playing in bar bands and I wanted to find a way of trying to break out.

'It was all live music and the music part of it was OK because I always liked The Beatles music and it was fun to play and try to sound like them.

'I do sound like Lennon even when I don't try to. It just happens that way, but I don't really think I look like him. I used to think I did. I used to have really long hair and wear little wire glasses so I guess I used to look a bit like him.'

Crenshaw's debut album *Marshall Crenshaw* on Atlantic included the track 'Soldier Of Love'.

Nicky Cuff Liverpool midget who performed in various local bands, mainly of the showband variety type such as The Connaughts. John once said that Nicky was his favourite comedian.

Allen Curran Liverpool sculptor who created a tribute statue of John. He began the work in January 1981 and worked hard to complete it for the unveiling at the Mersey Beatle convention at the Adlephi Hotel, Liverpool on 29 August of that year, spending about £1,000 on materials. 1,500 fans were present when the statue was unveiled by Victor Spinetti, with 'Imagine' playing in the background.

Describing the event, Jim Hughes of Cavern Mecca wrote 'The curtains open and in the light of a single spot you see a 14 foot high John Lennon, wearing his denims, holding that Rickenbacker and giving the peace sign V. The base reads: ''A Working Class Hero.'' There is a long moment of complete silence then, as one, 1,500 throats begin to roar.

'To witness such raw emotion is utterly phenomenal and for a moment in time, John is actually there. Many were overcome, but they cry for the *right* reason, they cry because John is here, not because John isn't.

'Cavern Mecca has another little job to do now — raise £10,000 by October 1983 to pay to have this magnificent work cast in bronze and erected in public here in the heart of Liverpool to remind the world that a truly great man still lives on. Allen has done his work and it is now up to the lovers of John Lennon everywhere, to make sure that this statue is not wasted.'

Bettina Derlin Blond, buxom *bierfrau* at Hamburg's Star Club which The Beatles opened in April 1962. During that year the group played at the club for three short seasons and Bettina, known as Betty, was one of John's girl friends. At her bar at the rear of the club she displayed photographs of the Liverpool bands. Among them were several pictures of John including one to which a Preludin packet was attached.

Jack Douglas American record producer. He was the engineer of John's albums *Imagine* and *Sometime In New York City*. He also recorded a number of unreleased albums with Yoko before being asked to co-produce *Double Fantasy*.

Dr Winston And Booker Table And The Maître D's Wacky name John used on the credits to his song

'Beef Jerky', which was issued as the flipside of 'Whatever Gets You Thru The Night' and as a track on the *Walls And Bridges* album.

Edwin Drummond Man who illegally climbed the Statue of Liberty in May 1980. On 8 December 1981 together with girl student Lia Simnacher he began to scale the side of a 41-storey skyscraper in San Francisco and between the eighth and ninth floors displayed a banner which read: 'Imagine No Arms'. A letter was distributed to the spectators in which he'd written: 'A year ago today, John Lennon was murdered. To us, the call of his music is to imagine a world without arms.'

John Dunbar One of the owners of London's Indica Gallery. In November 1966 when Yoko's *Exhibiton No 2* was being held at the gallery, he introduced John and Yoko to each other. Dunbar was married to pop star Marianne Faithful at the time.

John Dykin Liverpool man with whom Julia Lennon lived during the years in which Freddie Lennon was at sea, after the birth of John and also after the birth of another child whose father was a gunner in the army.

Having placed John with his Aunt Mimi and given her second child to a Swedish couple, Julia became John Dykin's common law wife and they had two daughters, Julia and Debbie.

In 1963, Dykin became restaurant manager of the Odd Spot Club in Liverpool's Bold Street, where The Beatles appeared four times. The following year he went to work in a hotel on the Isle of Man. Eddie Porter, who worked with him at both places, states: 'The reason

John (Lennon) called him "Twitchy" was because of a habit he had. He would press his nose back because it was badly scarred and needed a new bridge built.'

Following Julia's death, Dykin married a waitress called Rhona and at the end of 1969 both were involved in a car crash. They'd been returning to Liverpool following a trip to Wales for an interview about seasonal work in a hotel, when their Austin car crashed into a tree.

Both were taken to Sefton General Hospital, Smithdown Road. This was the hospital in which Julia was pronounced dead after her car accident. This also occurred near Penny Lane.

Rhona was treated for facial injuries and discharged. Dykin was admitted and died two weeks later. Rhona has since married a prison warder.

Bob Eaton Artistic director of the Everyman Theatre in Liverpool who conceived, wrote and directed the play *Lennon*, which made its debut at the Everyman in 1981. Bob writes: 'I was born in Chesterfield, Derbyshire on 19

Bob Eaton composed his own tribute to John.

September 1948, went to the local grammar school and, like millions of others, formed a beat group under the influence of The Beatles, called The Invaders. I studied drama at Manchester University and have worked as director, writer and actor in many northern theatres including ones at Stoke and Scarborough, the Contact Theatre Manchester and another in Lancaster.'

Bob became artistic director of the theatre at the beginning of 1981 and his first production was *Lennon*. He also travelled to New York in 1982 to direct the show in the off-Broadway Entermedia Theatre, where it received an enthusiastic reception during its nine-week run.

Electric Light Orchestra Generally known as ELO, a band conceived by Roy Wood of The Move in 1970. Following their debut album in 1971, he lost interest, but the band continued under the leadership of Jeff Lynne and became hugely successful. Their strong orchestral melodies are reminiscent of The Beatles in their Sergeant Pepper period. The group paid tribute to John during their American tour in the autumn of 1981 by performing 'Across The Universe' and 'A Day In The Life'. John once called the band 'The Sons Of The Beatles'.

Elephant's Memory New York band which, for a short time became John's backing band. The group were first brought to his attention by Jerry Rubin, who played him a tape of their music. They had performed two numbers on the soundtrack of the movie *Midnight Cowboy* a few years previously and, although there had been some minor line-up changes, the leader Stan Bronstein was still performing with the band in New York.

John was seeking musicians at the time and used them to back him on the album *Some Time In New York City*. They also appeared with him when he took over *The Mike Douglas Show* for a week, backed him on a few more TV shows, performed as his backing band on the One To One concert on 30 August 1972 and also on the *Jerry Lewis Telethon* the same year, providing backing on the numbers 'Imagine', 'Now Or Never' and 'Give Peace A Chance'.

The group also backed Yoko on the album *Approximate Infinite Universe* and on three singles: 'Now Or Never', 'Death Of Samantha' and 'Jose Joi Banzaie'.

As a way of showing his appreciation of the band, John and Yoko produced an album with them for Apple. Entitled simply, *Elephant's Memory*, it was issued in the US on Apple SMAS 3389 on 18 September 1972 and in Britain on Apple SAPCOR 22 on 10 November of the same year. The tracks were 'Liberation Special', 'Baddest Of The Mean', 'Cryin'', 'Black Sheep Blues', 'Chuck 'n' Bo', 'Gypsy Wolf', 'Madness', 'Life', 'Power Boogie' and 'Local Plastic Ono Band'.

Apple released three singles from the sessions. In America 'Liberation Special' coupled with 'Madness' was issued on 13 November 1972 followed by the release the following month of 'Liberation Special' coupled with 'Power Boogie'. At the same time, the British branch of Apple issued 'Power Boogie' coupled with 'Liberation Special'.

Their line-up in 1972 was: Stan Bronstein (sax), Adam Ippolito (keyboards), Rick Frank (drums), Gary Von Scyoc (bass) and Wayne 'Tex' Gabriel (guitar).

Bill Elliot Newcastle-born singer who was picked by John to sing lead vocals on 'God Save Us', a number he'd written specially to help the magazine Oz in its obscenity trial. Elliot later teamed up with another friend from Newcastle, Bob Purvis, who wrote a song called 'Lonely Man' with Mal Evans, who had also helped John produce Elliot's single. Mal brought the two boys to the attention of George Harrison and under the name Splinter they recorded a number of singles and an album for George's Dark Horse label. Their biggest hit was the number 'Costafine Town'.

Brian Epstein One of the most important people in The Beatles' life, the man who steered their career to success. As their manager, he had dedication and faith in the band and persevered when almost every record company in Britain turned the band down.

He first became aware of The Beatles in 1961 through reading *Mersey Beat*, the music paper in which he wrote record reviews. When he entered the Cavern to see them perform, he was aware of their background and of the exciting local musical scene which was teeming with talent at the beginning of the 'sixties.

Unfortunately, over a decade after his death, his image has suffered a battering from various Beatle biographers.

Philip Norman for instance in his book *Shout!* makes the claim that Brian fell in love with John the moment he saw him at the Cavern. This is more novelization than fact. The people who were actually around at the time refute this

Brian: much admired when he lived, much maligned after his death.

claim from a writer who never even met Brian or John and who was not around Liverpool at the time.

Brian genuinely wanted to manage The Beatles and build their success as a group because it became a vocation for him, a chance to prove himself. Obviously, the fact that he was a homosexual provided writers with an opportunity to make many speculations years after his death, when Brian could not deny what they had written. Similar remarks could be made following the death of John.

'We were in a daydream till he came along', said John. 'We'd no idea what we were doing. Seeing our marching orders on paper made it all official. Brian was trying to clean our image up.

'He said we'd never get past the door of a good place. He'd tell us that jeans were not particularly smart and could we possibly manage to wear proper trousers. But he didn't want us suddenly looking square. He let us have our own sense of individuality. We respected his views.'

John said 'Epstein fronted for The Beatles and he played a great part in whatever we did. He was theatrical — that was for sure. And he believed in us. But he certainly didn't package us the way they say he packaged us. He was good at his job, but to an extent he wasn't the greatest business man. He was theatrical and he believed.'

The most controversial episode concerning John and Brian was when the two went on holiday together to Spain within weeks of John's son Julian being born. The holiday is said to have sparked off a comment made by Bob Wooler at Paul's 21st birthday party which caused John to attack him.

In Peter Brown's book *The Love You*

Make, it is claimed that John slept with Brian on that holiday.

John said, 'I went on holiday to Spain with Brian. This started all the rumours that he and I were having a love affair, but not quite.

'It was never consummated. But we did have a pretty intense relationship. And it was my first experience with someone I knew was a homosexual. He admitted it to me.

'We had this holiday together because Cyn was pregnant and we left her with the baby and went to Spain. Lots of funny stories, you know. We used to sit in cafés and Brian would look at all the boys and would ask, "Do you like that one? Do you like this one?" It was just a combination of our closeness and the trip that started the rumours.'

Brian might not have been the best businessman in the world when it came to The Beatles' financial deals, although part of his success may be due to the fact that he was blazing trails. No group had been as amazingly successful in the British music industry before and there was no precedent with which Brian could compare the offers The Beatles received.

The decisions he made did not displease The Beatles at the time and he did steer their career in a way that made them the world's most successful rock group. He was creative, sensitive and didn't like discussing money.

However, he did take up an offer for them to appear in Kansas City on one of their days off because the money offered was the highest-ever fee for an artist to that date.

He was very conscious of prestige. He accepted a fairly low fee for the *Ed Sullivan Show* because he realized it had the power to really hurl them into the forefront in America. He was not afraid of making them change their minds about certain matters if he considered something would either benefit or harm their careers.

He convinced John that he should accept the MBE when John thought that by accepting it he would be selling-out to the establishment. When John received such hostile reactions in America to his comments in the famous Maureen Cleave interview, Brian set up a press conference in which John could clarify his original statements.

When he first signed The Beatles, Brian was manager of the family's record store in Liverpool. He then created Nems Enterprises and signed such artists as Billy J. Kramer, Gerry And The Pacemakers, Cilla Black and The Fourmost.

There was a great deal of criticism locally when he moved his office from Liverpool to London, but he wished to be near the heart of things.

Although he was a homosexual, it was said that he intended marrying a singer Alma Cogan, but she died of cancer. He bought the Savile Theatre in London's West End, hoping to turn it into a rock centre, but he was ahead of his time.

The last few years of his life may not have been entirely happy ones. His most exciting days were the ones with challenge when he had to fight on behalf of The Beatles.

Once they were at the top of the tree, things weren't quite the same. He died on 27 August 1967 of an accidental overdose of drugs. The Beatles were up in Bangor, Wales, at the time, having enrolled in a course of transcendental meditation with the Maharishi Mahesh Yoga. They were stunned by the news.

John commented, 'They said, "Brian's dead" and I was stunned. We all were, I suppose, and the Maharishi; we went in to him. "What, he's dead," and all that. And he was sort of saying, "Oh, forget it, be happy, like an idiot, like parents, smile." That's what the Maharishi said. And we did.

'I liked Brian and I had a very close relationship with him for years, because I'm not gonna have some stranger running things, that's all. I like to work with friends. I was the closest with Brian, as close as you can get to somebody who lives a sort of "fag" life, and you don't really know what they're doing on the side. But in the group, I was closest to him and I did like him.

'We had complete faith in him when he was running us. To us, he was the expert. I mean originally he had a shop.

'Anybody who's got a shop must be all right. He went around smarmin' and charmin' everybody. He had hellish tempers and fits and lock-outs, and y'know he'd vanish for days. He'd come to a crisis every now and then and the whole business would fuckin' stop because he'd been on sleeping pills for days on end and wouldn't wake up.'

Brian eventually went to sleep and didn't wake up again. He was buried in Liverpool at Long Lane cemetery on 29 August 1967.

Kenny Everett Zany British DJ born in Liverpool in 1944. He began to work for Radio London, a pirate station. In 1966 he went to the States with The Beatles, preparing a daily report on their activities.

He also contributed to *Beatles Monthly*. He was later to become a popular Radio One DJ and then enjoyed a spectacular success when making the move to TV.

His madcap shows (a collection of comedy sketches, pop star guest spots and sexy dance routines from Hot Gossip) established him both on ITV and BBC TV in the early 'eighties.

In October 1982 his autobiography *The Custard Stops At Hatfield* was published and it contained many anecdotes relating to The Beatles and Brian Epstein.

One of the incidents he mentions tells of the time he bumped into John and Terry Doran when they were coming out of a club called The Speakeasy. While the two of them coped with some waiting fans, Kenny slipped into their car. They apparently didn't notice him. They arrived at John's house in Weybridge and Kenny made himself known, at which John made a comment that sounded like, 'Life is a bacon butty'.

Ira Fieldsteel New York judge who ruled that John would have to leave the United States or be deported. Fieldsteel made this ruling in March 1973 after pressure was applied from American intelligence agencies. This followed suggestions from Senator Strom Thurmond and Attorney General John Mitchell the previous year that John would be used as a political pawn by leftwing activists.

So began John's battle to remain in America despite the hostility of the Nixon administration, which wanted him deported. There were various appeals and John was finally given his Green Card on 27 July 1976 by Fieldsteel, the judge who had ordered his deportation.

Peter Fonda Actor son of Henry Fonda and brother of actress Jane. He directed and starred in the cult 'sixties film *Easy Rider* and a movie about psychedelic drugs called *The Trip*. He invited The Beatles to a party in Hollywood following their Hollywood Bowl concert and was on an LSD trip when he talked to John.

John was on an LSD trip for only the second time in his life and remembered Fonda saying to him, 'I know what it's like to be dead. I know what it's like to be dead, man.' He based his song 'She Said, She Said' on the experience.

Paul Frees American actor who provided the voice of John for a series of 52 animation films of The Beatles, first screened by ABC-TV in America in 1965. Frees made no attempt to capture a Liverpool accent and the actual phoney British accent that he did use was one that John found amusing. Frees also provided the voice for George.

Nelson Gardener Dairy farmer of Bridgewater, Virginia. John and Yoko brought 103 cows from him after purchasing a cattle farm in New York state. Within a few days they purchased a further 71 Holsteins from Kenneth Kibler, another dairy farmer in nearby Luray.

David Geffen American record executive who when he formed his own label, Geffen Records, managed to sign up a number of major artists including John and Yoko. His label was to launch John's return to the music scene with the single '(Just Like) Starting Over' and the album *Double Fantasy*. Yoko was later to break with Geffen and sign with Polygram.

Gary Gibson Singer of Preston, Lancashire who bears an uncanny resemb-

Gary Gibson — a fan who resembles his idol.

lance to John. He is guitarist/vocalist with the group Cavern. Discussing the number of fans who mistake him for a resurrected John, he says, 'I try to let them down lightly. I smile and say "I'm not John Lennon at all — I'm Tom Jones!".'

Albert Goldman American writer and author of the best-seller *Elvis*, a book which upset most Elvis Presley fans because of its sensational revelations about the singer's personal life.

Goldman was a former writer with *Life* magazine and the *New York Times* and an associate professor of English and Comparative Literature at Columbia University.

As a rock writer, he interviewed John in the early part of the 'seventies for a magazine called *Charlie*. He is working on a book about John which has caused concern to fans who are afraid it may be slanted in a similar vein to the Elvis book.

Paul Goresh An American photographer who provided the cover picture for Yoko Ono's 'Watching The Wheels' single. He also took the shot of John signing an album for his killer, Mark Chapman.

Barbara Graustark Journalist with the American magazine *Newsweek*. Barbara was the first person to interview John after his 1975 appearance on the *Tomorrow* show when she was granted an interview with him early in 1980. This was printed in the 29 September issue of the magazine. An edited version of the interview was included in the paperback *Strawberry Fields Forever: John Lennon Remembered*.

John Green Pseudonym used by John during a brief visit to Cape Town, South Africa, during 1980.

John Green American astrologer who worked for the Lennons for six years at a salary of £13,000 per year and free accommodation. He first read the Tarot cards for Yoko in May 1974, during her temporary split from John. He was initially employed at £50 per week to give regular readings. Green's relationship with the Lennons ended over an argument about money and he later sold some highly salacious gossip about the couple to the newspapers. One feature, published in the *Sun* (London) in November 1981 under the headline 'Secret Sex Sessions Of Love Hungry Lennon', claimed that Yoko hired prostitutes to satisfy John's cravings, that he called her 'Mummy', and that he insulted her mercilessly in public, picking on her nationality and sexuality. Yoko denied Green's allegations, saying 'John is dead and can't fight back. Those things that John Green said just aren't true'. She commented on each of the accusations Green had made, refuting them all. However, 1983 was the year of the 'kiss-and-tell' books, and Green's contribution was called *Dakota Days*. It was published in America by St Martin's Press on 6 July 1983 and was also serialized in Penthouse.

Dick Gregory Black American comedian who John met at the airport when he was in Canada in December 1969 to discuss the planned peace festival. Dick became one of the several guests to join John at Ronnie Hawkins' home that month. John was particularly impressed, not only by Gregory's wit, but by his opinions on the peace movement. Gregory became one of the many celebrities to support John when the federal authorities were attempting to deport him.

John Gregson Late Liverpool-born screen actor, star of numerous British films, including *Genevieve*. Cynthia Lennon relates an anecdote concerning him in her book *A Twist Of Lennon*. John saw the actor outside Ye Cracke pub in Rice Street and looked around for something unusual for the actor to sign. He found an old boot and asked Gregson to autograph it, a gesture which quite amused the actor who signed the offending article across the stitching.

Bob Gruen American photographer who worked on several photo assignments for John following a series of shots he took at the Attica benefit night at the Apollo Theatre, New York in 1972.

David Guardine An American psychic who claimed that John sent a song to him at a seance. The song was called 'To Be One Again' and the lyrics were printed in the American weekly newspaper *The Examiner*, with the comment that it was 'John's last song'.

Jonathan Hague Former art student at Liverpool College of Art. Reminiscing about his life, Jonathan comments: 'I was born and brought up in Wales and I think the country bumpkin upbringing helped my relationship with John, him being the tough city lad showing me the city life, teaching me to drink etc.

'I spent the most time with John when we were both studying "intermediate" in our second year. This was a course ending in an examination for the National Diploma in Design. We were split into separate classes by crafts. John and I did lettering, together with Cynthia and a girlfriend of hers called Phyllis.

'John failed his "intermediate" because of lettering and at his second sitting he seemed to be beyond caring. I remember feeling very concerned because he was thinking of Hamburg. He once told me he would have finished college, but for intermediate — and then what would have happened to The Beatles?'

Jonathan has many memories of the art school days and says, 'I remember Arthur Ballard used to take us every Monday morning in a small room where our pictures would be hung on a wall. This was the 'composition' homework and he would give us a big crit on them, discussing each one individually.

'They were the usual subjects for such studies: the railway station, a restaurant, the docks, roadworkers etc.

'For some reason John would get away with presenting one of his cartoon drawings each week. For instance, he would have hundreds of little dockers climbing over a boat. And his railway station was just a man's foot disappearing down a staircase.

'He was always the entertainer. The atmosphere in the life class when we drew from live models was always like that of a church. Everyone would sit in silence taking their drawing seriously.

'John would start by making the tiniest noise, then create a snigger which he'd let grow louder, bit by bit, 'til he had the whole room erupting in bursts of laughter.

'I remember the metalwork teacher took John outside the room into the passageway one day to give him a ticking off because John had cut out some monster-type figure.

'I hear the teacher saying, "What do you think you will end up doing?"

'"I want to be a Pop star." The teacher groaned and said, "Be realistic!"

Jonathan obtained his ATD (a diploma necessary for becoming an art teacher). He continued: 'After ATD I obtained a British Council scholarship to the Hague for about 18 months, but stayed for three years. I took the scholarship as my last chance and worked every day — and with luck held a number of private gallery exhibitions there, one at the Gemeentee Museum itself. I sent John a catalogue.'

Jonathan received a letter from John, thanking him for his note:

"So there you are in Holland with all those clogs, eh? Glad you are now a FAMOUS PAINTER — just like Arthur Ballard said you would be!

'The catalogue looked good, seems you've forgotten all about Bratby! I still can't paint — but still do, if you see what I mean, ANYWAY — I'm pleased to hear from you. My address is not so special — but here it is.

J. Lennon
Kenwood, St. George's Hill
Cavendish Road
Weybridge
Surrey.

'If you write — try and use a similar type of envelope to the one you sent — you know BROWN — or your letter might get lost in the happy fan mail.

'See or hear you soon.

'Good Heavens.

'John. A band (Lennon).'

Jonathan continues: 'After I left Holland, which I've always regretted, I did a two-day a week teaching job at both Coventry and Birmingham art schools for five years. I had a number of private gallery exhibitions as well, plus paintings in the Royal Academy etc, and started seeing Lennon again, him showing me the Big City again: this time, London.'

When Jonathan was 29, John and Paul McCartney sponsored an exhibition of his work. He says: 'One day I took my paintings in a huge roll to his house and we spread them all over his sitting room. He liked them, hence the exhibition. He dragged Paul in on it, but I don't think Paul was very keen, although he didn't

mind putting up the money.'

The exhibition took place at the Royal Institute Gallery in 1968 and there was a diverse selection of paintings whose subjects included The Beatles, Mick Jagger, Vincent Van Gogh and the funeral of Sir Winston Churchill.

However, rather than boost Jonathan's career as a painter, it seemed to end it.

'After the exhibition, I gave up,' he says. 'I'm not sure why. The newspapers, TV etc . . . but I think I thought I was no good. So I drifted into antiques, which I still do for a living — better than teaching!'

Jonathan is an antique dealer living in Leamington Spa in a house John bought for him. In 1982 he decided to try his hand at painting again with a series of studies of John.

Hammrick and Leonard Canadian hypnotists who visited John and Yoko in Aalborg, Denmark on 29 December 1969 and hypnotized the couple in an attempt to help them to give up smoking.

Lonnie Hannagren Surgeon from Las Vegas who in 1981 bought a 1956 Bentley formerly owned by John. The car was painted in a psychedelic style, had purple leather seats, pink carpets and paisley curtains. He paid 325,000 dollars for the car when he purchased the vehicle from Ron Morgan, a Californian, who had bought it in January 1981, a few months previously, for only 50,000 dollars.

James Hanratty Man hung for murdering Michael Gregsten in the notorious A6 murder case in Britain. The killing took place in 1962 and many people doubted that Hanratty was the murderer. John and Yoko were approached by Hanratty's father who had spent several years attempting to clear his son's name. He convinced the duo of his son's innocence. They took such an interest in the case that they contemplated making a film about it. They also displayed a placard stating 'Britain Murdered Hanratty' on 11 December 1969 at the Royal Charity première of *The Magic Christian*.

Peter Harrison George Harrison's elder brother who was in the same class as John at Dovedale Primary School. He was subsequently employed by George at his gothic mansion, Friar Park, supervising ten gardeners and a botanist to maintain the beauty of the extensive gardens.

Norman Hartnell A leading British fashion designer and dressmaker to Queen Elizabeth II. He was John and Yoko's nearest neighbour when they resided at Tittenhurst Park.

Jay Hastings A Beatles fan who became a doorman at the Dakota Buildings in 1978 and established a friendship with John and Yoko. He was on duty the night that John was shot and rushed to his aid.

After phoning the police, he then sought out the killer, but Mark Chapman was simply standing in the street reading a book. When the police arrived they originally drew their guns on Hastings because his clothes were covered in blood, but a fellow doorman yelled out his identity to them.

Sam Havadtoy Interior designer who renovated Yoko's Palm Beach mansion in 1982. The press linked their names together romantically. Yoko first met Havadtoy when he was decorating her New York flat. Reports in October 1982 even suggested a marriage was imminent and Havadtoy's friend and associate Kerry Westbrookes told the press, 'Sam says the wedding is definitely on. He is more open about the relationship than Yoko, but she has changed her lifestyle completely since she has been with him.'

Ronnie Hawkins Rock singer born in Arkansas in 1935. He formed a group called The Hawks and moved to Canada in 1957. His backing group returned to the States, changed their name to The Band and backed Bob Dylan.

He settled in a house in Streetsville near Toronto with his wife Wanda. Their life was temporarily turned topsy-turvy in December 1969 when rock journalist Ritchie York arranged for John, Yoko and their entourage to stay with them for a short time on their ten-acre farm.

They were accompanied by several people including their personal assistant Anthony Fawcett and comedian Dick Gregory. Various journalists such as Ray Connolly and Ralph Ginsburg also turned up.

Extra phone lines were installed to enable John to call journalists and radio stations in different parts of the States on behalf of his 'Peace Campaign'. Hawkins was horrified some months later at the staggering phone bills he received.

A huge white Christmas tree with a cage containing two doves arrived, together with a girl to do the washing-up as the Lennons were into microbiotic foods and had brought their microbiotic cookbook with them.

They were at the farm for five days,

during which John signed 3,000 copies of his erotic lithographs for his 'Bag One' project.

Although the thought of paying the phone bills had never entered John's head, he was obviously appreciative of the Hawkins' hospitality and recorded a special promotional message for Ronnie's new single 'Down in The Alley'. A special single with John's spoken introduction on the A side and a longer chat on the flip was sent along to radio stations throughout the US and Canada.

Abbie Hoffman Noted American anarchic figure of the 'sixties whose first demonstration was in 1960 in protest at Caryl Chessman's execution.

He left his wife and children to become involved in controversial political activities and was one of 'The Chicago Eight' who were charged with conspiring to incite a riot at the 1968 Democratic convention.

He formed The Youth International Party, The Yippies, with Jerry Rubin and they sent out 30,000 Valentines, each with a joint (of marijuana) attached in 1969.

Hoffman was also author of the anarchic book *Steal This Book*. When John and Yoko arrived in America and Jerry Rubin became something of a political adviser to the couple, Hoffman also teamed up with them and had plans to use John as a front for a number of political stunts.

Dezo Hoffman Czechoslovakian-born pop photographer who worked for the *Record Mirror* musical weekly at the beginning of the 'sixties and was sent by the paper to Liverpool in 1962 to take some photographs of The Beatles.

Over the next few years he took several thousand shots of the group, had numerous private studio sessions and assignments with them and travelled to their various shows in Britain and abroad. In his book *With The Beatles*, published by Omnibus Press in 1982, he mentions that the close relationship he had with the band deteriorated following an argument he had with John on the set of *A Hard Day's Night* at Twickenham Studios in March 1964.

Dezo commented: 'Because he (John) was taking drugs, his paranoia was worsened. That day, he actually accused me of making a fortune out of The Beatles, while they saw nothing.'

Ida Holly Dark-haired Liverpool girl who was John Lennon's clandestine girl friend before his marriage to Cynthia became public. Bill Harry comments: 'I'd known Cynthia from Junior Art School and during the time she was at Liverpool College of Art, and while she was attending Beatles' gigs at places ranging from the Jacaranda to Aintree Institute.

'Then, for a while, she no longer appeared in John's company and when I met him frequently at the Blue Angel Club he was accompanied by Ida. I remember getting a lift home from him one night and he dropped Ida off near her parents' house in Croxteth.

'She was interested in the local beat scene. I fixed her up with jobs as a "commere" at some local venues and on the *Mersey Beat* Showboat to the Isle of Man. She later moved to London to try her luck as a model and changed her name to Stevie Holly.'

Deziah Holt Clairvoyant who in 1980 warned Yoko that both she and John should beware of contact with strangers by the name of Bell, Richard or Mark.

Aldous Huxley British writer and philosopher, author of such contemporary classics as *Brave New World* and *Crome Yellow*. John was very influenced by his work, which he discovered in 1966. Later he made the comment: 'I've always wondered what it was about politics and government that was wrong. Now, since reading some books by Aldous Huxley, I've suddenly found out what it's all about.'

Huxley also wrote *The Doors Of Perception*, a book about the effects of psychedelic drugs on the mind which, in some ways, could stimulate a person into experimenting with hallucinogenics.

Huxley was one of the 60 odd figures chosen by all four Beatles to appear as cut-outs on their *Sergeant Pepper* sleeve and it is likely that Huxley was John's personal choice. Huxley died in 1963.

Toshi Ichiyanagi Yoko's first husband, Japanese pianist-composer, who she met in New York in 1957 when she was 25 years old.

They lived for a few years in Greenwich Village, but the marriage didn't last and they were divorced six years later.

However, Yoko, apparently the dominant partner in the relationship, urged him to return to Japan to gain acclaim for his work. She said, 'He used to write Stravinski-type material, but he gradually changed after we met and now he's the foremost *avant-garde* composer in Japan.'

Nat Jackley Veteran Scottish comedian, dubbed 'the rubber man' because of his comedy contortions, particularly with his neck. He was one of the guest artists who joined The Beatles on their *Magical Mystery Tour* and John personally directed the scene in which Jack chased a group of bikini-clad girls around a swimming pool.

Sir Geoffrey Jackson British diplomat kidnapped by South American guerrilas in 1970 and tortured by sensory deprivation techniques. These consisted of 'Across The Universe' being played to him for numerous hours without a break. He reminisced about John Lennon in a Radio Four interview in May 1981.

Arthur Janov Instigator of a 'cure for neurosis' which he called primal therapy. Janov, an American psychologist, expounded his theory in a book called *The Primal Scream*. John received a copy of the book in the post, read it, was intrigued and passed it on to Yoko for her opinion.

Yoko approved of the ideas in the book. John contacted Janov by phone in Los Angeles and arranged for him to fly to England to supervise a course of primal therapy for himself and Yoko.

Janov explained that prior to their first session, they must not see each other for 24 hours and should retreat to separate rooms, cleared of distractions such as phones and TV sets, armed only with pencil and paper.

On his arrival, Janov began a course of sessions lasting three weeks, the first week of which was conducted at Tittenhurst Park where he visited John and Yoko for separate sessions each day. It was the first time the couple had been separated for two years.

For the following two weeks, John moved to the Inn on the Park Hotel in

London and Yoko booked into the nearby Londonderry Hotel. After the initial three weeks, Janov told the couple that they needed to attend his Primal Institute in California for several months in order to obtain further benefits and to join in the group sessions.

They flew to California and rented a house in Bel Air, attending sessions at the Primal Institute in Los Angeles for the next four months. The therapy resulted in John writing several songs, a number of them about his late mother, and they were featured on the *John Lennon/Plastic Ono Band* album, often referred to as his *Primal Album*.

Sir John Jasper Character played by John in the 'What A Night' sketch in the first half of *The Beatles Christmas Show* presented at the Finsbury Park Astoria, London from Tuesday 24 December 1963 to Saturday 11 January 1964. During the short melodrama, Sir John Jasper appeared brandishing a whip, twirling a false moustache and dressed in top hat and long black cloak. He tied the heroine Ermyntrude (George Harrison) to the railway lines as the snow fell (Ringo sprinkling paper over the actors) until all was saved by the arrival of Fearless Paul (McCartney) The Signalman.

Johnny And The Moondogs Temporary name used by John, Paul and George in 1959. They'd noticed an advertisement in the *Liverpool Echo* that Mr. Starmaker, Carroll Levis, was bringing *The Carroll Levis Discovery Show* up North. The finals were to be held in Manchester on the *Discoveries* show and there were to be some heats, one of which was to take place at the Empire Theatre, Liverpool.

The new Elizabethans.

John, Paul and George needed a name when applying for an audition and thought up 'The Moondogs'. Then, since John was the titular head of the group, changed it to Johnny And The Moondogs. There were a number of acts from the north-west appearing at the Liverpool heats including, according to some reports, Billy Fury.

Some people say that a group called The Gladiators won. Other sources report that the winners were a duo called Rikki & Dane (Allan Clarke and Graham Nash, who were to become leaders of The Hollies).

Johnny And The Moondogs, however, definitely came third. This meant they were entitled to appear in the finals in Manchester. The trio were particularly influenced by Buddy Holly at the time and during their appearance they sang 'It's So Easy' and 'Think It Over'.

At the end of the show each act was required to reappear and perform a few bars so that the audience's applause could be measured.

However, Johnny And The Moondogs were so short of money that they couldn't afford overnight accommodation at a hotel. So they had to set off to the station to catch the last train home before the finalé and missed the opportunity of being judged. The name was dropped later that year to be replaced by The Silver Beatles.

Jesus Christ John was very aware of the teachings of Christ. At the time of his bed-ins he said: 'We are all Christ — and we are all Hitler. We want Christ to win. We're all trying to make Christ's message contemporary. What would he have done if he had advertisements, records, films, TV and newspapers? Christ made miracles to tell his message. Well, the miracle today is communications, so let's use it.'

When John did use communications to get a message across, such as his belief that The Beatles were more famous in the modern world, in some instances, than Jesus — there was a terrible outcry. He was also censured when he used the word 'Christ' in the song 'The Ballad Of John And Yoko'.

John originally wanted both Christ and Hitler to be represented on the *Sergeant Pepper* sleeve, but his idea was vetoed.

Betsy Johnson American fashion designer who dedicated her autumn 1981 collection to John. She said, 'Just after his death, I was working on my collection. I flipped back to 1965, '66 and '67 and listened to all the Beatle songs. It inspired a whole new mood. I think we're getting back to romance, children, love and life together.'

Pauline Jones An ex-Essex University student who married John's father Freddie, even though at 56 to her 19 he was three times her age. Pauline was working for John at his Kenwood house when Freddie met her, a relationship which John encouraged. 'As long as they're happy, they can do as they wish.' The couple eloped to Scotland, married, settled in Brighton and gave John a half-brother, David. Following Freddie's death, Pauline retained possession of his autobiographical manuscript and in a woman's magazine claimed that she still contacted Freddie's spirit at seances. She later remarried.

Freda Kelly Irish-born, Liverpool-based Beatles fan who became their longest-lasting fan club secretary, taking over the position from her friend Bobbie Brown, the first secretary, in 1963.

However, if it hadn't been for the intervention of John Lennon, the story might have been completely different. Freda joined Brian Epstein's staff at Nems shop in Whitechapel in 1962 as a shorthand typist. The following year she had a mishap in the office which resulted in 30 of Brian's letters being erased from a dictaphone machine.

Brian was furious and sacked her on the spot. Fortunately for Freda, John Lennon was with Brian at the time and made him see the funny side of things, with the result that Freda was reinstated and went on to run their Fan Club.

Vincent Kelly Merseyside journalist who worked for the *Liverpool Echo*, the major newspaper in the area. He visited the Cavern in 1962 in order to interview The Beatles but took exception to a sarcastic remark made by John and, as a result, did not write his interview.

Jacqueline Kennedy Widow of assassinated USA president, John F. Kennedy, and Greek millionaire, Aristotle Onassis. As a special consultant of the American book publishers Doubleday, she gave support and encouragement to the project which resulted in the collection of *Rolling Stone* articles in book form: *The Ballad Of John and Yoko*.

J R Kirkwood Liverpool registrar who presided over the wedding of Alfred Lennon and Julia Stanley.

Allen Klein New York rock music accountant who harboured a dream of managing The Beatles because 'they were the best'. He'd desired the job even when Brian Epstein was alive. He saw his opportunity after Apple accountant Stephen Maltz informed the group of their company's dire financial state. This led John to remark in the newspapers that he was going broke.

Klein managed to phone John and flew to London for a meeting at the Dorchester Hotel with John and Yoko in January 1969. Klein had been born on 18 December 1931 in Newark, son of a Jewish butcher. His mother died when he was two years old and he and two of his three sisters were then placed in an orphanage.

The story of his early life which he related to the pair made a great impression on John and as Klein also showed an enthusiastic knowledge of The Beatles' music, he was sold on the man. The next day John sent a message to Sir Joseph Lockwood of EMI which read, 'Dear Sir Joe, from now on Allen Klein handles all my things.'

By February 1969 Klein was confirmed as manager by George and Ringo, with Paul McCartney being the only dissenting Beatle. The deal Klein had made with the group was for 20 per cent of any increase in their earnings.

He immediately became involved in a number of complicated manoeuvres. The first was the attempt to acquire control of Nems, which represented The Beatles' management company, deducting commission from their royalties.

Klein lost this first round and the company was taken over by Triumph Investments.

Klein next attempted to gain control of Northern Song on The Beatles' behalf but also lost this fight with the company being bought by ATV, Sir Lew Grade's company.

Klein did, however, renegotiate their royalty deal. He was in a strong position to do this as their EMI recording deal was coming to an end.

He was to claim that he had increased their earnings during the first 18 months of management to the tune of nine million pounds. This was true — but a great deal of money had come from the sale of their shares of Northern Songs to ATV, and Brian Epstein had been responsible for their having the shares.

Paul found he couldn't stand Klein handling his affairs. He received legal advice which pointed out that the only way he could rid himself of Klein would be by taking legal action against Klein and his fellow Beatles.

Reluctantly, he set the wheels in motion and The Beatles as a partnership were dissolved. Klein must have resented Paul's move very strongly as it has been suggested that he contributed some lines to John's 'How Do You Sleep?' number which was critical of Paul.

Klein had brought in Phil Spector to resolve their 'Let It Be' tapes, arranged a film role for Ringo, given George a first A side of a Beatles single with 'Something' and taken a controversial role in the financial dealings of The Concert For Bangla Desh venture.

It was ironic that John, in 1969, had remarked, 'He knew all about us and our music. I knew right away he was the man for us', because by 1973 when Klein's contract ended, the romance was over.

John and George had become disenchanted with the man and like Paul were suing him. Klein on the other hand was suing John for 200,000 dollars and by 1977, in a case concerning the royalty payments, Klein received a settlement of more than four million dollars.

Ed Koch When a Congressman, Koch worked hard to persuade the Immigration and Naturalization Service that John had contributed a great deal to music and the arts and should remain in America. He was Mayor of New York at the time of John's death. On Friday 22 May 1981 he presented the Hendel medallion to Yoko as a posthumous award for John. The Hendel medallion is a special New York award for outstanding cultural merit.

Kosaku Koishihara Buyer for the Japanese department store Seibu, who was the most prominent bidder at the Sotheby's 1982 Beatles auction on Wednesday 22 December. He spent £50,000 on 70 separate lots.

His largest purchase was the gold disc of *Sergeant Pepper's Lonely Hearts Club Band* for £13,000. He paid £2,200 each for two of John's 1965 drawings *The Vicar* and *The Motley Bunch*, and £2,800 for a bronze bust of John. All the purchases were scheduled to be resold at his department store.

Billy J. Kramer Liverpool singer who had several major hits in the early to mid 'sixties with Lennon and McCartney numbers such as 'Do You Want To Know A Secret?' 'Bad To Me', 'I Call Your Name', 'I'll Keep You Satisfied' and 'From A Window'. He also topped the British charts with the Mort Shuman /John Leslie MacFarland number 'Little Children'.

Billy (whose real name was William Ashton) was a popular local singer fronting a group called The Coasters when he was voted third most popular act in the *Mersey Beat* popularity poll.

Brian Epstein, who already managed The Beatles and Gerry And The Pacemakers who were one and two in the poll, paid Billy's manager, a pensioner called Ted Knibbs, a nominal fee to transfer the management.

The Coasters refused to turn professional so Brian secured the services of a Manchester group called The Dakotas to back him. Although the partnership seemed a success on the surface, Billy didn't get on with his new musicians.

He recalls how he originally came by the J in his name. Shortly after signing with Epstein, he was asked to call at the Nems offices. Brian was present with John Lennon. Billy was asked how he would like having a J added to his name. 'It was John's idea,' said Epstein. 'He thought it made the name flow better.'

The 'J' in Billy J. Kramer's name stands for Julian.

Billy agreed to the suggestion, but asked, 'What do I tell people if they ask me what the J stands for?'

'John has suggested Julian', said Epstein.

'But that's a pouf's name,' protested Billy, unaware of John's secret marriage to Cynthia and the fact that he had a son called Julian.

Denny Laine Former member of The Moody Blues who once toured with The Beatles. In later years he became a millionaire after Paul McCartney invited him to join Wings. On hearing of John's death he said: 'I can't imagine what Paul will be thinking. Me, I just don't know what to say. It is a tragedy. I'm heartbroken. His trouble was that he was too honest. Sure, he was outspoken and it's killed him. There will be a lot of people crying today. Many

youngsters looked on him as a hero. Somehow, he managed to bridge the generation gap. Now he's gone. And that has left my world with a big hole.'

Annie Leibovitz Major American rock photographer who began to work professionally in the field in 1969 following a course at the Art Institute in San Francisco. She became chief photographer for the prestigious *Rolling Stone* magazine and her first front cover contribution to that publication was a portrait of John.

This was taken as part of an assignment to provide shots for the famous Jann Wenner two-part 'Working Class Hero' interview in 1970. Of that initial session, she commented: 'It was the first time I had met a legend and it was at the beginning of my career. John was a real person and he seemed to make an effort at being a human, totally in control of the situation. Working with him broke all my fears and barriers. He provided a precedent for the way in which I have interpreted people since.'

Annie was the last person to take photographs of John. This was on Monday 8 December 1980 as part of another *Rolling Stone* assignment. The photographs were taken inside the Lennon's own apartments in the Dakota Building, one of the rare occasions on which John and Yoko allowed a photographer into their private world.

Her portfolio of photographs from this session and the ones taken the previous Wednesday were featured in the 22 January issue of *Rolling Stone*, with a front cover of John crouched naked over Yoko, kissing her on the cheek.

Of this now famous picture, Annie commented: 'I promised John that this would be the cover. It was taken a few hours before he died.' Annie's photographs of John are to be found in several publications, including *Shooting Stars: The Rolling Stone Book Of Portraits; The Ballad Of John And Yoko, Lennon Remembers* and *One Day At A Time*.

Alfred Lennon John's father was born in Liverpool on 14 December 1912, the son of Jack Lennon and Mary Maguire. Although there were six children of the union, there was no record of the couple having married. When Jack died of a liver disease in 1921, Alfred was nine years of age, and together with one of his brothers, was placed in the Bluecoat School, which took in orphans. He remained at the school until he was 15 and then left to take his first job as an office clerk. It was during this period, in 1927, that he met Julia Stanley, a 14 year old girl, in Sefton Park. He chatted her up and asked her to sit with him, and she told him she would on condition he got rid of his silly bowler hat. He immediately threw it into the lake. The couple then began going out together and continued doing so over a period of ten years, in between Alfred's voyages abroad.

At the age of 16 Alfred was drawn to the sea, and signed up as a ship's waiter in 1930. In between voyages he stayed at the Stanley house in Wavertree and taught Julia how to play the banjo.

It was Julia who finally suggested that they should get married and they did, at Mount Pleasant Register Office on 3 December 1938. No member of their family was present and after the ceremony the couple went to the Trocadero cinema where they spent their 'honeymoon'. Later that evening

Julia went back home to Wavertree and Freddie went to his digs, leaving the next day on a three-month trip to the West Indies. He was also away at sea in October 1940 when John was born.

While at sea, Fred had arranged to pay sums of money to the company he worked for, which Julia could collect from the branch in Liverpool. He was now a head waiter and as it was wartime and he was in New York city, was asked to report to a ship sailing for Britain. However, on this he was to be assistant steward, not head waiter and he bemoaned the fact to the captain, upset at being demoted. The captain suggested that he get drunk and miss the boat, which he did. He was then interred on Ellis Island until another ship, this time sailing for North Africa, was available. There was a certain

Fred, John's 'Dad, Pater, Father, Whatever'.

amount of stealing aboard the ship but Fred claimed he had nothing to do with this. When they reached North Africa he claimed that one of the cooks asked him to bring a bottle of Vodka from his cabin and while Fred was drinking from it a party of police arrived to investigate the thefts and arrested him for stealing the Vodka. He was jailed for three months and his money was stopped. Unable to provide Julia with any cash, he wrote her letters and suggested she enjoy herself by going out with other men. He later regretted the suggestion because she took him up on it — and he lost her.

In 1945 she gave birth to another son and had him adopted by a Norwegian couple. She also began living with another man and placed John with his Aunt Mimi in Menlove Avenue.

Docking in Southampton in the summer of 1946, Fred phoned Aunt Mimi and asked if he could take John up to Blackpool. Mimi felt she couldn't refuse this request from the boy's father and Fred picked up the five-year-old and took him to stay in a friend's flat at Blackpool.

During the few weeks they were in the northern seaside resort, Fred told John of his desire to take him to New Zealand. The idea appealed to Fred because his friend was emigrating to there and, at the time, Fred was earning money on the side through black market deals.

Julia arrived at the flat saying that John should come back with her to Liverpool. Fred asked the boy whether he wanted to go to New Zealand with him or return to Merseyside with his mother, and John opted for Fred's proposal. However, when Julia left the house he changed his mind and ran after her. Fred did not see his son again

'Ver is der Kaiser?'

for 20 years. When Julia returned to Liverpool she placed the boy in Mimi's care again.

In 1964, Fred had finally abandoned life on the ocean wave and was working as a porter in the Greyhound Hotel, Hampton, near London for £10 a week. The *Daily Express* traced him and wanted to set up a meeting between him and his now famous son.

Fred went along to the set of *A Hard Day's Night* and entered the dressing room. John wouldn't talk to him but asked him to leave his address. John sent a letter to the Greyhound with a note to 'Dear Alf, Fred, Dad, Pater, Father, Whatever' with £30 enclosed.

John began to send Fred a regular £12 a week and the ex-seaman moved into a flat in Kew, basking in the limelight as a minor celebrity, having his life story printed in the weekly magazines and gracing the London nightspots. He even found himself with a manager,

Tony Cartwright, who co-wrote a song with him called 'That's My Life', which was issued as a single in December 1965 by Pye Records on their Piccadilly label. The company issued a press handout which read:

'Fifty-three-year-old Freddie Lennon, father of John, has made his first record. It is entitled "That's My Life (My Love And My Home)".

'Mr Lennon has been an entertainer in an amateur capacity for most of his life. He comes from a musical family, for his father was one of the original Kentucky Minstrels, and taught him to sing when he was young.

'Most of Freddie's childhood was spent in an orphanage, for he was born into a large family and in those difficult times parents could not afford to feed so many children. At the orphanage, Freddie always took a major part in concerts, played his harmonica to the other children and generally showed an inclination towards the stage. He once sang at a theatre but the orphanage authorities were dismayed at the thought of one of their boys going on to the stage, so Freddie's early dreams were quickly dampened.

'After leaving the orphanage at the age of 15, Freddie worked in an office, but the call of the sea was strong, and he joined his first ship as bell boy at the age of 16. He stayed at sea for 25 years and travelled the world.

'Freddie was always connected with entertainment on board ship, and has acted as compere, produced numerous concerts, sang in New York clubs and even conducted an orchestra in Lisbon. He has many interesting stories to relate about his adventures at sea.

'At the age of 25 Freddie married, and his son John was born three years later. He was the only child.

'When he left the sea 12 years ago, Freddie took a job as a waiter, and later worked in holiday camps at northern resorts. He came to live in London seven years ago. Over the years, Freddie was always interested in songwriting, but he never took it seriously. Six months ago he met Tony Cartwright, who is now his manager. Together they wrote "That's My Life (My Love And My Home)" — a story about Freddie's life. The song was taken to a music publisher, accepted and recorded.'

By the close of 1967 the two were reconciled and Fred often dropped around to John's house in Kenwood. At the time John had a student working for him as a secretary. Her name was Pauline Jones, she was 19. Fred at 56 was almost three times her age.

During the Christmas period, the sly and cunning John manoeuvred Fred into Pauline's bedroom and the two fell in love. Pauline's parents were furious and had her made a ward of court, but the two eloped to Scotland where they were married. They then went to live in Brighton with John paying the rent for their flat and had a son whom they called David.

Fred and Pauline decided to take David along to see John at his mansion in Tittenhurst Park. John was in a foul mood and tossed them out, seemingly upset at the idea of seeing his half-brother, which may have set off painful memories.

Years later, when Fred was dying, John spoke to him by phone from America on several occasions, although Fred could hardly speak a word in return. When Fred died John offered to pay for his funeral, but Pauline rejected the offer.

Charles Lennon Alfred Lennon's brother and John's uncle. Charles lives in Mossley Hill, Liverpool and is a regular visitor to Cavern Mecca, in addition to appearing at the annual Liverpool conventions. A friendly and convivial person, he was once told by John during a visit to Weybridge: 'Uncle Charlie, whenever you're confronted by the press you have two left feet and a stub of an arm.'

Cynthia Lennon She was born in Blackpool in 1939 where her parents had moved temporarily from Merseyside (a prime target for bombers) during the war. Her two brothers, Tony and Charles, had been evacuated to Wales. The family returned to their home in the Wirral, across the River Mersey from Liverpool.

Having failed her eleven-plus exam, Cynthia managed to pass an entrance examination to the Junior Art School. She left the school following the death of her father but resumed her art studies at Liverpool College of Art when she was eighteen.

It was during her periods in the lettering class that her romance with John took root, although he teased her cruelly. When Cynthia told John that she was pregnant, he proposed and the couple were married at Mount Pleasant Register Office on 23 August 1962.

For a time they were able to live in Brian Epstein's flat in Falkner Street. But as John was performing with the band most of the time, it was decided that for her to be left alone in a state of pregnancy was not advisable. She moved in with John's Aunt Mimi. The arrangement didn't last long as Cynthia claimed she was frightened of John's aunt.

Cynthia gave birth to Julian at Sefton General Hospital in April 1963, and later that month John went on holiday to Spain with Brian Epstein.

It had been a frustrating time for Cynthia because she'd had to keep the romance quiet in the early days of The Beatles' rise to fame in Liverpool for fear that local girl fans would beat her up.

By the time the group were achieving more renown, she was advised to remain in the background and when they were married, the affair was hushed-up. In fact, even the birth of Julian was kept from the media and Cynthia had to avoid meeting the press in the early months of Julian's life.

The news eventually leaked out and Cynthia went to live with John in London, initially in a flat in Knightsbridge. This proved to be inconvenient and the couple moved to a dream house in Weybridge.

For a few years life must have seemed ideal: a lavish home, security, adulation (there was a Cynthia Lennon fan club), a famous husband, a growing son, holidays in tropical environments and special trips with The Beatles to such places as India in the company of other celebrities. It must have seemed too good to last, and it was.

Cynthia felt the beginning of the end was heralded by John's introduction to LSD. But it was the combination of several factors, the main one being the appearance of Yoko Ono on the scene.

Cynthia arrived home from a holiday in Greece to find Yoko in her home with John. She felt weak, helpless and embarrassed. Part of the problem was Cynthia's inability to summon the strength of will to fight a person as dominating as Yoko. It was as if she acknowledged defeat without a fight.

There was a brief reconciliation, but Yoko was determined to get her man. When Cynthia was on holiday in Italy, Alexis Mardas was sent to tell her that John wanted a divorce.

It was finally arranged — but on Cynthia's terms — not John's. Cynthia retained the custody of Julian and obtained a financial settlement. The divorce was finalized in November 1968 and within two years on 31 July 1970 Cynthia remarried.

Her new husband was an Italian restaurateur Roberto Bassanini, with whose family Cynthia was staying two years previously when John's ultimatum had been delivered to her.

The marriage didn't last long and within a few years Cynthia was married again, to businessman John Twist.

For a while they lived in Ruthin, Wales, quite close to Merseyside. Julian attended the local school and Cynthia went into business as part-owner of a restaurant.

Her third marriage also turned sour and following John's death Cynthia attempted to seek some creative satisfaction by returning to her love of art. Julian left home and moved to London. Cynthia reverted to the name of Cynthia Lennon and toured America with her paintings making many new friends including May Pang, one of John's former mistresses. Returning to England, Cynthia once again moved south, settling in Wiltshire where she was able to work on some further books following the success of her autobiography, *A Twist Of Lennon*.

David Henry Lennon John's young stepbrother, first son of Alfred and Pauline Lennon. He has a younger brother, Robin.

Jack Lennon The paternal grandfather John Lennon never knew. An Irishman, he left for America where he became a member of The Kentucky Minstrels. He returned to Liverpool but died in 1921 when Freddie Lennon was only nine years old.

Julian Lennon John's first son and the first child born to any member of The Beatles. The Beatles were currently promoting their new single 'Please, Please Me' at the time and John's marriage to Cynthia had been kept secret from the world in general.

Accompanied only by her friend Phyllis, Cynthia was rushed to Sefton General Hospital in Smithdown Road, Liverpool and gave birth to Julian at 7.45 am on Monday 8 April 1963.

There was some difficulty at the actual birth as the umbilical cord was wrapped around the child's neck, but he proved to be a healthy baby. Cynthia then requested a private room and John visited her there a week later.

When Cynthia left hospital with Julian she returned to Menlove Avenue where she had been staying with John's Aunt Mimi. When Cynthia's mother returned from Canada six months later, they decided to return to Trinity Road, Hoylake, their previous home.

In November Julian was christened at Trinity Road parish church, although John was unable to attend. His full name is John Charles Julian Lennon.

The first christian name was chosen in honour of John, the second in memory of Cynthia's father and the third in memory of John's mother Julia. News of the marriage and the birth of Julian eventually found its way into the press. The three were able to unite as a family at last and move into a flat in

Emperor's Gate, Kensington, London.

This proved inconvenient and they later moved to St. George's Hill Estate in Weybridge, Surrey where Julian attended the local prep school.

When Julian was four years old he brought home a picture of a school friend which he'd drawn and called it 'Lucy In The Sky With Diamonds'. This inspired John to write a song of the same name.

At one time there was a kidnapping threat and Julian was guarded day and night, both at home and at school.

Yoko Ono entered the picture and John and Cynthia's marriage was doomed. Alexis Mardas conveyed a message to Cynthia that John was going to divorce her and take Julian away from her. Paul McCartney was particularly upset by the split and felt sorry for Julian, an emotion which led him to his composing 'Hey Jude'.

After the divorce, John had access to Julian who joined his father and Yoko on numerous occasions, visiting the filming of The Rolling Stones' *Rock and Roll Circus* and joining them on a trip to Scotland with Yoko's daughter Kyoko in June 1967.

Later that same year another of his drawings was immortalized, this time as the sleeve of *Christmas Time Is Here Again*, The Beatles' Christmas record issued in December.

In 1970 Cynthia married hotelier Roberto Bassanini, but the marriage was a brief one and they parted shortly afterwards. The divorce came through in 1973 and she married businessman John Twist in 1976. They settled in Ruthin, North Wales where Julian attended the local school and Cynthia teamed up with Angie McCartney, ex-wife of Mike McGear, to open a venture called Oliver's Bistro.

During the remainder of the 'seventies, Julian led a more-or-less normal life, out of the limelight, attending the local school and making friends in Ruthin. Julian's life was shattered when John Twist had to tell him that his father had been murdered, and he lay on the floor in a state of shock for hours.

Yoko wanted him to come straight to New York, but said that she didn't want Cynthia to come with him, so he was accompanied by one of his Ruthin friends, Justin.

Julian's life completely changed after the tragedy. Cynthia and John Twist were estranged. Cynthia changed her name back to Cynthia Lennon and began to tour America with her paintings, also leaving North Wales for a new home in Wiltshire.

On returning from America, Julian had decided that the time had come for him to leave home and he moved to Chiswick in London. He became a favourite topic of the gossip columns, attracting dolly birds like moths to a flame. He'd had girl friends in Ruthin such as Sally Hodson and a girl called Amanda, but the models who pursued him in London were totally different.

He'd been befriended by old Etonian Kim Kindersley who took him round all the fashionable clubs, from Tramps to Stringfellows. At Tramps he was approached by Stephanie La Motta, who became one of a series of girls he hit the headlines with.

He was given a 19th birthday party at Stringfellows, which received considerable press coverage with models such as Sian Adley-Jones stripping to the waist. For the next few years, models found that a date with Julian ensured them press coverage.

Some examples include Kate Latto, featured in a *Daily Mirror* story in January 1982 under the heading 'Julian's Blonde'.

Two months later the *Sunday Mirror* was featuring 'The New Girl For "So Shy" Lennon' in a story which began: 'This beautiful blonde is the new girl in Julian Lennon's life. Model Jordana . . . has been wined and dined . . . by (Julian) since they met at a London night club.'

The stories continued and a topless Debbie Boyland was featured in the *Sunday People* in April 1983 under the heading 'Love And Sun For Lennon' in a story beginning: 'Delicious Debbie Boyland and her lover Julian Lennon . . . are Barbados-bound.'

His club exploits caused controversy, such as the occasion when he was photographed with a blonde holding a gun to his head at L'Escargot Club.

In the years immediately following John's death, Julian seemed only newsworthy for his partiality for blonde birds. His musical career seemed to be almost non-existent, despite the fact that he'd been signed up by Tariq Siddiqi.

When he was 18, Cynthia had said he could play the guitar better than his father. At one time he had a band called The Lennon Drops and in April 1982 the London *Evening Standard* in a story entitled 'Julian's Chilling Debut' wrote that Julian was about to 'astonish the world with the release of a chillingly brilliant début record.'

The number was 'I Don't Wanna Feel It Any More', which John himself had actually recorded during the *Double Fantasy* sessions but had never released.

In March 1983 reports appeared in the British press that Julian had joined

Julian, looking remarkably like his father, steps out with his Mum.

Quasar, a group led by Paul Inder, son of Lemmy of Motorhead.

Paul was also managed by Siddiqi. In May 1983 there was some controversy because Siddiqi organized the group's appearance on the roof of the old Apple building in Savile Row.

Even Paul Inder's mother couldn't stomach this blatant use of Julian and said, 'The whole idea of using the memory of The Beatles and using John Lennon's son in this way is sick.'

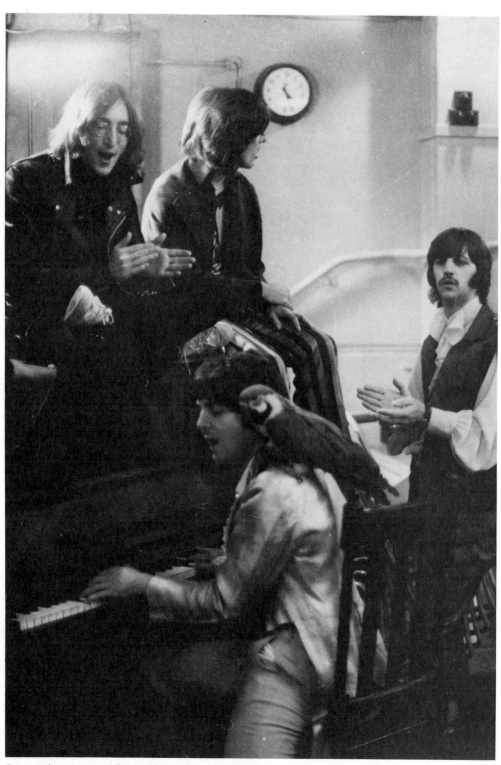

Remember Long John and His Silver Men?

In the years following John's death, there was always controversy regarding his inheritance. Some papers described him as 'The heir to John's vast fortune — estimated to be more than £50 million'.

However, Julian began to bemoan the fact that he was broke and began offering to tell his story to newspapers.

A series did appear in the *News Of The World* in January 1982 in which Julian talked to Polly Hepburn. The headline ran 'All You Need Is Love. The Beatles Said It, But I Wish Dad Had Shown Me Some.'

Julian claimed that John had offered him marijuana when he was only 12 years old, described his visits to John in America and said boys often threatened to beat him up because he was the son of a Beatle, and other rather innocuous stories.

Yoko granted him an allowance of 100 dollars a week, a sum which was criticised when the news leaked out. Julian said: 'Yoko decided to give me a hundred dollars a week some time ago, but it is not mine by right. The papers say I'm heir to a fortune worth millions, but Yoko has total control of everything.'

'I will get half the trust fund cash, about two hundred thousand dollars, when I am twenty-five. The other half goes to Sean.'

Yoko replied to the criticism by saying, 'Poor Julian is probably very confused. It all has to do with Cynthia. She is not getting any money from John's estate, rightly, and she is very hurt by this. It's hard for Julian to please his mother without saying bad things about me.

'John never gave him any allowance. Julian was complaining that he didn't

Sean must be glad that John changed his mind and didn't christen him

George Washington United States of America Citizen Lennon.

have enough money to be able to buy beer so I said "How much would cover that?" Am I wrong? How much do most kids his age get? Should he grow up differently from other kids?"

Robin Lennon Second son of Alfred and Pauline Lennon. His mother Pauline remarried and is now Mrs Pauline Stone.

Sean Lennon The only offspring of John and Yoko was born on John's 35th birthday, 9 October 1975 at New York Hospital. Yoko had had three miscarriages before the birth of their son, which was obviously one of the high points in their lives. John was to say, 'I feel higher than the Empire State Building.' At one time he considered calling his new born child George Washington United States Of America Citizen Lennon.

The couple had almost given up hope of having a child together, but decided to try again on the advice of an acupuncturist. John said: 'We went through all hell trying to have a baby, through many miscarriages and other problems. He is what they call a love child in truth. Doctors told us we could never have a child. We almost gave up. We were told something was wrong with my sperm, that I abused myself so much in my youth that there was no chance. Yoko was 43, and so they said, no way. But this Chinese acupuncturist in San Francisco said, "You behave yourself. No drugs, eat well, no drink. You have a child in eighteen months." We had Sean and sent the acupuncturist a Polaroid of him before he died, God rest his soul.'

Having experienced a childhood without any direct parental care, and harbouring a guilt for letting his career take precedence over seeing his first son Julian grow up, John decided that he would spend virtually his entire waking life in the company of Sean. He did this for a period of time which lasted five years.

In the Dakota apartments, John became a househusband, caring for Sean, feeding him, teaching him, and doting on him while Yoko went out to work, controlling the couple's many business interests. For the first year of Sean's life, John took Polaroid shots of his son every single day. When Sean began to draw, John had all the sketches framed. He was finding a satisfaction in life he had never experienced before.

John's life revolved around Sean's meals. He would rise at six in the morning to plan breakfast. The two would have this at around seven-thirty, when they would both 'communicate'.

Then at ten o'clock when Sean was involved in other things, John would be planning the next meal.

He didn't mind the role-reversal of having Yoko take care of business while he looked after the home. He'd finally ridden himself of that chauvinism so associated with males from the north of England.

It was during his holiday in Bermuda with Sean that John finally decided to resume a musical career. However, fate tragically brought this to a chilling end.

Sean is left with memories, the treasure of five years of a close intimacy rare between father and son. Nothing will compensate him for his loss. Life must have seemed puzzling for such a child, growing up in a world in which he was forever surrounded by bodyguards. Despite the dramatic suffering he must have gone through, he continued developing the way John would have wished, into a 'beautiful boy'.

Sidney Lennon One of John's uncles who emigrated to Ontario, Canada in 1967. When contacted for an interview for the *Detroit Free Press* following John's death in 1980 he was 72-years-old. He claimed that he and his wife looked after John in their home in Liverpool for about nine months when John was four-years-old, shortly before John's mother, Julia, placed her son in the care of his Aunt Mimi.

David Leon Actor who portrayed John in the film *Beatlemania*.

Arthur Lewis A Labour MP who, following the Montague Square police raid in October 1968, questioned the Home Secretary in the House of Commons as to the necessity of having such a large force of police and dogs to raid the flat where John and Yoko were staying. Lewis considered the force excessive and mentioned that the cost of the operation to the police was £178 1s.7d.

John Lindsay Mayor of New York when John and Yoko were opposing efforts to deport John from the US. Lindsay supported John's cause and requested that the proceedings be halted.

Brett Livingstone-Strong American sculptor who carved a marble statue of John, which was erected and unveiled in Los Angeles in the summer of 1981.

Sir Joseph Lockwood Head of EMI Records in Britain during The Beatles' years. The group met him on numerous occasions and when John and Yoko had been 'busted' whilst at Ringo's Montague Square flat, John phoned Sir Joseph from Marylebone Police Station to ask his advice. He was told to plead guilty.

When John finally decided to take on Allen Klein as his manager, he sent a message to Lockwood in January 1969 saying, 'Dear Sir Joe, from now on Allen Klein handles all my things'.

Long John And The Silver Men

Name suggested to John, Paul and George by Casey Jones, leader of Mersey band Cass And The Cassanovas, after they had decided to dispense with The Quarrymen title. Cass didn't like the name 'The Beatles' and told them they should have the name of a group leader up front. This was the fashion in those days with bands such as Cliff Richard And The Shadows. The group didn't like his suggestion, but retained the word 'silver' and called themselves The Silver Beatles.

Virginia Lust New York actress who was featured in John and Yoko's film *Fly*, shot in an attic in the Bowery at a session lasting a full one and a half days.

It has been suggested that Virginia was sedated to enable her to lie still for interminably long periods while flies were filmed crawling over her naked body by a macro lens.

Virginia's nude form was intimately explored in this short film, originally three-quarters of an hour long but pruned to 19 minutes.

The camera tracks a fly crawling around her toes and moving up her legs, into her pubic hair and examining her vagina. Different flies were used as the exploration continued over her body, moving from her abdomen to her breasts and to her face.

Rod Lynton Session musician invited to the studios in Tittenhurst Park in the autumn of 1971 to work on the 'How Do You Sleep?' track on the *Imagine* album. Of the three nights spent working on the number, Lynton commented, 'I was phoned from Apple and asked to bring down some rhythm guitarists. So I took down some friends of mine, Ted Durner of Wishbone Ash, Andrew Cresswell-Davies of Stackridge and John Tout who played piano with Renaissance.

'John played vibes, but the rest of us made up a rhythm section. His studio adjoined the kitchen, but he also had a separate control room with some of the finest equipment I had ever seen.

'There were never more than eight of us in the studio at the same time. He had Klaus Voorman playing bass, Alan White on drums, Nicky Hopkins on piano, George Harrison slide guitar and John Barham on harmonium.

'When we weren't wanted for one particular song, we just sat it out in the kitchen at a long pine table down the middle of the room, stacked high with chicken, ham, tongue and salad. You just helped yourself if you felt a bit hungry.

'We all had the run of the house when we weren't working. In between some numbers we played billiards in John's library. He had a full size billiards table in there with thousands of books lining one huge wall from floor to ceiling.

'It really shook me up when we

started recording "How Do You Sleep?" because I had grown up admiring The Beatles and there I was standing there playing rhythm guitar, and I heard John's voice coming over the speakers, putting down Paul.

'That really pulled me up with a jolt. Until that moment, I don't think it had really sunk in that I was playing with John, who had always been my idol.

'When I first started to play, Yoko came round the room, sat on the floor opposite me, looking very intense, and I was worried at first because I thought she didn't like me.

'She was just sitting there, staring at me, but I learned afterwards that Yoko does that. She sits thinking very deeply and it can be unnerving if you have never seen her do it before because her eyes are so intense.'

James McClain Ex-convict who became a Pentecostal minister having become a born-again Christian during his spell in Lewisburg Prison for bank robbery.

He became John's bodyguard during the last few months of John's life. As a security guard at the Hit Factory, the studio where John was recording *Double Fantasy*, he was asked to become bodyguard for John and Yoko. He asked if he could guard them round the clock, but John said he'd only be required at the studio. McClain commented: 'If only I had been there, maybe I could have helped.'

McClain has cut a gospel album and says: '(John) doesn't know how much he helped me. He left a big impact on me as far as songwriting is concerned. He found out I was a musician and I sang him a few bars of gospel.'

John told James he liked his voice and looked forward to hearing his record.

Steve McDowell Art dealer from Seattle who, together with Ken Kinnear, manager of Heart, bought four *Bag One* sets at a cost of 300,000 dollars and arranged for them to be used as a touring exhibit in a hundred American cities. One twelfth of the admission price was donated to the Spirit Foundation. The lithographs proved too much for the police department at Providence, Long Island, and they closed the exhibition when it opened in their jurisdiction.

Marshall McLuhan This renowned authority on communication and the media died in the 'seventies. The Canadian-born lecturer/author was also noted for his books concerning communication such as *Understanding Media* and *The Medium Is The Message*. Whilst a professor at the University of Toronto, he invited John to visit him on 19 December 1969 to participate in an interview which was filmed by CBS Television. John and McLuhan spent 45 miutes discussing numerous subjects from peace to music as the camera whirred. As John left, McLuhan escorted him to the door with the words, 'These portals have been honoured by your presence'.

Keith McMillan Originally a dancer with the Royal Ballet, Keith took to photography. His first contact with John came when Anthony Fawcett with whom he'd worked previously on art assignments, called him to take photographs for the Acorn Catalogue being compiled for the National Sculpture Exhibition at Coventry Cathedral.

He was then commissioned to take pictures of the actual event. Keith also took the official photographs for the 'You Are Here' exhibition and currently works as a freelance for the major British magazines.

Norman Mailer Prominent contemporary American writer who was one of the many celebrities who spoke up in defence of John at the hearing at the Immigration and Naturalization Service Building in New York on 27 July 1976 when John was finally granted his green card. Mailer appreciated John's talent and stated that it would be a pity if America lost it. Following John's death, he told *Rolling Stone* magazine: 'We have lost a genius of the Spirit.'

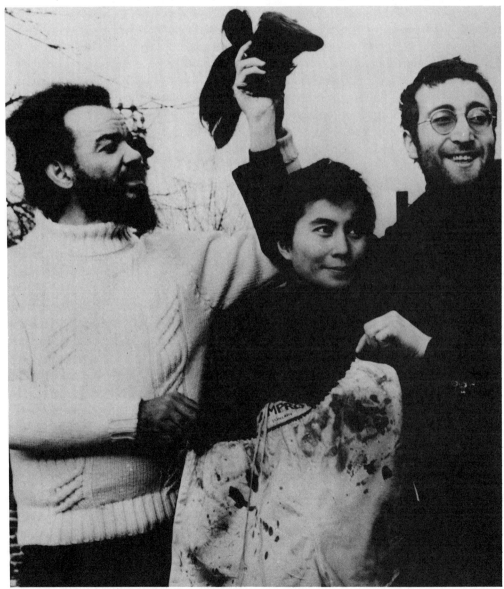

The best of the crop — Lenono hair for Michael X.

Michael Abdul Malik Controversial figure known as Michael X, a Black Power revolutionary in Britain, who was one of the several causes with which John and Yoko involved themselves. They met him in 1969 and were interested in his project of organizing a centre for Black Culture in London, which he called The Black House. They gave him moral and financial support in the venture, and cut their hair short and donated it to him on 20 January 1970.

Soon afterwards, The Black House was burnt down in a mysterious fire. Michael X was arrested and charged with robbery and demanding money with menaces. He'd already had experience of being 'inside', having spent a term of three years in jail, and jumped bail in January 1971. The Lennons had provided the bail for Malik, but despite this, they continued to support him.

He moved on to Trinidad where he started a commune and the Lennons visited him there. The commune burnt down in February 1972. But it proved a more serious case than that of the burning of The Black House, as two corpses were discovered in the rubble. One of them was Gail Ann Benson, daughter of an ex-Member of Parliament, Captain L.F. Plugge.

Malik was convicted of her murder in 1975. John Lennon paid for a lawyer, William Kunstler, to fly to Trinidad to defend Malik and he also wrote to the authorities in Trinidad to plead for Michael X's life. To no avail. Michael X was hung in 1975.

Years later, a bizarre story began to link various threads to produce a conspiracy theory. Gail Ann Benson first met Michael X's friend Hakim Jamal at The Black House. The couple then began to live together and travelled first to Morocco, then to Paris. In Paris they associated with film star Jean Seberg and it was rumoured that they were involved in a *menage-à-trois* with her. Gail and Hakim next went on to Trinidad to join Michael X.

Jamal left them to go on a trip to America and while he was away Benson and X became lovers. Three weeks later her body was found. The next year Jamal was murdered in Massachusetts and Jean Seberg was discovered dead in her car in 1979. The following year John was killed.

By overstretching their imaginations, some people in America began to suggest that the deaths of Hakim, Seberg and Lennon were connected by a conspiracy to avenge the death of Gail Ann Benson.

Jayne Mansfield Pneumatic blonde promoted by Hollywood as another Monroe, and most famous among Rock fans for her performance in *The Girl Can't Help It*. May Mann, in her biography *Jayne Mansfield*, claims that on The Beatles' first American tour John Lennon mentioned that the one film star he wanted to see was Jayne Mansfield. A rendezvous between the star and the group took place at the Whiskey A Go Go on Sunset Strip. Mann further claims that John was annoyed when Jayne brought her husband along and said: 'I just wanted to be alone with Jayne. I've dreamed about it.'

Other sources suggest that it was Paul, not John, who made the original request. Perhaps May Mann got the two mixed up because the famous photograph of the meeting at the Whiskey pictures Jayne and John sitting together.

In fact, when The Beatles were staying at the Hollywood suburb of Bel Air it

We took the wrong turning, actually. We were looking for the cloakroom.

was Jayne, dressed in a mauve cat suit, who dropped in to see them. John was the only member of the group present and she tugged John's hair and squealed, 'Is this real?' to which John replied, dropping his eyes to her most famous features, 'Well, are *those* real?'

Mao Tse-tung Communist Chinese leader known as Chairman Mao who since the end of the Second World War led Communist China. He ruled the vast country until his death in the 'seventies. Mao (together with John and President Kennedy) was one of three prominent 20th century figures to be selected by the BBC for their television documentary, *Man Of The Decade.* John also had a daring mock-up photograph made of a naked Chairman Mao dancing with an equally naked President Nixon for display on his *Some Time In New York City* album.

Alexis Mardas Blond, Greek electronics expert, first introduced to John by John Dunbar. His initial gimmicky inventions amused The Beatles, who were also intrigued by his claims of electronic wizardry and descriptions of inventions which he would be able to conjure up if he had the money. When Apple was established, Magic Alex (as he came to be called) was engaged to head the Electronics Division. He was 27 at the time.

He was apparently an engaging chap whose head was bursting with ideas. Unfortunately, few of them ever actually saw the light of day. They included a force field, a sonic screen, paint that glowed, a computerized telephone that dialed on vocal command, transistorized speakers without wires, and radios in the shape of apples. One of his 'toys' which amused John was a 'Nothing Box', which produced a series of flashing red lights.

The Electronics Division of Apple was literally a one-man-band, yet it devoured tens of thousands of pounds, whilst Alexis led a life of comparative luxury in a £20,000 house that John had bought.

He travelled with The Beatles to Rishikesh. It was he who told John that the Maharishi had made advances to Mia Farrow, with the result that John confronted the guru and left India. The fact that John trusted Alexis is evident. He preferred to accept the Greek's insinuations and refused to tell the Maharishi of what he was accusing him.

John was later to send Magic Alex off to Greece for a holiday with Cynthia, Donovan and Donovan's friend Gypsy. When the group arrived back at Kenwood, Yoko was there. Cynthia went off for a holiday to Italy with Julian and her mother and John heard further rumours from Alexis, who told him that Cynthia was having an affair with an Italian.

John sent Alexis across to Italy to tell Cynthia that he was divorcing her, taking Julian from her and sending her back to live in Hoylake with her mother. As it turned out, he discovered that Alexis' suggestions were unfounded and as Yoko had become pregnant, John agreed to a divorce on Cynthia's terms.

At Apple, Magic Alex had promised The Beatles he would provide them with their own space-age recording studio, complete with a 72-track recording machine. They were naturally impressed as they had been recording on a four-track in Britain.

There was already an eight-track in America and technology was ready to introduce a sixteen track machine. But a 72-track! They were all keen for Alexis to get on with the job.

However, time went by and nothing transpired. The group wanted to record 'Let It Be' in their own studio, so they turned to George Martin for advice. George, who referred to Alexis as a sycophant, told them he could bring in a mobile recording unit. He did so and he installed it in their Savile Row premises.

When Allen Klein entered the picture he swiftly gave Magic Alex his marching orders.

Margo Surname unknown. A German girl who reputedly dated John in Hamburg. George Tremlett in *The John Lennon Story* quotes a musician named Tony Dangerfield who was in Hamburg at the time.

'John used to go round with a big fat chick called Margo, who used to go everywhere with him,' says Dangerfield. 'He pulled her out of the audience one night — all the English musicians had German chicks. It was like a colony of English yobboes and German chicks.'

George Melly Liverpool jazz singer who penned John's obituary for *Punch* magazine on 12 December 1980. George and John had met on several occasions, although they nearly came to blows once at a publisher's party over George's review of *In His Own Write*. George also appeared on a television show with Yoko.

When Derek Taylor was involved with WEA Records he struck up a friendship with George and promoted the singer on the label. During a trip to Los Angeles with Derek, George once again met John and the two of them spent the night reminiscing about Liverpool and discussing a Liverpool wrestler called Jackie Pye.

Annie Millward John's maternal grandmother.

Jeff Mohammed When John first entered the art college, he teamed up with a couple of kindred spirits, one of whom was Jeff Mohammed. They got up to mischief in much the same way that John and Pete Shotton had done at Quarry Bank School. John, commenting in *The Authorised Biography* on his initial attempts to woo Cynthia, mentions the class Christmas party of 1958, saying, 'We had a class dance. I was pissed and asked her to dance. Jeff Mohammed had been having me on, saying "Cynthia likes you, you know". As we danced I asked her to come to a party the next day. She said she couldn't. She was engaged.'

In his *Playboy* interview, John mentioned that he had heard that Jeff had died.

David Moore Milkman for John, Cynthia and Julian Lennon when the trio lived in Weybridge, Surrey. Moore said, 'I see most of my customers every day, but I have seen the Lennons only once. To satisfy my own curiosity, I have always tried to get John to pay the bill over the doorstep, but the cook always comes to the door and says they will send a cheque to the head office. When I did see him, it was rather a shock. Living in a mansion like that, I expected him to be dressed really smart — but all he wore was a black roll-neck jumper and jeans.'

Ron Morgan Man who brought John's Bentley for 50,000 dollars. He exhibited the car for ten weeks in Las Vegas before sending it on a tour of the US.

John Munro Canadian Minister of Health in 1969 when John and Yoko visited the country. Following their meeting with Prime Minister Trudeau, the duo went for a conference with Munro and members of his department and the press. Among the topics for discussion was the generation gap and the use of soft drugs.

Bas Muys Dutch singer who impersonated John Lennon on the hit 'Stars On 45' Beatles' medley single.

David Nutter British Photographer who was regularly commissioned to take photographs of John and Yoko on behalf of Apple, including shots of them at EMI Studios signing with Allen Klein and around the Apple building. One of his most important sessions was the John and Yoko wedding, of which he commented: 'I got this James Bond type phone call asking me to pack my bags and camera and catch the first plane to Gibraltar. No names were given and I had to try and guess who it was. I had one camera and one lens and when I found out it was for John I was as nervous as hell.'

Tommy Nutter Fashionable West End tailor to the stars. Cilla Black was one of the original investors in his business, which is situated in Savile Row, close to the former Apple building.

Apart from The Beatles, Nutter's regular clients included Twiggy and Elton John. Nutter has related how John and Yoko arrived in his shop one day to try on their identical white wedding suits. Much to the amazement and eye-popping interest of the customers and passers-by, the duo stripped naked in the shop in order to try on their new clothes.

Claes Oldenburg American conceptual artist and Pop Art painter whom John and Yoko met for the second time at one of his London exhibitions.

Keisuke Ono Yoko's younger brother born in December 1936.

Setsuko Ono Yoko's younger sister born in December 1941.

Yoko Ono Yoko, whose name means 'Ocean Child', was born in Japan on 18 February 1934 (although some sources claim it was 1933). Her parents were Eisuke Ono and his wife Isoko, both of whose families were prominent in the Japanese banking world. Her brother Keisuke was born in December 1936 and her sister Setsuko in December 1941. When Yoko was 2½ years old she was taken to America, as her father was working in a bank over there. Isoko returned to her home country with her children when Japan invaded China, for she was afraid of anti-Japanese feeling in America. She went back to San Francisco with her children for a short time and Yoko attended school there. The family then had to return to Tokyo in 1943 due to the impending war.

As her family was rich and influential, Yoko didn't suffer the hardships of many of the Japanese people during the war; she continued with her education, becoming fluent in English. After the war the family returned to America, settling in the high-class Scarsdale area outside New York where Yoko attended the Sarah Lawrence School in 1953. The

Yoko: the Ocean Child.

19-year-old girl didn't like the school and left in her third year to live in Manhattan with a young Japanese composer and musician, Toshi Ichiyanagi, whom she married. The marriage was short-lived, although during it Yoko gave signs of the strength of character and leadership evident in her later life. She encouraged Toshi in his musical career and talked him into returning to Japan where he received a degree of acclaim. The couple were divorced in 1963.

Yoko continued living in Chambers Street in New York, becoming part of an artistic sect called Fluxus, composed of painters, musicians and writers. She began to hold concerts and art exhibitions of her own, gaining a reputation as a creative conceptual artist. She married a film producer, Tony Cox, and they had a daughter named Kyoko. In September 1966 the family moved to London to further Yoko's career. Even at this time it was very much a case of

Yoko being the strong partner, advancing her career while her husband looked after the child. Yoko began to involve herself in 'happenings' in London and also gained a degree of notoriety in the media for her film *Bottoms*. She had also, by this time, had a small book of conceptual ideas called *Grapefruit* published in a limited edition in America.

It was during the preview of her exhibition at the Indica Gallery on 9 November 1966 that the famous meeting with John took place. Yoko was relatively unaware of the phenomenon which The Beatles had become and was initially unimpressed when the gallery's co-owner John Dunbar urged her to speak to the 'millionaire'. The much reported incident of hammering in the imaginary nail took place and each realized that they had found a kindred spirit. In September 1967 John was to sponsor her 'Half-Wind Show', which she subtitled 'Yoko Plus Me'.

It was in May 1968 when Tony Cox and Kyoko were in France, that John invited Yoko to the house in Weybridge. He suggested they go upstairs to make experimental tapes, which they were to call 'Two Virgins'. Yoko reported: 'It was midnight when we started and it was dawn when we finished and then we made love.' John's wife Cynthia arrived home to find Yoko in a dressing gown. She left. There was a brief attempt at a reconciliation, but it didn't work out and Cynthia began divorce proceedings. John and Yoko moved into Ringo's London flat and Yoko began involving John in her conceptual creations, beginning with their acorn sculpture idea at Coventry Cathedral. The two were first seen in public when

John takes the cake from Yoko on his 31st birthday.

they attended the premiere of the play *In His Own Write* on 18 June. The press took an immediate dislike to Yoko, and thus began the snide and hurtful comments which were to continue for more than a decade and were among the number of reasons which clinched the couple's decision to live in New York.

In July, John held an exhibition called 'You Are Here — To Yoko From John, With Love'. Yoko was pregnant at the time, and when she was admitted to Queen Charlotte's Hospital later that month, John took to sleeping on the floor next to her bed. Unfortunately she had a miscarriage — and was to have two further ones before she eventually bore John a child. Before the year's end they had issued their *Two Virgins* album, telerecorded The Rolling Stones' *Rock & Roll Circus* and appeared on stage at the Albert Hall in the 'Alchemical Wedding'. The two were to

At home on the streets of New York.

John is leading by a tie.

continue to work jointly in the creative and business fields, making records and films together, forming companies such as Bag One and Lenono, with Yoko appearing on 'b' sides of John's singles, on his albums and also recording five LPs in her own right.

In 1969 they continued to dominate the headlines, appearing on stage during a jazz concert in Cambridge and getting married in Gibraltar on 20 March — which they celebrated by holding their 'Bed-In For Peace' in Amsterdam. By May of that year John had officially changed his name to John Ono Lennon and the couple had moved into a large estate in Ascot called Tittenhurst Park. Following a trip to Montreal, the couple took John's son Julian and Kyoko on a visit to Scotland during which the car crashed, but no one was seriously hurt.

The Wedding Album, Live Peace In Toronto and The War Is Over occupied the remaining months of 1969, and in 1970, the year which they christened Year One, they gained further notoriety when John's lithographs, some of them showing him in intimate sexual embrace with Yoko, were seized by the police. They also underwent Primal Therapy in America. In 1971 Yoko and John appeared with Frank Zappa at the Fillmore East in New York, and began their efforts to obtain custody of Kyoko. It was during their search for Yoko's daughter that they decided to remain in America, settling in New York and beginning a battle for John to obtain his Green Card. They made various films and records over the next few years, but the major event in their lives was the birth of Sean Ono Lennon on 9 October 1975. Sean had been born following

their reunion after a period of eighteen months during which John had left Yoko to live with May Pang.

John decided to spend the next five years looking after Sean while Yoko attended to the couple's business affairs. While John reared Sean in their apartments in the Dakota Building, Yoko worked in the Lenono office on the ground floor of the building, turning their money into a vast fortune of over one hundred million dollars, with various astute business ventures which included buying farms and breeding cattle.

After the fatal shooting, Yoko remained at the Dakota, having to employ bodyguards to look after Sean on a round-the-clock basis. She administered the huge funds which were donated on John's behalf to the Spirit Foundation, sending the money to various charities. She also began work on securing a memorial to John in Central Park, to be called Strawberry Fields.

Interior designer Sam Havadtoy became her constant companion and rumours of their impending marriage have persisted. She became involved in consultations regarding TV movies of her life with John, but in 1983 became so sickened by the number of kiss-and-tell books which attempted to cheapen the relationship she'd had with John for so many years, that she left New York in September 1983 to settle in San Francisco.

May Pang Chinese-American girl who first met John and Yoko while working in Allen Klein's office in New York. It was in the latter part of 1970 and John and Yoko asked her to enter their employ, and she began involving herself in their movie production company.

She then became their secretary. When John had turned 33 years of age, he suddenly fled to Los Angeles with May and for the period described as his 'eighteen months Long Weekend', she became his mistress.

She also continued to act as his secretary and helped to organize some of his West Coast recording projects. She was credited as production co-ordinator of the *Walls And Bridges* and *Rock 'n' Roll* albums.

When John returned to Yoko, May resettled in New York where she became professional manager of United Artists Music.

Following John's death she became friendly with Cynthia Lennon and accompanied her to some conventions and exhibitions of Cynthia's artwork. Her book *Loving John — The Untold Story* written with Henry Edwards, was published in America by Warner Books in October 1983.

Kenneth Partridge British interior designer whom John and Cynthia employed to furnish their Kenwood house in St George's Hill from top to bottom.

Joe Pecorino Actor/musician who took the role of John Lennon in the 1977 New York show *Beatlemania*. The other lookalikes were Mitchell Weissman (Paul McCartney), Leslie Fradkin (George Harrison) and Justin McNeill (Ringo Starr). There were 29 Lennon-McCartney numbers featured in the show by The Beatle lookalikes and five additional backup musicians.

David Peel American musician who first met John in New York in 1971 and started a Beatles Liberation Force. He was with a friend, Howard Smith, in the Limbo Shop in the East Village when he was introduced to John. He met him several times in the company of Jerry Rubin and Abbie Hoffman, and John arranged for him to record for Apple. His album *The Pope Smokes Dope* on which he was backed by The Apple Band was issued in April 1972 and the tracks included 'Keep John Lennon In America' and 'The Fat Budgie'. The latter was the poem from John's second book *A Spaniard In The Works*, to which Peel had added music. The LP also featured a Lennon/Ono composition 'The Ballad Of New York City'.

Peel also ran his own record label, Orange Records, and his releases included the albums *Bring Back The Beatles* (ORA 004) and *John Lennon For President* (ORA 005). He also had a band called The Lower East Side which he sometimes called The Lower East Side Ono Band.

Thelma Pickles Attractive student at Liverpool College of Art while John was in attendance. For a short time she was one of John's girl friends and later related her impressions of John's character and charisma in those art college days to the Beatles' authorized biographer, Hunter Davies.

'I knew he could be famous at something,' she commented 'but I didn't know what. He was so different and original. But I just couldn't see what he could be famous at. Perhaps a comedian, I thought.'

Thelma was later married to Roger McGough, one of Liverpool's premier poets, who was also a member of the popular and successful trio The Scaffold, of which Mike McGear, Paul McCartney's brother, was a member.

William Pobjoy Sympathetic headmaster at Quarry Bank High School. He was appointed in 1956 when he was 35, during John's fifth year at the school. John was surprised that Mr Pobjoy made a genuine attempt to communicate with him, took an interest in his music and didn't treat him as a tearaway.

John and Pete Shotton were, in fact, a pair of troublemakers at the school, but the headmaster only caned John once. When John failed all his O levels, Mr Pobjoy was surprised and disappointed. Aware of John's latent talent in art, he sought to help him further. He later said: 'I thought he was capable of passing (his exams). He only failed them by one grade. This was probably one of the reasons I helped to get him into art college. I knew he was good at art and felt he deserved a chance.'

Mr Pobjoy then arranged for Mimi Smith, John's aunt, to visit him at the school to discuss John's future. He suggested to her that he would attempt to find John a place at the college if she would agree to support him during his first year there.

Aunt Mimi agreed, William Pobjoy made the arrangements and John began his first term at Liverpool College of Art in September 1957.

Martin Polden John's defence counsel at Marylebone Court, London on 28 November 1968 when John was fined £150 with 20 guineas costs after pleading guilty to possessing cannabis. Roger Frisby, the prosecutor, accepted Yoko's plea of not guilty. Polden commented: 'He (John) is a public figure, but he stands before you in a private capacity. I hope by accepting that he did make efforts to cleanse himself that you will see the charge in its true perspective.'

Steve Potter Massachusetts dairy farmer who at an auction in Syracuse, New York on 2 July 1980 bought a single Holstein-Friesland cow belonging to John and Yoko for 265,000 dollars. This was the largest amount paid for a Holstein cow up to that date.

Tony Powell One of Cynthia Lennon's two brothers, the other was named Charles. Together with his wife Margaret he attended Cynthia and John's wedding.

Princess Margaret Sister of Britain's Queen Elizabeth. John's name for her was Priceless Margarine. The Princess was present at the Royal Variety Performance on 4 November 1963 when John, acting on the advice of a veteran comedian on the show, decided to make a humorous comment.

'On this next number I want you all to join in. Would those in the cheap seats clap their hands. The rest of you can rattle your jewellery.' It had the desired effect and the wit of Lennon was widely quoted.

The Princess also attended the world première of A Hard Day's Night at the London Pavilion on 6 July 1964 and returned to the cinema the next year on 29 July for the world première of Help!. She visited Twickenham Studios on 4 March 1969 to watch Ringo Starr and Peter Sellers during the making of The Magic Christian and also attended the world première of the film at the Odeon, Kensington on 12 December 1969.

The Quarrymen John's first band, a skiffle group. Skiffle was a phenomenon which occurred in Britain in the early fifties. It was a type of music based on American folk and railroad songs, performed on simple instruments: washboard, tea-chest bass, guitars and drums. The music engulfed Britain for a few years, throwing up hit recording acts such as Lonnie Donegan, Nancy Whiskey and Chas. McDevitt And The Vipers.

There were numerous skiffle bands on Merseyside including the Darktown Skiffle, the Gin Mill Skiffle and the Ed Clayton Skiffle Group. John formed the band while he was in the fifth form of Quarry Bank School and their name was adopted from the school's own song in which there was a line, 'Quarry Men strong before our birth'.

The initial personnel comprised John and his close friend Pete Shotton. John played guitar and Pete was the rather reluctant washboard player.

They were soon joined by other friends, including Ivan Vaughan who occasionally played tea-chest bass in place of Nigel Whalley, Eric Griffiths on bass guitar, Rodney Davis on banjo and Colin Hanton on drums.

Once the group had begun playing at local youth clubs there were one or two line-up changes. Nigel Whalley assumed the informal post of manager and Len Gary took over on tea-chest bass. Visiting cards were printed, emblazoned with the message: 'Available for engagements. Country. Western. Rock 'n' Roll. Skiffle. THE QUARRYMEN.'

Ivan brought along his Liverpool Institute schoolfriend Paul McCartney to the Saturday afternoon gig at the St Peter's church village fete in Woolton. The date was 6 July 1957 and Paul remembers the smell of beer on John's breath.

Paul joined them to play a few numbers and John was impressed by the fact that he knew how to tune a guitar and was able to write out the complete lyrics to some of the popular songs. Paul was asked to join the group when Pete Shotton was making his exit, following an incident in which John smashed the washboard over Pete's head. There were no hard feelings and Pete was relieved to be leaving.

The line-up changed and by the time the group made their debut at the Casbah Club in Heyman's Green, West Derby, they had a basic line-up of John, Paul and George (who had joined them in August 1958) with occasional drummers. There had been one or two temporary name changes but The Quarrymen name was finally abandoned and they became, for a short time, the Silver Beetles, the Silver Beatles and finally, with the inclusion of Pete Best in 1960 and their debut in Hamburg, The Beatles!

The Reverend Fred and Ada Gerkin Names used by John and Yoko when they were travelling in the 'seventies.

Lisa Robinson American journalist who interviewed John shortly before his death. She was also interviewed on the US TV programme *The Tomorrow Show* on 9 December reminiscing about John's years as a househusband.

Todd Rundgren Philadelphian guitarist who formed The Nazz in 1968 before making a number of solo albums such as *Runt* and *Runt, The Ballad Of Todd Runtgren*. He recorded 'Strawberry Fields Forever' on his 1976 album *Faithful*.

John called him Turd Runtgreen following a short feud between the two of them conducted in the pages of *Melody Maker* when, in the 14 September 1974 issue, Rodd began the attack with a tirade laced with four-letter words: 'John Lennon ain't no revolutionary. He's a f****** idiot. Shouting about revolution and acting like a ****. It just makes people feel uncomfortable.' John sent a lengthy letter answering the criticism, which was printed in the 28 September issue. He said: 'I think the real reason you're mad at me is because I didn't know who you were at the Rainbow, LA.'

Jerry Rubin American radical of the 'sixties who was involved in the Berkeley Vietnam Day Teach-In in 1965. He was one of the defendants in the Chicago Eight Trial and co-founder with Abbie Hoffman of the Youth International Party.

When he read that John and Yoko were in New York, he contacted them and introduced them to Abbie Hoffman. He spent some time with them discussing American politics and claims that they then made him their political adviser.

As a result, the couple became involved in a number of political causes such as a campaign to free the imprisoned John Sinclair, leader of the White Panthers. When John and Yoko appeared on a benefit concert for Sinclair at Ann Arbour, Jerry Rubin played congas during their set. He also advised them on the political figures they were to interview when they were offered their own short series of spots on the TV Programme *The Mike Douglas Show*.

The influence of Rubin is evident in the contents of *Sometime In New York City* and John's involvement with the radicals contributed to the campaign to have him deported from the US.

Bertrand Russell Famous British philosopher and pacifist who died in February 1970. In 1969 when John was involved in his peace campaign, he wrote a letter to Russell asking for his help. Russell replied, congratulating him on the way he was using the media to present his views on peace and also for his stance on Vietnam and Biafra.

David Stuart Ryan Author of the book *John Lennon's Secret*. A European copy director for Time-Life Books, David had been writing for publications such as *International Times* in the 'sixties, had won the International Poetry Contest in 1974 and had published a novel about the demise of the swinging sixties called *The Affair Is All*.

Of his Lennon book, his blurb commented: 'John Lennon's Secret was researched in London, Liverpool and via phone in the USA. The author knew many of the people and places mentioned in the book during the 'sixties — the arts lab, where John and Yoko held their first joint exhibition, UFO, Electric Garden, Michael X etc.'

Robert Ryan Late American film actor whose movies included *The Dirty Dozen* and *The Tall Men*. John and Yoko moved into the apartment he vacated in the Dakota Building after the death of his wife through cancer. John and Yoko reputedly held a seance soon after moving in and contacted the spirit of Mrs Ryan. Yoko then got in touch with the Ryans' daughter, Lisa, to tell her how her mother was progressing on 'the other side', but the gesture wasn't appreciated.

Peter Sanders Artist who drew figures for a TV series of cartoons on The Beatles' songs in 1964. He did many sketch studies of John with such observations as: 'pulls funny faces, especially after giving orders, which he immediately wipes off'; 'John never sits, he slouches'; 'John moves with fast, jerky, almost aggressive movements'; 'When facing front he uses a sly, sideways look to talk to somebody' and 'John, especially when delivering important lines, really looks the leader. Feet apart, hands on hips, chin up, looking down his nose with a slightly mocking expression'.

Nicholas Schaffner New York author who specializes in writing books about The Beatles and their world. His first work was *The Beatles Forever*, an encyclopaedic biography of their life, illustrated with 400 photographs. He followed with *The Lads From Liverpool*, a basic biography written with the younger reader in mind. His *The British Invasion* concerned the heyday of the first wave of British bands to hit America in the 'sixties. In 1983 his collaboration with John's childhood friend Pete Shotton was published in America by Stein & Day, entitled, *John Lennon: In My Life*.

Fred Seaman Acted as aide to John and Yoko. After leaving their employ he was arrested for stealing various items from the Dakota apartment, including John's diaries. He was sentenced to five years probation in July 1983. All of the diaries, with the exception of the diary for 1980, were returned to Yoko. Judge Jeffrey Atlas ordered Seaman not to reveal their contents under threat of a seven year jail sentence. Seaman's book *Living With Lennon* was published in America by Simon & Schuster in January 1984.

David Sheff Young journalist commissioned by G Barry Golson, *Playboy's* executive editor to conduct a Playboy interview with John Lennon in 1980. The Boston-born Sheff had to submit his time and place of birth to enable Yoko to check his horoscope before she granted him permission for the series of interview sessions to take place. Sheff spent three weeks with John and Yoko in September 1980 during which he taped over 24 hours of material. The edited interview appeared in the issue of *Playboy* dated January 1981 issued in America the day before John was killed.

A fuller version of the tapes' contents was published in book form by The Playboy Press in America in 1981 and by New English Library in England during the same year, under the title *The Playboy Interviews With John Lennon And Yoko Ono*.

Don Short *Daily Mirror* show-business columnist of the 'sixties who tracked The Beatles all round the world in search of a good story. Although he covered the entire pop music scene, he seemed particularly to like covering three subjects: The Beatles, the Miss World contests and the location filming of the James Bond films. In fact, he went on to write a book about the Miss World contests, in addition to ghosting Britt Eckland's bestseller *True Britt*. He left the *Mirror* to form his own highly successful freelance agency, Solo.

When John took his second LSD trip

I think he's got a Spaniard in the works.

in Hollywood, he later reported: 'There was a reporter, Don Short. We were in the garden; it was only our second one (LSD trip) and we still didn't know anything about doing it in a nice place and keeping it cool.'

Then they saw the reporter and thought, 'How do we act?'

'We were terrified waiting for him to go, and he wondered why we couldn't come over. Neil (Aspinall), who had never had acid either, had taken it and he would have to play road manager. We said, "Go get rid of Don Short," and he didn't know what to do.'

Anthony Fawcett in his book *One Day At A Time* relates how, when Apple was being planned at Wimpole Street, John and Yoko, Paul and Neil Aspinall were in a room drinking coffee and checking the proofs of The Beatles' biography when one of the *Daily Mirror's* top show biz reporters appeared in the doorway with his photographer.

John and Paul, both apparently horrified at the unannounced intrusion, muttered in unison, 'Get 'im out.'

'Just a quick photo, boys,' he pleaded, while the photographer took aim.

'And what's all this big business you're getting into?' I was surprised when John shouted at him sarcastically, 'Get out, we're not telling you anything.'

Nevertheless, the very next day a complete page of the *Daily Mirror* carried a story 'The Big Business Beatles' with a large by-line for Don Short.

A few days after John's death, a week-long series of articles on John began on 11 December in the *Sun* newspaper, under the by-line 'By Don Short — The Man who shared his secrets.'

The series was syndicated and a small excerpt entitled, 'The Lighter Side Of John Lennon' was contained in the Proteus book *A Tribute To John Lennon 1940-1980.*

Pete Shotton Blond-haired childhood friend of John whose reminiscences are to be found in his book *John Lennon: In My Life*, published by Stein and Day in America in the autumn of 1983. The book was written in collaboration with Nicholas Schaffner, author of *The Beatles Forever* and *The Lads From Liverpool.*

John and Pete first met when they were seven years old and the encounter turned into a rough and tumble fight because Shotton, knowing that John's middle name was Winston, teased him by calling him 'Winnie'. As Pete lived in Vale Street, quite close to John's house in Menlove Avenue, they took to playing together after school and forming a gang.

When John entered Quarry Bank Grammar School at the age of 12, Pete was in the same class and the two became almost inseparable for a time, playing truant together and engaging in various mischievous pranks. They were also members of the choir of St Peter's Church in Woolton and of its Sunday school and Youth club.

In 1956, John formed a two-man skiffle band of himself and Pete. It was the first line-up of The Quarrymen with Pete on washboard. The group was then enlarged. Apparently, Pete's heart was never entirely into playing with the band and he didn't mind too much when his musical career came to an abrupt end as John, drunk at a party, smashed the washboard over Shotton's head.

The close relationship waned with Pete's departure from the group, to be replaced by John's partnership with Paul. However, John and Pete kept in touch with each other over the years and John put up the money for his friend to run a supermarket in Haylings Island in 1966.

He later arranged for Pete to be put in charge of the Apple Boutique although the latter position didn't turn out to be a success and Pete returned to the supermarket.

Johnny Silver Name John was purported to have used during a brief period when The Silver Beatles used pseudonyms in an attempt to smarten up their image, perhaps inspired by the Larry Parnes method of creating new names for each of his discoveries, such as Johnny Gentle, with whom they toured.

Whilst backing Gentle, Paul called himself Paul Ramon, George was Carl Harrison and Stu Sutcliffe adopted the name Stu Da Stael.

In Hunter Davies' authorized biography, he mentions that John denied he used the name Johnny Silver, but the other members of the group said he did.

John took the trouble to write a letter to Roy Carr and Tony Tyler for a new edition of their book *The Beatles: An Illustrated Record*. He sent a clipping from a gig at the Neston Institute on Merseyside immediately following their Johnny Gentle tour (they were now calling themselves The Beatles) which seems to bear him out. 'I was *never* . . . repeat *never* known as *Johnny Silver*. I *always* preferred my own name,' he wrote.

Frank Sinatra American singer/actor and one of the major International stars of the twentieth century. On hearing of John's death, he commented: 'It was a staggering moment when I heard the news. Lennon was a most talented man and above all, a gentle soul. John and his colleagues set a high standard by which contemporary music continues to be measured.'

John Sinclair American founder of The White Panthers. A poet, but also a radical and one of the numerous people looked upon with disfavour by the Nixon administration. The chance to put him behind bars came when an undercover policewoman managed to entice him into giving her two joints of marijuana. As a result, he was sentenced to ten years in prison. Jerry Rubin explained John Sinclair's predicament to

John and asked him to appear at a benefit at the University of Michigan in Ann Arbor on 11 December 1971. John and Yoko turned up at the demonstration and soon began to voice their feelings at the unfairness of the sentence. Public pressure began to mount and Sinclair was released on a legal technicality. John also penned a song about him which is included on the *Some Time In New York City* album.

George Smith A father figure to John. George was married to John's Aunt Mimi, who took John into her home as a small boy when his mother Julia went to live with a waiter. Uncle George became the closest thing to a father John ever had. George ran his own dairy business in Woolton village, and the relationship he had with his nephew was very comforting. He bought John his first mouth organ. John was deeply shaken when, in 1953, George died suddenly of a haemorrhage

Howard Smith American talk show host. John appeared on his WPLJ radio programme on 6 June 1971.

Kris Smith American sculptor who produced a limited edition of a sculpted bust of John, 9 inches high, in 1981. A portion of the purchase price was donated to The Spirit Foundation in respect of Yoko Ono Lennon and to John's memory.

Mimi Smith One of the five Stanley sisters, another being Julia, John's mother. Mimi was Julia's elder sister and was quite excited by the birth of John, even venturing out during an air-raid to walk to the hospital to see her new nephew.

Mimi married a dairy farmer, George Smith, and moved from the family home in Newcastle Road to join her husband at the pleasant semi-detached house Mendips in Menlove Avenue, near to her husband's business in Woolton.

The couple never had a child of their own and were therefore delighted when the opportunity of rearing John presented itself. John was five years old when Julia placed him in the care of her sister.

The marriage between her and Alfred Lennon had long since been judged a failure and she'd had another child which she'd given away and now wanted to live with a man called John Dykin.

Freddie had in fact intended to take John to New Zealand. John had stayed at his Aunt Mimi's place on and off for some time and Freddie had asked to have John with him for a short holiday in Blackpool, to which Mimi consented.

When the New Zealand plan came up, Julia went to Blackpool and brought John back, placing him with Mimi for good. Mimi and George then brought up John as their own son.

Mimi often despaired at John's rebellious nature and at his poor school results, although teachers always impressed upon her that John had talent as an artist.

At his junior school, when handing Mimi a bundle of John's drawings, the teacher commented: 'The perspective is amazing for a boy of eleven.'

Tragedy struck when Uncle George died of a haemorrhage in 1953 and Mimi had to take on the task of bringing up the strong-willed boy herself.

There was friction between them, for John was stubborn and rebellious and Mimi was anxious to bring him up in a responsible fashion, with sensible middle-class values.

Perhaps there was a bit of cruelty involved, too, as when she gave away his pet dog as a punishment.

It was Mimi who took Mr Pobjoy's advice and agreed to let John have an opportunity of studying at Liverpool College of Art. By this time she was aware of his interest in music. This didn't please her all that much, although she had bought him a guitar at Frank Hessy's for £18 when he was seventeen. She later threatened to throw this instrument into the dustbin.

John's interest in The Beatles gained her disapproval. She felt that the group would draw him away from his studies. She went to see the group at the Cavern and didn't like them. She told John, 'The guitar's all right as a hobby, but you'll never make a living out of it.' Later, John had this phrase engraved on a silver plaque and presented it to her.

Mimi was able to present John with an 'I told you so' speech when he returned from Hamburg penniless after promising her that he would be well paid. His days at Mendips were coming to an end. He shared flats with fellow students and then married Cynthia. While John was on the road Cynthia stayed with Mimi for a while but, by all accounts, preferred to return to the company of her own mother.

When The Beatles' success in Britain grew, John was determined to express his gratitude to Mimi for the love and dedication she had given to him in his formative years, and he bought her a home in Poole overlooking the harbour.

When he was awarded the MBE he sent his medal to Mimi because he knew she would appreciate it. He later asked for its return so that he could send the medal back to the palace.

Mimi was 67 years old when John died. She was saddened and appalled by the various smears which cropped up about John in subsequent books and articles. She decided to speak up on his behalf (to set the record straight) in a series of articles in the *Daily Star* newspaper in February 1981. She mentioned that John had phoned her the night before he died, that he had always asked for books, rather than toys, on his birthdays; that he paid for guitar lessons at five shillings a time out of his pocket money and that he tithed a tenth of his income each year to a charity for spastic children.

An insight was given into that magic moment when John charmed the media with his comments at the Royal Variety Show. Apparently, John already had a ready wit when he attended pantomimes in Liverpool. When a fairy who was a bit older than the others appeared on the stage, the eleven-year-old John shouted out, 'She's a bit old for a fairy, isn't she?' and when the principal boy strode on to the stage, John shouted, 'Why, he's got my wellies on!'

The Smothers Brothers Popular American duo. Tommy Smothers was among the celebrities John recruited for his backing choir on *Give Peace A Chance*, recorded in a Montreal hotel bedroom. Tommy was also at one time in 1969 interested in appearing with Ringo Starr in a film called *Captain Blood*.

In 1974, during John's long weekend (the period during which he left Yoko and moved to the West Coast with May Pang) John would regularly go on carousing sprees with hard-drinking friends such as Harry Nilsson and Keith Moon. It was at the Troubadour Club in March, accompanied by Nilsson, that he hit the world's headlines following an incident which occurred after he'd begun to heckle The Smothers Brothers. The duo had been appearing at the club as part of a Smothers Brothers revival and John, high on brandy Alexander's, shouted out, 'Dickie, you're an asshole.' Some scuffles and ugly scenes followed. John was to admit that he'd always liked Tommy, but he considered Dickie was 'a wimp'.

Sissy Spacek Leading American actress who starred in such films as *Coal Miner's Daughter* and *Carrie*. In 1969 under the name Rainbo she issued a single in which she was critical of the full frontal nude shot on the cover of the *Two Virgins* album. It was entitled 'John You Went Too Far This Time', coupled with 'C'mon Teach Me To Love'. The single was issued on Roulette 7030.

Phil Spector Born Harvey Philip Spector in New York on 25 December 1940, he became a millionaire before he was 21 because of his success in the recording industry.

He wrote and produced the number one hit 'To Know Him Is To Love Him' with the trio The Teddy Bears, of which he was a member, when he was 17.

Over the years he produced a series of hits such as 'He's A Rebel', 'Da Doo Ron Ron', 'You've Lost That Loving Feeling' and 'River Deep, Mountain High' for artists such as The Crystals, The Righteous Brothers and Ike And Tina Turner.

The man who had been called a 'teen genius' didn't have much success in the recording field in the middle and late 'sixties and had become somewhat reclusive.

He'd married Veronica 'Ronnie' Bennett of The Ronettes (who had toured with The Beatles in 1965) and lived in Los Angeles. In 1969 Allen Klein asked him to come to Apple to salvage something from the 24-hours of tapes which had become known as the 'get-back' tapes.

On 26 January 1970 John asked him to produce *Instant Karma* which he'd written that day and wished to record immediately. When the get-back tapes were issued as the album *Let It Be*, Spector came in for a lot of criticism and Paul McCartney considered that he'd ruined the track 'The Long & Winding Road'.

Spector went on to produce several albums and singles with both John and George Harrison. They included John's albums *John Lennon/Plastic Ono Band*, *Imagine* and *Some Time In New York City* and also *All Things Must Pass* and *The Concert For Bangla Desh* for George.

Among the singles he was involved with were: 'Instant Karma', 'Power To The People', 'Happy Xmas (War Is Over)', 'You Can't Catch Me', 'Sweet Little Sixteen', 'Bony Moronie', 'Just Because', 'Bangla Desh', 'Deep Blue', 'Try Some Buy Some', 'You', 'God Save Us' and 'Do The Oz'.

'Try Some Buy Some' and 'You' were numbers written by George Harrison which Phil attempted to use to revive his wife's career, but they didn't work out and George later used the backing tracks and sang lead vocals on the numbers himself.

When John went to Los Angeles in October 1973 he tried to persuade Spector to record an album of his favourite rock numbers. Spector had become an eccentric figure, rarely leaving his Santa Monica beach home and it took John an entire month to talk him into involving himself in the venture.

There are many stories concerning the sessions at Record Plant West including tales that Phil used to fire off a gun in the toilets, that he just didn't bother to turn up at the studios most of the time and he eventually ceased to attend the sessions, after taking possession of all the tapes.

At the time there were only nine incomplete songs on tape. John was unable to contact Spector, who'd left no telephone number and refused to admit anyone to his home.

Months passed during which John recorded a Harry Nilsson album and returned to New York.

He commented: 'There was a rumour that he had this dreadful car accident and with Phil one never knows if it really happened, or if it didn't happen, or if it just happened in his head.'

A few days before John began work on his *Walls And Bridges* album, Al Coury, president of Capitol Records, managed to secure the tapes by paying Spector two hundred thousand dollars and ten boxes of tapes were delivered to John. He found them almost unusable and there were only four tracks he considered he could include on an album, which was eventually issued as *Rock 'N' Roll*.

Victor Spinetti Welsh-born actor, writer, director and producer who was the only person apart from the Fab Four themselves, to appear in all three of their 'acting' films: *A Hard Day's Night*, *Help!*, and *Magical Mystery Tour*. He also appeared with John in the film *How I Won The War*.

Discussing how his long association

with The Beatles began, he explained: 'The lads saw the production I was in, *Oh What A Lovely War* and they said, "We want you in our film" and that was it!'

He followed his *Hard Day's Night* role as a panicky television director with the mad scientist character in *Help!* He was then asked to appear in *Magical Mystery Tour* of which he said, 'They wanted me to play the courier on the bus in *Magical Mystery Tour* so I would be travelling with them all the time. But I couldn't because I was doing a show in London, so I could only join them from London and go back there to do the show. Otherwise I would have loved to have gone on that whole trip, it would have been marvellous.

'I had to write my own script. I've got a letter from John somewhere saying, "We want you to be in this", and I said, "What can I do?" and he said "Well, write it yourself. You know, just do your own bits." I said, "Okay", so I did the drill-sergeant thing that I had done in *Oh What a Lovely War*, where I was portraying the kind of establishment figure who was telling them to get their hair cut, pull themselves together and behave like responsible people. In other words, be killers!'

By that time Victor was a close friend of all four members of the band, attended a number of their recording sessions and can be heard tap-dancing on their 1967 Christmas disc!

Victor next produced and co-authored a special stage version of John's two books. He said, 'A girl from Detroit called Adrienne Kennedy who wrote a play which was put on at the Royal Court Theatre came to see me when I was in London doing *The Odd Couple* and asked me to be in it. And I read it

and said, "Well, you know, if you are going to put this on stage you will have to do more than you have done". And I told her what I felt about a person growing up and his own reactions to family situations, schools etc. Because it's very autobiographical, the whole thing.

'And so she said, "Come and tell Ken Tynan", and I told Ken Tynan and he said, "Come and tell Laurence Olivier", and I told Laurence Olivier, and he said, "My dear baby, direct it for us!" So then I said to Adrienne, "Have you had permission from John to do this, turn it into a play?", and she said "No!".

'I said, "But you have to!" So I rang him up and asked him, and he said, "Yeah, okay. You got permission." And then he came to a rehearsal and became interested, and then we worked together on the script.

'At the rehearsal he in fact cried and said, "These were all the things that I was thinking about when I was 16," and he got involved in it and eventually we spent quite a bit of time together working on the script, writing out those little extra things that one needed for it.'

A book of the play, credited to Victor, Adrienne and John was published in 1968 by Jonathan Cape.

Incidentally, before the play was staged, John invited Victor to join himself and Cynthia on a six-day holiday in Casablanca in January 1968.

George Stanley John's maternal grandfather who used to take him for walks around Liverpool's Pier Head area when John was four years old.

Freddie Starr Leading British comedian who was one of the handful of Mersey Beat singers who achieved success and maintained it for more than 20 years. His first claim to fame came when he appeared as a tearaway in the film *Violent Playground*. He then became one of the lead singers with Howie Casey And The Seniors, the first Liverpool group to go to Hamburg and the first Mersey Beat group to have a record released in Britain.

He appeared on many bills with The Beatles and led several of his own bands on Merseyside, including Freddie And The Delmonts and Freddie Starr And The Midnighters. However, it was as a comedian that he achieved fame, becoming one of the highest-paid cabaret acts in Britain and host of his own TV series.

A few days after John's death, Freddie happened to mention to a British national newspaper that he'd heard some unreleased tapes by John Lennon in Lennon's former home at Tittenhurst Park, now owned by Ringo Starr.

When the newspaper checked, John Hemingway, one of Ringo's aides, denied that there were any Lennon tapes at the mansion. When they got back to Freddie, he told them that he had not only seen the tapes but had actually played them.

He then commented, 'When I went back to Tittenhurst the other night, after John's death, the tapes were gone and somebody there said they had been sent to America.'

Jim Steck Disc jockey who interviewed John in 1964 and whose interview is contained on Side 1 of the Charly Records 1981 re-release of the 1964 album *Hear The Beatles Tell All*.

William Stout American graphic designer who drew the original cover illustration for an album of Beatle tribute songs entitled *Beatle Novelties* issued by Rhino Records in America in 1982. John's assassin Mark Chapman was featured among the drawings of fans and there was a great deal of protest at this. Following accusations of bad taste, the cover was withdrawn and replaced by a photograph of Beatles memorabilia. Harold Bronson and Gary Stewart of Rhino Records arranged for Bill Stout to present his point of view in a statement which was printed in the fanzine *Good Day Sunshine*. It read:

'Recently there has been a tremendous amount of controversy over the new Rhino Records' release of *Beatlesongs*, an innocuous collection of novelty songs by Beatle fans about their heroes. The controversy stems not from any of these songs but from my cover for the LP, which is a group portrait of fans at a Beatlemania convention.

'Depicted is a complete range of Beatles' fans: a wide-eyed nostalgic, there because of her affection for the lovable mop-tops and their music: the greedy dealer who couldn't care less about The Beatles (but cares lots about money); a guy who had *his* 15 minutes of time because he looked like Ringo; a little girl too young to be a first-wave Beatles fan but who doesn't want to miss any of the fun; a guitar player hoping some of the magic will rub off if he owns an original piece of a Beatles instrument; and the rest of the assortment that make these friendly gatherings.

'The fans stand behind a large banner embellished with 'We Love You Beatles!' The banner is held by two young men. One of them is the assassin of John Lennon. Because of this, many stores are (or were) stocking the record in your good ol' "plain brown wrappers". There are a few stores that have refused to stock it at all.

'I will not attempt to explain the black humour behind the cover concept, because attempts to dissect such humour always evaporate that fragile vapour of funniness. Instead, let me give you my *serious* reasons for producing what *Cashbox* magazine described as "the sickest cover design concept seen in quite a while".

'When I decided that the cover design was to be a scene of Beatle (mania) conventions, the thought of putting Lennon's alleged assassin on the cover streaked through my mind. "My God," I exclaimed to one of my studio-mates. "Wouldn't that be the absolute *worst* in bad taste?"

'The more I thought about it however, the more I realized one terrible truth: in the darkest depths of a thing called fandom, John's assassin is the ultimate Beatles fan. He collected paraphernalia of, and in his own mind (according to psychiatrists at the time) became one of, The Beatles. He completes the range of fans shown on the cover.

'This observation compelled me morally to include him, and present him as a warning to hard-core fans everywhere (only hard-core fans would recognize him ... the president of Rhino Records didn't even realize whose idiot grin that was). It is my sincere hope that fans who might see a bit of this man in themselves will re-evaluate their obsession in terms closer to reality.

'At the risk of sounding obvious to non-fans: musicians aren't really gods here on earth in human form. Show these *people* you admire and respect them by purchasing their products but *not* by intruding upon their lives, their fair share of breathing room.

'Now, I have to confess that in my art school days John Lennon was my guide to sartorial splendour and to this day I maintain a complete collection of his recorded works. But I never believed that the arrogance of an intrusion by *this* fan would enhance his life. The folks most upset by the covers are the humorless lot who *do* see a bit (or more?) of John's assassin inside their obsessive little heart-of-hearts.

'The rabid would-be eccentrics can take heart. In an unprecedented move by a heretofore brave little company, *Beatlesongs* is being reissued with the back cover of Beatles' paraphernalia on the front cover. I have refused to alter the particular face on the original cover as requested by Rhino Records, so it will *not* appear (revised) on the backcover in place of the photo now being used for the front.

'The *Beatlesongs* cover was created out of anger, a sense of loss and a sense of John's own sardonic humour. A friend of mine went into a six-month depression upon the assassination of John Lennon. When I showed him the (first) *Beatlesongs* cover, he looked at it and replied with a statement that puts to rest in my mind any arguments over taste: "It's so true".'

Millie Sutcliffe Mother of Stuart Sutcliffe. Whilst Stuart and John were involved in adventures in Hamburg, Rod Murray was having great difficulty in coping with the rent of the Gambier Terrace flat and eventually had to vacate the premises.

He contacted Mrs Sutcliffe asking if she could arrange to pick up Stuart's personal possessions, and she hired a van. While she was supervising the movement of Stuart's gear, Rod suggested she take John's possessions in store, too.

She found a cupboard full of his old boots and clothes, although she says they were in a terrible state. She also took a dresser belonging to John with some of his personal items, but she never looked at them to check the contents.

She stored John's stuff in a corner of one of the rooms in her Ullet Road, Aigburth flat. When her husband came home from one of his sea trips, he wanted to know what the items were. She told him they belonged to John Lennon and he said, 'What're we storing his stuff for?' and threw them out.

On 8 November 1964 Bill Harry was visiting The Beatles backstage at the Empire Theatre, Liverpool and suggested to John that the two of them should visit Mrs Sutcliffe in her Aigburth flat after the show. They arrived unannounced at the door and she was thrilled.

Both John and Millie enjoyed the visit and she showed him the range of Stuart's work she had displayed around the flat. She asked him to select whatever of the works he wanted and he picked a blue abstract oil painting from Stuart's Hamburg period.

Mrs Sutcliffe also gave him *How To Draw Horses*, a book he'd won at Quarry Bank School and had lent to Stuart several years previously. She also gave him a small press clipping from a local paper, containing the very first mention of The Beatles prior to their *Mersey Beat* coverage.

John was later to send the clipping to Roy Carr and Tony Tyler, who used it in their book *The Beatles: An Illustrated Record*. It read:

'ROCK' GROUP AT NESTON INSTITUTE

'A Liverpool rhythm group, The Beatles, made their début at Neston Institute on Thursday night when northwest promoter Mr. Les Dodd presented three-and-a-half hours of rock 'n' roll.

'The five-strong group, which has been pulling in capacity houses on Merseyside, comprises three guitars, bass and drums.

'John Lennon, the leader, plays one of the three rhythm guitars, the other guitarists being Paul Ramon and Carl Harrison. Stuart Da Stael plays the bass and the drummer is Thomas Moore. They all sing, either together, or as soloists.

'Recently they returned from a Scottish tour, starring Johnny Gentle, and are looking forward to a return visit in a month's time.

'Among the theatres they have played at are the Hippodrome, Manchester; the Empire, Liverpool and the Pavilion, Aintree.'

Following Stuart's death, Millie struggled for years to recover some of Stuart's lost works. Her husband died and she moved south. Her two daughters, Joyce and Pauline had married. Joyce remained on Merseyside, Pauline became a social worker in the south. Following an exhibition she organized at the South London Art Gallery in July 1976, Millie requested that the paintings be taken to her daughter's flat until she moved from the damp premises she lived in to better accommodation in Sevenoaks. She is currently attempting to catalogue Stuart's work and trace many of the lost paintings.

Stuart Sutcliffe Born in Edinburgh on 23 June 1940, he was the son of Charles and Millie Sutcliffe. When his work took him to Liverpool, Mr Sutcliffe Senior arranged for the family to follow.

Stuart had two younger sisters, Joyce and Pauline. His mother had taught art at elementary school. Stuart attended Prescot Grammar School and then entered Liverpool College of Art. It was during his art school days that he and John became the best of friends. Stuart was invited to join John's band as either drummer or bass guitarist.

Initially, he couldn't afford any musical instruments, but he entered a painting for the annual John Moore's Exhibition at the Walker Art Gallery in 1959 and sold it for £60. This enabled him to buy a Hohner President bass guitar.

He couldn't play it, didn't receive any professional tuition and had to learn as he went along. Paul, who played rhythm guitar (John also played rhythm at the time) wanted to be the bass guitarist, and there was some friction. In fact, reports indicate that Stuart received a great deal of abuse during his time as a member of the band. John referred to this by saying, 'We'd tell Stu he couldn't sit with us, or eat with us. We'd tell him to go away, and he did.'

During their tour of Scotland with Johnny Gentle, all but John changed their names temporarily. Stuart chose Stu Da Stael. Despite the ribbing, Stuart had a great influence on the group, particularly in the case of John.

He was intense, though introverted, and read books by the philosopher-mystics.

He was already regarded as a potentially brilliant artist by the masters and students at the art college. He'd moved away from his family's home at 37 Aigburth Drive to be close to the art college and rented a flat at 7 Percy Street.

Later, he shared a flat with John and Rod Murray at 3 Gambier Terrace. He painted some unusual and distinctive murals in the basement of the Jacaranda Club in Slater Street, although the club manager Allan Williams didn't think much of them at the time.

Stuart's influence on The Beatles wasn't musical. He gave them an added dimension with his aura of mystery, brooding looks and intelligence. It was Stuart who suggested that they call themselves Beetles, although John added the 'a'. It is said that he thought of the name in tribute to Buddy Holly's backing group The Crickets. His mother thinks it was because he was often called a Beatnik because he wore very tight jeans, winkle pickers and at one time had a goatee beard.

She says: 'Stuart's influence on them has been played down as if he was not a potent member of the formation. At the time I was amazed that he was going around with them and threatened to withdraw my financial support. I thought I was doing my duty, but he started buying paints rather than food. Stuart went round like an orphan of the storm. So I relented and agreed to come and see his group.

'John knew I was coming, the others didn't. Harrison spotted me and said, "Stuart, your Mum's here."

'They thought I'd come to create a scene. But it was a pleasant surprise. I thought their music was out of this world. Afterwards, Stuart said, "What did you think of it, mother?" I couldn't express the feeling of pleasure the music gave me.'

Mrs Sutcliffe mentioned that Stuart's influence on their image was an important one: the leather look, the original Beatle haircut, even the collarless suit were all a product of Stuart's influence, she says. 'I remember when Stuart had the black leather suit and Astrid was wearing it all the time. In fact, Astrid liked it so much that Stuart hardly had a chance to wear it at all.

'As for the Cardin suit, Stuart had it on the very last time he came home. It was a velvet Cardin suit. He took his sister Pauline down to the Cavern to see John and the next day Pauline said to me, "Those Beatles hate Stuart, especially Paul McCartney."

'They were saying, "Oh, you're wearing your sister's suit, Stuart," mocking the suit the way they mocked his Beatle haircut.

'They always made Stuart out as a softie, but it was the other way round. Stuart had a strong character and in the important things John abided by what Stuart said.

'As for the haircut, it started when Stuart's hair was falling down and sticking out. One night Astrid had been moaning about his hair and then took him into the bathroom and cut it. He told me, "They (The Beatles) laughed at it. I defied them and kept it that way."'

Mersey Beat readers looked upon Stuart as a James Dean-type character. When the group went to Germany, it was Stuart who initially aroused the interest of the students who came to see them such as Astrid Kirchnerr, Klaus Voorman and Jurgen Vollmer.

Stuart and Astrid fell in love and when the group returned to Hamburg in 1961, Stuart decided to remain. He'd been extremely upset when he'd been refused the opportunity of returning to Liverpool College of Art. When the chance came for him to resume his studies in Germany, he took it.

Two of his German friends, who were also artists, recommended that he seek a place at the State High School of Art Instruction in Hamburg. For a while he worked in Gustaf Seitz's sculpture department until the official authority came through for him to commence work under Eduardo Paolozzi, who had arranged for Stu to receive a grant.

When discussing Stuart in the 1967 book *Art In A City* Paolozzi said: 'He was a very perceptive and sensitive person and very restless.' He also said, 'There is that sort of marvellously desperate thing about the whole Liverpool business now. I always felt there was a desperate thing about Stuart in his life . . . I was afriad of it.'

When Stu left The Beatles, Paul was very pleased. He took over on bass guitar. Although they had had many arguments in the past (at least one of them physical) they now became friends. John kept writing lengthy letters to Stuart and harboured the hope that he would eventually return to the band.

In 1962 he had made a life for himself in Hamburg, lived in the attic of Astrid's family home in Altona and was turning out an incredible volume of work, despite persistent and agonizing headaches, for which doctors couldn't find an explanation.

He and Astrid planned to marry in June of that year. The handsome blonde girl was two years older than Stuart and was a highly talented photographer. Her photographs of The Beatles had proved to be quite impressive.

At the age of 21, Stuart collapsed and was taken to hospital. He died of cerebral haemorrhage in an ambulance with

Astrid by his side. The date was Tuesday 10 April 1962 and The Beatles were due in Hamburg the same week to appear at the Star Club.

Astrid had sent two telegrams to Mrs Sutcliffe. The first read, 'My Stuart is dying', the second 'My Stuart is dead'. The second cable arrived before the first.

While John lives on in his music, Stuart survives also in his painting. There have only been a few exhibitions of his work — at the Walker Art Gallery in Liverpool and at the South London Gallery. There is a painting of Stuart's which is part of the permanent exhibition at the Walker Art Gallery entitled 'Hamburg Painting No. 2'.

Thisbe Shakespearean character from *A Midsummer Night's Dream* portrayed by John in a short excerpt of the play which The Beatles performed for Jack Good's TV production *Around The Beatles*. The show was first screened in Britain on 6th May 1964. Paul portrayed Pyramus, Ringo was Lion and George appeared as Moonshine.

Strom Thurmond Republican senator from South Carolina. He sent a dossier on John to John Mitchell, Richard Nixon's attorney general, suggesting that John be deported.

Ken Townsend General manager of Abbey Road studios. When he was chief technical engineer he worked closely with The Beatles and credits them with creating an atmosphere of experimentation which led to a revolution in recording methods.

In an attempt to facilitate some of The Beatles' experiments in the fields of double tracking, he invented a machine which he called ADT (Artificial Double Tracking). In his book *Abbey Road*, Brian Southall tells how John Lennon persisted in calling the machine Ken's Flanger, with the result that 'flanging' has become a standard technical term used in recording studios throughout the world.

Pierre Trudeau At an historic meeting on 22 December 1969, John and Yoko had a private meeting with Pierre Trudeau, the Prime Minister of Canada. When John had been working on his acorns-for-peace idea, he'd commented that he would like to meet the Canadian premier and present him with an acorn for peace.

Trudeau heard of this and commented: 'I don't know about acorns, but if he's around I'd like to meet him. He's a good poet.'

John was in Canada at the time and arrangements were made for the meeting, with an agreement that there would be no advance publicity. John wore a cape over his Pierre Cardin suit when he left to meet the Prime Minister at his office.

They talked together for 51 minutes, covering many subjects. Trudeau described his visit to China and asked John many questions concerning the peace movement, contemporary youth, The Beatles and John's books and poetry.

After the meeting, John said, 'Trudeau was interested in us because he thought we might represent some sort of youth faction. We spent about 50 minutes together, which was longer than he had spent with any head of state, which was the great glory of the time.' He later added: 'If there were more leaders like Mr Trudeau, the world would have peace.'

Bill Turner A friend and fellow pupil from John's Quarry Bank schooldays. He was interviewed by Bill Harry for *Mersey Beat*. His story appeared in 'The Mersey Beatle' section of the paper under the heading 'The Daily Howl', which was the main subject of the interview.

Bill explained: 'Whilst we were at Quarry Bank School John produced a book called *The Daily Howl*. It was an exercise book filled with his stories, poems, drawings and cartoons.

'He used to show his work to a bloke called Pete Shotton before he let anyone else see it. Pete was his best mate at Quarry Bank and I think John wrote *The Daily Howl* mainly for him.

'I remember it was at the time Davy Crockett was all the rage and one of the poems was 'The Story Of Davy Crutch-Head'. He also took a current hit song called "Suddenly There Was A Valley' and he incorporated this into a story which went: "Suddenly there was a valet who rode up riding. . ."

'There were quick flashes in the book such as a weather report: "Tomorrow will be Muggy, followed by Tuggy, Wuggy and Thuggy."

'He had an obsession for Wigan Pier. It kept cropping up, mainly in a story called *A Carrot In A Potato Mine*, and the mine was at the end of Wigan Pier.

'One of his favourite cartoons was a bus stop scene. I remember he wrote under the sign which said "Bus Stop" — "Why?" And he had a flying pancake at the top of the cartoon and below it there was a blind man wearing glasses leading along a blind dog — also wearing glasses.

'At one time *The Daily Howl* was confiscated by one of the teachers and it went all round the staff before he got it back at the end of term.'

Ugly George New York cable television man who goes out on the city streets to interview people and attempts to talk girls into divesting themselves of their clothing. His soft-porn show is then televised during the evening. In 1980 he bumped into John and Yoko and interviewed them for his show.

Canon Verney Canon of Coventry Cathedral at the time of John and Yoko's 'Two Acorns' event in November 1968. When John and Yoko arrived at the preview with their sculpture, the canon told them that a decision had been made by the cathedral authorities forbidding them to exhibit in the main area of the exhibition.

He explained that the area was consecrated ground and during ensuing arguments let it be known that the cathedral authorities did not like to be associated with a couple who were 'living in sin'.

After they had planted their acorns outside the consecrated ground they left, having passed on a number of their catalogues to be distributed among the visitors. The canon refused to allow them to be given out.

Jurgen Vollmer Jurgen was a student at Hamburg Art College when The Beatles first travelled to Hamburg in 1960. A fellow student, Klaus Voorman, together with Klaus's girlfriend, Astrid Kirchherr, persuaded Jurgen to join them on a trip to the St. Pauli district to listen to some rock and roll music by Liverpool bands.

The club was the Kaiserkeller and Jurgen saw The Beatles for the first time and was intrigued.

Recollecting the trip, Jurgen said that John was 'the obvious leader of the group ... a typical rocker ... the Brando type.' The Liverpool band and the German exis (existentialists) formed a close bond and both Astrid and Jurgen took photographs of The Beatles, which the group brought back to Liverpool to give to Bill Harry to be published in *Mersey Beat*.

The photographs were impressive, containing a mood and atmosphere unlike any rock photographs published elsewhere in Britain. They are a unique record of that first Hamburg trip and were reprinted in various American magazines over the years.

In 1961, Jurgen moved to Paris and when John received a birthday gift of money from an aunt in Edinburgh, he used the cash to enable both Paul and himself to travel to the French capital to see Jurgen again.

Of this particular trip, Jurgen remarked: 'I gave both of them their first Beatles haircut in my hotel room on the left bank. John wanted a corduroy jacket like mine and a sweater, with cut off sleeves like I wore, which was collarless and vest-like.' This seems to indicate that the Pierre Cardin collarless look, which they were to adopt for a short time and the famous mop-top hairdo, had their origins in the influence of Jurgen.

In 1981 Jurgen had a book of his photographs published in Paris and New York. Among them were the pictures he took of The Beatles in Hamburg. The Paris edition was published by Editions de Nesle and the American by Google Plex Books. Entitled *Rock 'N' Roll Times*, the book is divided into two parts. The second part consists of his photographs of Paris youngsters, intriguingly bearing captions of rock-and-roll songs to describe them, including a series of pictures of youngsters in the act of making love.

John was able to pen a short note for the book in which he wrote, 'Jurgen Vollmer was the first photographer to capture the beauty and spirit of The Beatles ... we tried very hard to find someone with his touch after we returned from Hamburg ... nobody could.'

The book's cover, featuring John in a doorway, was also used as the cover for John's *Rock 'n' Roll* album.

Cecil Walker Registrar who conducted the wedding between John and Yoko at Gibraltar on 20 March 1969.

Fred Walter Butcher who supplied meat for John and Cynthia when they lived in Weybridge. When asked about John, he commented: 'I have never seen John — only his wife, and that was on the day they moved in, she drove down here in her mini and bought two pork chops. That was the last I saw of her. Now, the cook does their shopping — and we never see them at all.'

Peter Watkins British film director with a cult following. His movies include *Performance*, starring Paul Jones and Jean Shrimpton, a sci-fi rock story and *Panic In Needle Park*, another film set in the near future. His most controversial work was *The War Game*, a film he produced for BBC-TV showing the effects of a nuclear holocaust on London.

It was felt to be too horrific for showing on television and has been screened at a number of independent cinemas since the mid-sixties. His sequel was called *The Peace Game* (or *The Gladiators*).

John acknowledged that it was a letter which Watkins sent to him which finally convinced him actively to work for his peace campaign. The lengthy missive covered aspects of media manipulation and pointed out that John and Yoko, as prominent media figures, had a responsibility which they should use to advocate peace in the world.

He concluded with the question, 'What are you going to do about it?' The letter had a profound effect on John who three weeks after he received it decided to go ahead with Watkins' suggestion by launching his first 'Bed In'.

Jon Weiner History professor at the University of California whose researches for a book on John Lennon uncovered previously unreleased material about the attempt to have John deported from America.

Under the American Freedom Of Information Act, Weiner was able to study in 1983 FBI and Immigration files which had previously been unavailable to the public. He discovered that former President Richard Nixon supported a campaign to discredit Lennon and have him deported before the Republican Conference in 1972.

The President actually believed that John's activities in America could cost him the election. John was involved with a number of American radicals at the time, and was being used to gain publicity for various causes such as that of freeing John Sinclair. Nixon was told that John could be used to spearhead a mass anti-Nixon demonstration before the Miami Convention.

The late J Edgar Hoover, head of the FBI, had been instructed to obtain evidence against John which could lead to his arrest on drug charges and subsequent deportation proceedings. As a result, John's New York apartment was bugged and the FBI sent reports of John's daily activities to the CIA, the Secret Service and Bob Haldeman, presidential aide to Nixon.

Carol White British actress who rose to fame in the early 'sixties with the starring role in a TV play about the plight of the homeless called Cathy Come Home. She appeared in several other films, notably Poor Cow before moving to America where she remained during the 'seventies. She returned to Britain at the beginning of the 'eighties with her third husband Mike Arnold and in November 1982 her autobiography Carol Comes Home was issued by New English Library.

In it she relates how she first met John in a Chelsea boutique and was having a chat with him when Yoko, who had been trying on a black mini-dress, came up, ignored her and said to John: 'Well, what do you think of it?' John said, 'Not a lot' and she retorted, 'You never like anything' and stormed back to the changing room.

Carol admitted that she didn't like Yoko. She was biased by the fact that she preferred John's first wife, Cynthia.

Milton Wiess Californian psychiatrist who attempted to analyse John in 1974 but gave up in despair, commenting: 'If I was doing this as a job I'd have to send him two bills — one for each personality!'

Paul Williams A senior producer at BBC's Radio One, he was responsible for setting up the famous John Lennon-Andy Peebles interview. Originally, he and Andy, together with executive producer Doreen Davies, had planned to travel to America to interview David Bowie, a project which was subsequently broadcast on 5 January 1981.

Arrangements were made for them to meet John and Yoko at the Hit Factory on 6 December 1980 and the interview continued for a total of three hours, with Paul and Andy carrying on their conversations with John and Yoko over dinner.

Imagine their shock and horror when they arrived back in London on the morning of 9 December to be informed of John's murder. They spent the day editing excerpts from the interview, which were broadcast immediately. They then arranged for the full five-part series to be broadcast on Sundays from 18 January 1981. The broadcasts have since been aired on several other occasions.

Shelley Winters Blonde American movie star who was a close neighbour of the Lennons in the Dakota Building. Following John's shooting, she took to wearing disguises whenever venturing outside, commenting: 'I wear a wig and dark glasses and am driven around in a little Toyota, so I don't look like a movie star.'

Bob Wooler Living in Garston, on the outskirts of Liverpool, Bob Wooler was working as a clerk in the local railway dock office when he became interested in music performed by the Mersey outfits in the 'fifties.

For a time he was manager of a skiffle group called The Kingstrums, but he eventually found he was more suited to compèring the shows put on by local promoters. As a compère-cum-disc jockey, he worked part-time for promoters such as Wally Hill of Peak

Promotions, appearing at Holyoake Hall (Smithdown Road) and similar places. Bob also promoted his own shows for a time at Hambleton Hall.

With his mellifluous voice, his love of the local scene, his sense of organization and astute knowledge of the bands, he became a prominent figure on the scene and did much to aid the struggling Silver Beatles.

Another promoter he worked for was

Bill and Virginia Harry join John for a chat at the ABC, Blackpool.

Brian Kelly, who ran dances at venues such as Aintree Institute and Litherland Town Hall. Bob was soon recommending The Silver Beatles to him and Brian commented: 'I was organizing a dance at Litherland Town Hall to be held on Boxing Day 1960 but I was short of a group. On Christmas Day I received a phone call from Bob Wooler who said, "I've found a group for you at the Jacaranda and they're free. They want £8. Will they do?"

'"Not at that price they won't," I said. "A group won't increase my attendance enough to warrant that." Bob told me that they were called The Silver Beatles and that they played at the Casbah, Heyman's Green. We finally agreed to pay them £6.'

That particular gig, coming so soon

after their first trip to Hamburg, was to boost the reputation of the virtually unknown band in local circles. Kelly was quick to jump in, and recalled: 'On their first appearance I was completely knocked out by them. They had a pounding, pulsating beat which I knew would be big box office. When they had finished playing, I posted some bouncers on the door of their dressing room to prevent other promoters who were in the hall from entering. I went inside and booked them solidly for months ahead.'

Bob, although already convinced of the group's talent, was surprised at how much they had improved during their season in Hamburg. He was to write about that night in his column 'The Roving I' in issue No. 5 of *Mersey Beat*, dated 31 August.

He'd been invited by Bill Harry to write a column for the newspaper not only because of his knowledge of local group activities, but also because of his intriguing style of writing. Bob had a particular type of wit and created what were called 'Woolerisms', a range of phrases for people, places and events such as 'the best of cellars' (The Cavern) and 'the Nemperor' (Brian Epstein). His column, following the continual plugging of The Beatles in the paper since its first issue, did much to fuel interest in the group among the growing readership.

He wrote: 'Why do you think The Beatles are so popular? Many people many times have asked me this question since that fantastic night (Tuesday 27 December 1960) at Litherland Town Hall when the impact of the act was first felt on this side of the river.

'I consider myself privileged to have been associated with the launching of the group on that exciting occasion, and grateful for the opportunities of present-ing them to fever-pitch audiences at practically all of the group's subsequent appearances prior to their last Hamburg trip.

'Perhaps my close association with the group's activities, both earlier this year and since their recent re-appearance on the Merseyside scene, persuades people to think that I can produce a blueprint of The Beatles' success story.

'It figures I suppose, and if, in attempting to explain the popularity of their act, the following analysis is at variance with other people's views, well that's just one of those things. The question is nevertheless thought provoking.

'Well, then how to answer it? First some obvious observations. The Beatles are the biggest thing to have hit the Liverpool rock 'n' roll set-up in years. They were, and still are, the hottest local property any rock promoter is likely to encounter.

'I think The Beatles are No 1 because they resurrected original style rock 'n' roll music, the origins of which are to be found in American negro singers. They hit the scene when it had been emasculated by figures like Cliff Richard and sounds like those electronic wonders, The Shadows and their many imitators. Gone was the drive that inflamed the emotions. This was studio set jungle music purveyed skilfully in a chartwise direction by arrangement with the A & R men.

'The Beatles, therefore, exploded on a jaded scene. And to those people on the verge of quitting 'teendom — those who had experienced during the most impressionable years the impact of rhythm 'n' blues music (raw rock 'n' roll) — this was an experience, a process of

The Fab Four . . . and all that jazz!

regaining and reliving a style of sounds and associated feelings identifiable with their era.

'Here again in The Beatles was the stuff that screams are made of. Here was the excitement — both physical and aural — that symbolized the rebellion of youth in the ennuyé mid-'50s. This was the real thing. Here they were, first five and then four human dynamos generating a beat which was irresistible. Turning back the rock clock. Pounding out items from Chuck Berry, Little Richard, Carl Perkins, The Coasters and the other great etceteras of the era. Here they were, unmindful of uniformity of dress. Unkempt like long hair. Rugged yet romantic, appealing to both sexes. With calculated naïvety and an ingenuous, throw-away approach to their music. Effecting indifference to audience response and yet always saying "Thank-you". Reviving interest in, and

commanding, enthusiasm for numbers which had descended the charts way back. Popularizing (more than any other group) flipside items — example, "Boys". Compelling attention and influencing, wittingly or unwittingly, other groups in the style, choice and presentation of songs.

'Essentially a vocal act, hardly ever instrumental (at least not in this country), here they were independently-minded, playing what they liked for kicks, kudos and cash. Privileged in having gained prestige and experience from a residency at the Hamburg Top Ten Club, during the autumn and winter of last year. Musically authoritative and physically magnetic, example the mean, moody magnificence of drummer Pete Best — a sort of teenage Jeff Chandler. A remarkable variety of talented voices which song-wise sound distinctive, but when speaking, possess the same

naïvety of tone. Rhythmic revolutionaries. An act which from beginning to
end is a succession of climaxes. A
personality cult. Seemingly unambit-
ious, yet fluctuating between the self-
assured and the vulnerable. Truly a
phenomenon — and also a predicament
to promoters! Such are the fantastic
Beatles. I don't think anything like them
will happen again.'

The first Top Ten list of Mersey
groups ever published was Bob's own
personal choice, which he listed in Issue
No 7.

'Well here it is then, my list of what I
rate to be the ten most popular rock
groups on Merseyside — excluding the
Bluegenes, of course,' he wrote. 'They
are beyond comparison. They are in a
class of their own.'

1 The Beatles
2 Gerry And The Pacemakers
3 Rory Storm And The
   Hurricanes
4 The Remo 4
5 The Strangers
6 Johnny Sandon And
   The Searchers
7 Karl Terry And The Cruisers
8 Mark Peters And
   The Cyclones
9 Ray And The Del Renas
10 The Big Three

In addition to his writing activities for
Mersey Beat, Bob composed most of the
copy for the advertisements placed by
promoters both in *Mersey Beat* and the
Liverpool Echo. They were concise,
lively and contained many puns.

Apart from his compering duties, Bob
advised groups on stage presentation,
discussed their musical repertoires with
them and often recommended numbers
for them to learn. Bob's collection of
American singles, which he carried

Six cups go into four quite nicely.

around with him to the venues in a portable record case, led to a lot of bands playing the numbers which Bob had searched for and selected himself, songs such as Chan Romero's 'Hippy Hippy Shake', Chuck Berry numbers and the like. This was a contribution of his which has largely gone unrecorded.

When Allan Williams decided to launch a new Liverpool venue styled on the Hamburg clubs, which he called The Top Ten Club, he asked Bob to become resident compere. Bob agreed and gave up his full-time job. As luck would have it, the club in Soho Street burned down scarcely more than a week after its opening and shortly prior to a two-week season there by The Beatles. Having sacrificed his security. Bob had immediately to find a regular income. Williams suggested that he manage The Beatles.

Fortunately, the Cavern was to provide what Bob was looking for and he became DJ at the club in 1960, a job which lasted for seven years. The fact that The Beatles looked to him for advice was indicated when they asked him to attend their meeting with Brian Epstein, who was keen on becoming their manager. 'They thought Epstein was fly and wanted my advice,' Bob said. When the meeting took place, Epstein was perturbed by Bob's presence and demanded to know who he was. 'It's me Dad!' said John.

Bob was, in fact, something of a father figure, having been born in January 1932. He'd been promoting The Beatles at their Cavern gigs and by the time of their last appearance at the club on Saturday 3 August 1963, was able to check the Cavern's records and discover that the group had appeared there for a total of 293 times.

The Beatles appeared at the Cavern 293 times.

The most dramatic event which concerned John and Bob Wooler took place at Paul's 21st birthday party on 18 June 1963. The boys had been touring with Roy Orbison and had arranged for the party to take place at Paul's Aunt Jinny's house in the Huyton area. Guests included The Fourmost, The Scaffold and Billy J. Kramer and, as the party progressed, quantities of drink were consumed and Bob made a comment to John. The exact words are not known, but John later said, 'I think he called me a queer.'

Such a confrontation was inevitable. John had a hot temper which he couldn't control when he was drunk. Bob had a reputation for a cutting wit which often rubbed people up the wrong way. Bob was obviously aware of Brian Epstein's homosexuality and was also aware that John had gone on holiday with Brian to Spain in April.

When the comment was made, John went berserk and began to beat the DJ savagely. 'I battered his bloody ribs for him. I was pissed at the time,' he said. When Bob tried to protect his face by covering it with his hands, John kept on kicking him until the skin was ripped from Bob's knuckles.

Bob had to be taken to hopsital. He intended to sue John and finally agreed to an out-of-court settlement of £200.

A few months later, Bob announced their final appearance at the Cavern. Their phenomenal success had taken even him by surprise. Somewhat in awe of their new-found superstardom he announced them simply with the words, 'It's The Beatles!'

From that first meeting when John had introduced Bob to Epstein as his father, Brian had decided to use Bob's knowledge of the local scene and employed him to promote a number of concerts for Nems Enterprises at various venues including The Tower Ballroom and the Queen's Hall, Widnes.

When The Beatles moved to London, Brian employed a number of his friends, causing an exodus of Merseyside people to the London offices of Nems. Bob wasn't among them. He remained at the Cavern until 1967. He became Ray McFall's right-hand man, managed bands such as The Carolls and, for a short time, was married to Beryl Adams, Brian Epstein's former secretary who had been in love with Brian when she worked for him at the Whitechapel branch of Nems.

With the closing of the Cavern, Bob took on various DJ jobs in the north and worked for a time as a bingo caller at the former Locarno ballroom. In the 'seventies he presented an occasional promotion in Liverpool and worked on several projects with Allan Williams, primarily Beatle conventions. By the 'eighties he was escorting visitors to the 'Pool on special Magical Mystery Tours of The Beatles' former haunts.

Anne Yorke Australian photographer based in Toronto who teamed up on several occasions with Canadian rock journalist Ritchie Yorke. Anne covered the Lennons' Canadian Peace Trip in December 1969 and a selection of her photographs of that particular tour are featured in the book *One Day At A Time*.

Frank Zappa Notorious American musician born in Baltimore in 1940. Founder of The Mothers Of Invention who recorded a number of hit albums, including *Ruben And The Jets* and *Weasels Ripped My Flesh*.

He came to John's defence following the American outcry over John's remarks to Maureen Cleave. Zappa stated that he considered John's comments were correct.

For a time, Zappa lived in London where he wrote and starred in the film *200 Motels* in which Ringo Starr also appeared in the role of Frank Zappa.

When he returned to America, Zappa made one of the last appearances at the Fillmore East before the famous rock venue closed. The date was 6 June 1971 and John and Yoko joined him on stage to perform several numbers which were recorded. Four of them appear on the *Some Time In New York City* album: 'Scumbag', 'Well. . .Baby Please Don't Go', 'Jamrag' and 'Au'.

Are we making an exhibition of ourselves?

There are places I'll remember . . .

Liverpool College of Art.

Places

Strawberry Field.

Amsterdam Hilton Luxury hotel at 138 Apollolaan, Amsterdam, Holland. The setting for John and Yoko's first Bed-In commencing 26 March 1969 and lasting for seven days. Immediately following their marriage in Gibraltar, they were aware that the wedding was going to result in a great deal of press activity and decided to utilise it themselves. Nestling into Suite 902, they invited up to 40 reporters at a time to interview them.

John commented, 'We sat in bed and talked to reporters for seven days. It was hilarious. In effect, we were doing a commercial for peace on the front page of the papers instead of a commercial for war.

'We were on the seventh floor of the Hilton, looking over Amsterdam. It was very crazy; the press came expecting to see us fucking in bed; they all heard John and Yoko were going to fuck in front of the press for peace. So when they all walked in (about 50 or 60 reporters flew over from London, all sort of very edgy), we were just sitting in pyjamas saying, ''Peace Brother'', and that was it.'

When the hotel's management heard the news of John's death, they turned out all the lights in the building as a mark of respect, with the exception of Suite 902 which, from the seventh floor, shone like a beacon over the city.

Bermuda British Caribbean island colony to which John took his four-year-old son Sean on holiday in June 1980 during his term as a housefather while Yoko remained in New York attending to business matters. During this holiday,

Welcome to the honeymoon!

while visiting the botanical gardens, he saw the Double Fantasy orchid and gained the inspiration to return to his career in music.

In September 1982 Yoko sent Sean on a fortnight's holiday to Bermuda accompanied by three bodyguards, but she herself remained in New York, once again to attend to business matters.

112 Chambers Street Address in Greenwich Village, New York in which Yoko lived in a loft with her first husband, Toshi Ichiyanagi, whom she met while attending the Sarah Lawrence School. Yoko presented several events and concerts for a group of artists called Fluxus at the attic flat.

Château Champlain Hotel Canadian hotel in Montreal where John and Yoko held a press conference on 21 December 1969.

Chrysler Arena 5,000 seater stadium in Ann Arbor, Michigan where John and Yoko appeared in December 1971 at a John Sinclair benefit concert. Other acts on the bill included Stevie Wonder, Allen Ginsberg, Phil Ochs, Commander Cody and David Peel. John and Yoko wore 'Free John Now' T-shirts and performed four numbers on stage in a 15 minute set: 'Attica State', 'Sisters O Sisters', 'Luck Of The Irish' and 'John Sinclair'. They were backed by three acoustic guitar players and Jerry Rubin on congas.

The Conservative Club One of more than 300 social clubs in Liverpool during the 'fifties. Local groups were booked into the Conservative Club, situated in the Norris Green area, by promoter Charles (Charlie) McBain. It

was the time in 1957 that Paul McCartney first played officially on stage with John Lennon's group and he fluffed it. He appeared at the gig as The Quarrymen's lead guitarist, but was so bad that John told him he'd have to become another rhythm guitarist like himself.

Coventry Cathedral The former cathedral was the victim of Hitler's blitz on Britain when Coventry was virtually levelled in World War II. A new cathedral was built, an exceptional modern architectural structure.

When the National Sculpture Exhibition was planned for presentation in the cathedral grounds in November 1968, John and Yoko expressed their interest in being represented and arrangements were made through their assistant, Anthony Fawcett.

The duo's 'sculpture' was in fact two real acorns which they hoped would be planted in the grounds and allowed to grow into a massive oak tree. This, in perhaps a hundred years or more, would be a potent symbol of their love.

John is reported as saying, 'One faced east and the other faced west, to symbolise that East and West have met through Yoko and me', a quote very similar to one attributed to Yoko.

As it turned out, the Canon of the Cathedral wouldn't allow their sculpture to be planted in the cathedral grounds. Their acorns were planted nearby, then stolen, and armed guards had to be hired when a further 'sculpture' was planted.

Ye Cracke Small pub situated in the narrow Rice Street in Liverpool, branching off Hope Street — the nearest public house to the Liverpool College of Art.

Ye Cracke, the art college watering hole.

This is the pub John frequented whilst at college. There he'd meet teacher Arthur Ballard in a main room called The War Office. This is the room where John originally showed Bill Harry a sample of his poetry, which led to Bill asking John to write his own version of The Beatles' story. This appeared in the premier issue of *Mersey Beat*. It was a meeting place for The Dissenters and John was often to spend his leisure time here with his school mates, imbibing a half-of-bitter, the cheapest drink the impoverished students could afford.

The Denise René Gallery French art gallery situated in Paris which held an exhibition of *Bag One*, John's erotic lithographs, in February 1970.

Dorinish An island off the coast of County Mayo in Ireland which John and Yoko bought in 1970. They heard of a group of hippies who had nowhere to live and invited them to settle on the isle. One of the hippies, Sid Rowle, commented: 'John Lennon phoned us and said he had an island which we could use. We went to see him and Yoko Ono, and he said we were quite welcome to use the island for as long as we liked.'

Dovedale Primary School Situated at Dovedale Road, Liverpool 18. The first school John attended, enrolling at the age of four. The headmaster Mr Evans rather astutely commented: 'This boy's as sharp as a needle. He can do anything as long as he chooses to do it. He won't do anything stereotyped.' John also admitted to being reasonably well behaved at Dovedale in comparison with his rebellious attitude at Quarry Bank School. He said, 'I'd been honest at Dovedale, if nothing else, always owning up. But I began to realise that I was foolish.' Ivan Vaughan was among the friends he made at the school. When John passed his Eleven Plus examination he moved to Quarry Bank Grammar School.

Dreamstreet Farms Company from whom John bought four farms: one near Stamford, one in Delhi and two near Franklin, Pennsylvania in the lowlands of the Catskill Mountains.

Dromoland Castle Hotel Irish hotel in which John, Cynthia, George and Patti decided to spend a brief holiday. They hired a six-seater plane and flew from Manchester Airport in an attempt to keep their trip secret from the press. The suite they occupied had formerly had President Kennedy as a guest, and the quartet looked forward to a relaxing break.

Unfortunately, by the second day the press caught up with them and to prevent photographers getting pictures of Patti and George together, John and George set off for the airport and Cynthia and Patti were smuggled out of the hotel in a laundry van.

Dovedale Primary School.

Elgin Theatre New York theatre which held a three-night festival of films by John and Yoko in 1971.

13 Emperor's Gate Address in Kensington, London, quite close to the Royal Albert Hall, which provided a temporary home for the Lennons in 1964. Once it had been revealed publicly that John was married to Cynthia and was the father of a little boy, Julian, the family decided to find a place in which to live in London.

Photographer Bob Freeman suggested that they could apply for the flat on the top floor of the building in which he lived. Unfortunately, the premises proved unsuitable once Beatle fans had discovered the address soon after John and his family had moved in.

There were six flights of stairs (no lift) which Cynthia had to negotiate with a small boy, only to be greeted by hordes of fans as she tried to leave.

There was also disturbance from the noise of the Underground railway to the rear of the premises. Opposite to the flat was a students' hostel, whose occupants would always be trying to peek into the Lennons' flat or trying to attract their attention.

Entermedia Theatre Off-Broadway theatre on 2nd Avenue and 12th Street, New York which presented a seven week production of Bob Eaton's play, *Lennon*, in the late summer of 1982. The younger Lennon was portrayed by David Patrick Kelly and the elder by Robert LuPone. There was a cast of seven in the two-and-a-half hour production, five males and two females playing a variety of roles. The music was supervised by Mitch Weissman, who was associated with the *Beatlemania* stage show. *Lennon* was produced by Sid and Stanley Bernstein in association with Abe Margolis and Dennis Paget.

Everyman Theatre Formerly the Hope Hall Cinema, it was situated in Hope Street, as was the Liverpool College of Art. The Everyman was converted into a theatre in the 'sixties. It became a popular cultural centre on Merseyside and encouraged local poets and playwrights. In 1974 it held the world premiere of Willy Russell's play *John, Paul, George, Ringo And Bert* for a six week run before its move to London's West End. On 21 October 1981 it presented the musical play *Lennon*.

36 Falkner Street Address of a flat rented by Brian Epstein in the Liverpool 8 district, quite close to the College of Art. When John and Cynthia were married on 23 August 1962, Brian offered them the use of the ground floor flat, which also had a small garden.

They were grateful for a place, which was smartly furnished in contrast to the 'bedsit' where Cynthia had stayed. But they found the new flat inconvenient at times because the bedroom was separated from the rest of the flat by a hallway, which was used by all the other tenants in the house. Cynthia offers one or two amusing anecdotes about the flat in her book *A Twist Of Lennon*, but their stay there was relatively brief.

After several weeks, Mimi Smith didn't like the idea of a pregnant Cynthia being alone in the flat while John was away on the road, so she invited her to move into Mendips.

3 Gambier Terrace Gambier Terrace is a handsome Georgian terrace directly facing the Anglican cathedral. Situated less than a hundred yards from the Liverpool College of Art and Liverpool Institute, it also houses the Junior Art School and a nurses' home.

John's schoolmates, Rod Murray and Stuart Sutcliffe, had both rented flats at No 7 Percy Street, to the rear of Gambier Terrace. When John and Rod teamed up to share the flat at No 3, Stuart soon joined them.

The premises were quite large and John often had Cynthia stay with him, while Rod had his girl friend Diz as a fairly regular flatmate. Stu had no girl at the time and slept on a camp bed in the smallest of the rooms.

As students, they couldn't afford proper furniture and the elegance of the flat was often rendered tawdry by their erratic life-style and Stu's painting equipment.

However, the premises were never as bad as those described in 'The Beatnik Horror' article in the *Sunday People* newspaper in the summer of 1960. The paper had decided to expose beatniks and deliberately angled stories to present beatniks as filthy layabouts.

The particular issue in which a photograph appeared of the main room in the Gambier Terrace flat showed it to be in an appalling mess, with objects strewn about the floor. Among the five people lying around are Allan Williams and Stu Sutcliffe.

This was a put up job as the *Sunday People* reporters had been spending some time at the Jacaranda, and Allan Williams, ever helpful to the press, had decided to use John and Stu's flat to facilitate the needs of the *Sunday People* story, deliberately roughing-up the flat to provide the sort of picture they were after.

The Beatles sometimes rehearsed at the premises and they brought Royston Ellis, the beat poet, back to the flat after backing him at a Poetry-To-Beat session at the Jacaranda. John Lennon once put Bill Harry up in the bath overnight after a late-night chat session.

When The Beatles left for Germany, Rod Murray was saddled with the entire rent bill, which he couldn't afford, so he had to move out. Mrs. Sutcliffe collected Stu's and John's possessions and Rod moved into a cheaper flat nearby. Among the items he'd taken with him from Gambier Terrace was a copy of John's *Daily Howl*, and he was able to return this in exchange for some of the rent money which John had owed him.

Gibraltar British colony in Mediterranean, known as The Rock, with a population of less than 30,000. John and Yoko decided to get married here after consulting Peter Brown. They were unsuccessful in arranging for their wedding to take place on a cross-channel ferry as the captains of ferries no longer perform marriages. The couple's trip to Europe on a cross-channel ferry was halted because of passport queries, so they flew to Paris. From Paris they phoned Peter Brown in London and asked him if he could discover a convenient place for them to have a speedy and secret wedding. He called them back to suggest Gibraltar. John later said: 'We chose Gibraltar because it is quiet, British and friendly.'

On 20 March 1969 they flew from Paris on a private jet, accompanied by Peter Brown and photographer David Nutter, who were the only witnesses to the ceremony.

The jet, piloted by Captain Trevor Coppleston, landed in Gibraltar at 8.30

And here's the piece of paper to prove it.

am and the party arrived at the British consulate building at 9 am. John and Yoko were in their white period and Yoko was dressed in white knee socks, white mini-dress and white wide-brimmed hat. John wore white jacket, white pullover and white trousers and both wore white tennis shoes. The three-minute ceremony was conducted by the registrar, Cecil Wheeler. The couple then chose to spend their honeymoon at the Amsterdam Hilton, where they held a 'bed-in'.

Golspie Hospital John and Yoko took Julian and Kyoko for a brief holiday in Scotland on 1 July 1969. John, who hadn't done much driving (he only learned to drive when he was 24) was at the wheel when the car plunged into a ditch. Fortunately, the main impact was absorbed by the engine and front suspension and injuries to the occupants were minor.

John had to have 17 stitches, Yoko 14 and Kyoko 4. They were taken to Golspie Hospital and detained. Yoko was found to have an injured back and concussion. They'd arranged a press reception for their Plastic Ono Band single on 3 July but were unable to attend and a few days later flew back to London by jet.

Hornsey College of Art Students from this college had their own comment to make about John's work on 1 July 1968. That's the date when they sent a rusty, old bike down to his 'You Are Here' exhibition in London, with the message, 'This exhibit was inadvertently left out'. John put it in the exhibition.

Indica Gallery which opened in Mason's Yard in London's West End in the mid-sixties. It was run by Peter Asher, Miles and John Dunbar. Paul McCartney designed the shop's wrapping paper and presented the design to them as a gift.

Asher, Jane's brother, had hits with Lennon/McCartney material as part of the duo Peter & Gordon, and later worked for Apple.

Miles, who rarely uses his first name Brian, was a contributor to *International Times* and now works for Omnibus Press, for whom he has written several Beatles books, including *John Lennon In His Own Words*.

Dunbar was a Cambridge graduate married to Marianne Faithful. At the

I asked her if I could hammer a nail in.

104

preview of Yoko's exhibition when John asked Yoko if he could hammer a nail in the exhibit 'Hammer A Nail In', Dunbar said to Yoko, 'Let him hammer a nail in. You know, he's a millionaire. He might buy it.'

Apart from introducing John to Yoko, Dunbar also introduced John to Alexis Mardas, who later launched Apple Electronics and was known as Magic Alex.

Yoko's exhibition was entitled *Unfinished Paintings And Objects By Yoko Ono*.

Inn On The Park Luxury hotel in London's West End, close to Park Lane, where John and Yoko lived for a short time while Tittenhurst Park was undergoing extensive renovations.

John Lennon Boulevard Street in Madrid, Spain renamed in honour of John by the city's mayor on 7 December 1981. A wall in the street features a gigantic mural inspired by the *Yellow Submarine* film.

John Lennon Drive One of four Liverpool streets named in honour of The Beatles, the others being Ringo Starr Close, Paul McCartney Way and George Harrison Close.

For some years, a number of Beatle friends and fans had been attempting to persuade the council to pay tribute to the Fab Four by naming streets after them. Bob Wooler had even written to the Lord Mayor about this.

However, the council were not interested and claimed that such a practice had been abused in the past. Following John's death, more positive approaches were made to the council's Highways Committee to enable the local builders, Wimpey Homes, to name four streets

after The Beatles in one of the new estates they were building.

Once again the idea was turned down. Eddie Porter and Jeff Gilbert then formed The Beatle Street Campaign and together with members of Cavern Mecca, they carried mock street signs to another meeting of the Highways Committee.

The Committee finally voted 10 to 9 in favour of the idea and the decision was ratified by the full City Council on 17 July 1981, although one councillor opposed saying, 'The only member of The Beatles I would honour would be George McCartney.'

The estate with the Beatle street names is in Liverpool 6 and the first homes were opened on 27 November 1981 at a ceremony attended by the then Minister for the Environment, Michael Heseltine, MP and Sir Trevor Jones, MP, Derek Hatton, MP and Joseph Dwyer, head of Wimpey Homes. Three blocks of flats have been added to the estate. Their names are Epstein Mews, Apple Court and Cavern Court.

John Lennon Street Name given to a new road in the village of Sentmenat in Catalonia, Spain in 1981.

Junior Art School School in Gambier Terrace (where John was later to rent a flat) attended by Cynthia Powell, Bill Harry and Les Chadwick (one of The Beatles earliest photographers).

Kenwood Name of the mock-Tudor house in Cavendish Road, Weybridge, Surrey (the stockbroker belt) to which John, Cynthia and Julian moved in 1964 when John became the first Beatle to buy a house. It cost £40,000. The Lennons lived there until 1968 when the

The Junior Art School.

affair with Yoko (Cynthia found John and Yoko in her home; this upset her greatly) eventually led to John and Cynthia splitting up.

Living in the flat in Emperor's Gate had proved intolerable and they'd made up their minds to buy a house. When they were invited to dinner at the Weybridge house of The Beatles' accountant they decided they loved the area, particularly its seclusion. They chose a house on a hill surrounded by its own woods in the exclusive St George's Hill Estate.

They employed interior decorators to fit out the house, a job which took nearly nine months, during which the Lennons lived in a staff flat at the top of the house. They employed a woman called Dot to help Cynthia on a day-to-day basis; a driver called Jock and a married couple (a cook and a house-keeper). Eventually, retaining Dot, they made staff changes until they found people who suited them better.

The house provided a degree of privacy with its electronically controlled gates. It was furnished with antiques, there was a four-car garage, a swimming pool, film projection equipment, five television sets, walls full of books and a room with two pianos: a Broadwood and a Bechstein.

Kurioso City Japanese city which set up a John Lennon memorial museum.

Lady Mitchell Hall Venue in Cambridge, England where John and Yoko made their first public performance together at an *avant-garde* concert, which was recorded. The couple appeared there on 2 March 1969 and excerpts from the recording were used on the *Unfinished Music No 2. Life With The Lions* album.

Le Bourget French airport near Paris. John and Yoko flew there from Gibraltar shortly after they were married. Journalists were waiting for the couple and John told them, 'We got married in Gibraltar because we tried to get married everywhere else first. I set out to get married on the car ferry and we would have arrived in France married. But they wouldn't do it. We were no more successful with cruise ships. We tried embassies. But three weeks' residence in Germany, or two weeks in France, were required. Gibraltar was a bit small for us to move about for a honeymoon. The wedding was quiet and British.'

Le Roy's Tavern On The Green New York restaurant situated in Central Park. John and Yoko booked the venue for Sean's fourth birthday party, attended by children from the Dakota building, accompanied by their parents. Yoko ensured that every one of the children received an expensive gift, and the entertainment included a magician and clowns.

The Lee Nordness Gallery American art gallery, situated in New York, which held an exhibition of *Bag One*, John's erotic lithographs, in February 1970.

The Lennon Centre A health clinic proposed to be set up in Liverpool. In 1982 the regional health officer of the area, Dr. Duncan Egdell, announced that Yoko had agreed to provide the initial funds to launch a trust for a clinic to be set up, probably in the Liverpool 8 district, called The Lennon Centre. Dr. Egdell did not know how much Yoko proposed to donate in order to launch the fund, which would be augmented by an appeal for contributions from the public. But he estimated that the centre would cost in the region of half-a-million pounds. Commenting on Yoko's offer, Sir Trevor Johns, then leader of Liverpool's City Council, said 'It is a marvel-lous gift and it says a great deal about the kind of person Yoko Ono really is.' The idea of the centre has now been scrapped as Yoko has withdrawn her financial support. Her excuse: a 'protest' against the Falklands war!

Les Ambassadeurs Exclusive and fashionable London club near Park Lane. John and Yoko were among the guests invited there on 4 May 1969 when Ringo Starr and Peter Sellers hosted a celebrity-filled party to celebrate the completion of *The Magic Christian*.

Lewis's Liverpool's premier department store in Ranelagh Street in the city centre. The corner entrance doors opposite the Adelphi Hotel were a favourite rendezvous for couples. This is where John would often arrange to meet Cynthia during the early days of their romance.

Rearing high above the doors was a controversial statute of a well-endowed naked man, by the eminent sculptor Jacob Epstein. Adding to Cynthia's embarrassment at meeting beneath such a sculpture was the fact that, to please John, she used to dress quite sexily, often wearing short, tight skirts, fishnet stockings and high-heeled shoes.

Liverpool Institute Grammar school (adjoining Liverpool College of Art) in Mount Street. The pupils included Ivan Vaughan and Len Garry, both of whom were in John's Quarrymen group, Paul McCartney, George Harrison in a lower form than the others, being much younger, and Neil Aspinall. One of the tutors at the school was Alfred Smith, brother of George Smith, who was married to John's Aunt Mimi.

Lewis's — the statue where lovers met.

Liverpool College of Art.

When John, Paul and George were finally in a group together, following their appearances at the Casbah Club, the two institute boys used to sneak into the art college at lunch-times to rehearse in 'the life rooms.

When The Silver Beatles had the opportunity of touring Scotland for two weeks as a backing band for Johnny Gentle, Paul was in the midst of his studies for his GCE exams in which he was to sit six subjects. He preferred to be on the road, told his father he was going on two weeks' holiday and went on the tour, neglecting his studies, which resulted in his passing only one O level.

Paul held a concert in Liverpool for the teachers and students of Liverpool Institute in 1979, when Wings gave a performance at the Royal Court Theatre.

Mathew Street Narrow alley in the centre of Liverpool. It housed some warehouses and a couple of pubs until it gained character in 1957 when Alan Sytner opened the Cavern in the cellars of one of the warehouses. When the Cavern was destroyed and a car park covered the site, local sculptor Arthur Dooley created his famous *Four Lads Who Shook The World* piece and placed it high on the brick walls of the street.

Following John's death, another piece was placed next to the sculpture. This was a statuette of a baby holding a guitar with a halo and the words 'Lennon Lives' above it, and plaque with the lyrics to 'Imagine' placed beneath it.

John's death also aroused more interest in The Beatles' birthplace than at any other time and a multi-million pound complex the Eleanor Centre has been planned for the street, including the renovation of the Cavern on its former site, and a Beatles Museum.

Mathew Street is already the home of Cavern Mecca, The Beatles Museum and Information Centre run by Jim and Liz Hughes at 18 Mathew Street.

Mendips Name of the semi-detached house where John went to live with his Aunt Mimi and Uncle George in 1945. Situated at 251 Menlove Avenue in the suburb of Woolton, three miles from Liverpool City Centre, it was a pleasant house, built in the 'thirties with leaded

Mendips.

windows and a porch in which John spent many hours practising with his guitar. Overlooking the busy Menlove Avenue the house, with its small garden, was where John lived until he rented a flat temporarily in Gambier Terrace.

After John and Cynthia were married, when Cynthia was still expecting Julian, Mimi invited her to move into the house with her. Her husband George had died some years previously. Although Mimi Smith seemed quite content in Mendips, John bought her a luxury bungalow near Bournemouth in 1965 and she moved south.

64 Mount Pleasant A former Georgian town house, which for many years was a register office. Fred Lennon, a ship's waiter, married Julia Stanley there on 3 December 1938. Their son John was married in exactly the same room at the office on 23 August 1962.

His pregnant girlfriend, Cynthia Powell, wore a purple and black two-piece suit and John wore a black suit. Also in attendance were the best man, Brian Epstein and Paul McCartney, George Harrison and Cynthia's brother Tony, with his wife Margaret.

Where two sets of Lennons were married.

The Register Office was taken over by the Merseyside Community Relations Council in the 'seventies.

New York City The Beatles first arrived in New York in February 1964 and their first experience of America must have been exhilarating with the fervour of the fans and the onset of Beatlemania in America.

John was to fall in love with the city and together with Yoko packed most of his possessions from Tittenhurst Park and moved over to New York in August 1971, initially settling in the St Regis Hotel.

John was 30 and remained in New York for the rest of his life buying apartments in the Dakota Building, which he made his home and where he remained a virtual recluse for five years while rearing Sean.

John was to say, 'If I'd lived in Roman times I'd have lived in Rome. Where else? Today, America is the Roman Empire and New York is Rome itself.'

John also explained: 'I think for me it has to do with Liverpool. There's the same quality of energy, of vitality in both cities. New York is at my speed. It's a twenty-four-hours-a-day city, it's going on around you all the time, so much so that you almost stop noticing it ... I like New York because they have no time for the niceties of life. They're like me in this. They're naturally aggressive, they don't believe in wasting time.'

New York also took John to its heart and when the federal authorities were attempting to deport him, the city's mayor, John Lindsay, spoke up for John. A later mayor, Ed Koch, was also supportive of John and after his death agreed to rename part of Central Park Strawberry Fields.

John found New York vibrant and exciting and soon got to know the people, initially coming under the influence of the political activists who inspired his political album *Some Time In New York City*. Eventually he got to know the ordinary New Yorkers who he met on the streets during the daily round of his life.

9 Newcastle Road Two-bedroomed terraced house in Wavertree Liverpool. It was the cause of some controversy in 1981 when an estate agent advertised it as John's birthplace, offering it for sale at an inflated price. John's Aunt Mimi said that it was her mother's home where John spent a couple of months when he was a baby.

Oxford Street Maternity Hospital Liverpool hospital in which Julia Lennon gave birth to John at 7 am on the morning of 9 October 1940 during an air raid. At one time the baby had to be placed underneath the bed. One bomb fell directly outside the hospital. It was only natural in such circumstances, with the feelings of patriotism very strong, that Julia should give her son the middle name of Winston. Immediately John was born, his Aunt Mimi Stanley was informed by telephone and she hurried the two miles from her home to the maternity hospital to see him.

Quarry Bank High School Grammar school in Harthill Road, Allerton, Liverpool 18, which was founded in 1922. Former pupils had included Labour ministers Peter Shore and Bill Rodgers, but their most famous pupil was undoubtedly John, who began to attend Quarry Bank in 1952.

Ed Koch, Mayor of New York City, one of John's staunch supporters.

In the place where I was born . . .

Quarry Bank: where the music began.

His academic record was not one he could be proud of and he was noted for the antics he took part in with his best friend, Pete Shotton. An incoming head-master, William Pobjoy, took an interest in the rebellious pupil and although his exam results were disastrous, (he didn't get any 'O' level passes), John was able to find a place at Liverpool College of Art, with Mr Pobjoy's support. It was whilst at Quarry Bank that John formed his first outfit, The Quarrymen.

Queen Charlotte's Hospital Prominent London Maternity Hospital in Hammersmith. Ringo and Maureen's three children were born there. In early November 1968 Yoko had been in a hospital for blood transfusions, and it was established that she was pregnant. The baby was due at the end of December, but Yoko had to enter Queen Charlotte's in late November.

John took a sleeping bag and camped at the side of her bed. They had various personal problems at the time including the forthcoming court case over the cannabis found in the Montague Square flat and John's divorce from Cynthia.

Whilst in the hospital, John recorded the baby's heartbeat, which was subsequently included on the album *Unfinished Music No 2. Life With The Lions*. Tragically, on 21 November Yoko suffered a miscarriage.

Queen Elizabeth Hotel Here in Montreal, Canada, John and Yoko held a 'Bed-In'. They arrived accompanied by Derek Taylor on Monday 26 May 1969 and booked into suite 1742, having been granted permission to stay in Canada for ten days. Being unable to obtain an American visa, John decided that he could talk to the American media from Canada. Whilst in the hotel he conducted over 60 interviews with journalists and by phone with radio stations in the US.

He had many visitors and on 31 May ordered an eight-track portable recording machine to be delivered to his room to enable him to record 'Give Peace A Chance', with a number of his guests taking part in the chorus. They included disc jockey Murray The K, comedian Tommy Smithers, Rosemary and Timothy Leary, Rabbi Feinberg and the Canadian chapter of the Hari Krishna Temple.

The Rajah Court A nightclub and discotheque complex in Tokyo which on its opening night organized a charity auction in which various items with a John Lennon association were auctioned, including lithographs and photographs. The club raised over £2,000 which was donated to the Spirit Foundation.

Reece's Part of a complex at the corner of Parker Street and Leigh Street in Liverpool's city centre which housed a food store, restaurant and ballroom. On 23 August 1963, a rainy day, Brian Epstein hosted the wedding reception for John and Cynthia Lennon and guests Paul McCartney and George Harrison at the restaurant on the first floor. Arriving from the register office, they were too late to beat the lunchtime crowds of office workers as they ate a set lunch comprising soup, chicken and trifle. The premises were unlicensed and the couple were toasted in water.

Rosebery Street Liverpool street in which John and his skiffle group The Quarrymen performed from the tailboard of a lorry in the summer of 1957. A photograph which was taken of the band at the time is the earliest known picture of the group.

St Regis Hotel Hotel in Manhattan where John and Yoko stayed initially on their move to New York in 1971. The couple resided on the 17th floor.

St Peter's Parish church in Woolton, a suburb of Liverpool, which John attended. He went to the Sunday school, sang in the choir, was a member of the church's youth club and was confirmed when he was 15. His group The Quarrymen played at the youth club dances. On 6 July 1957 they appeared at St. Peter's village fete, where Paul McCartney met John for the first time.

Sefton General.

St Peter's Church.

Sefton General Hospital Situated in Smithdown Road, Liverpool 15, Julian Lennon was born here at 7.45 am on Monday 8 April 1963. Cynthia was rushed to hospital with her friend Phyllis. An ambulance had taken them to Sefton General in the middle of the night. The two girls were dressed only in their nightclothes, protected from the cold by their dressing gowns.

There was some initial difficulty at the birth because the umbilical cord was wrapped around Julian's neck.

Poor Phyllis wasn't allowed to stay at the hospital and had to set off home in her flimsy nightclothes and slippers — a bizarre figure because she still had her hair in curlers! After walking for two miles she managed to catch a taxi.

Sotheby's Prominent London auction house which had held a number of popular sales of Beatles memorabilia including numerous items pertaining to John. A major sale took place on 22 December 1981 and among the huge amount of material were various signed copies of John's books, photographs, posters and records. A pen and ink self-portrait with the words 'to dear mike love from dear john lennon goodbye and see you round the world or somewhere if not england or the disunited states with a ***' sold for £8,800.

Other items included John's and Cynthia's marriage certificate which went for £462 and a Two Virgins nude in perspex and plastic which sold for £4,620. Five of John's stage jackets, a stage suit, black knitted tie and his Raleigh Super Moped brought in £2,860; a radiogram he'd once owned in Liverpool raised £418; a Steinway upright piano fetched £8,250 and one set of his Bag One Erotic lithographs from a limited edition of 300 brought in £5,060.

South Ocean Boulevard Area of Palm Beach where John and Yoko bought a neo-Spanish house from Mrs Jock McLean for almost a million dollars early in 1980. The house had seven bedrooms, two swimming pools and 150 feet of beach front.

Strawberry Fields Area of New York's Central Park which was renamed in tribute to John. On 19 August 1981 Yoko sent out a letter to various people outlining plans for this section of the park. She wrote, 'In memory of John Lennon, New York City has designated a beautiful triangular island in Central Park to be known as Strawberry Fields. It happens to be where John and I took our last walk together. John would have been very proud that this was given to him, an island named after his song, rather than a statue or a monument.

'My initial thought was to acquire some English and Japanese plants and give them to the park commission to be planted in Strawberry Fields. But somehow that idea was not quite in the spirit of things. Then I remembered what John and I did when we first met over ten years ago. We planted an acorn in England as a symbol of our love. We then sent acorns to all the heads of state around the world inviting them to do the same. Many responded saying that they enjoyed the experience. So in the name of John and Yoko and the spirit of love and sharing, I would like once again to invite all countries of the world this time to offer plants, rocks and/or stones of their nations for Strawberry Fields.

'The plants will eventually be forests, the rock will be a resting place for travel-

Strawberry Fields, New York style.

ling souls, the bricks will pave the lane John and I used to walk on and the circle where we used to sit and talk for hours. It will be nice to have the whole world in one place, one field, living and growing together in harmony. This will be the nicest tribute we could give to John. The acorn we planted a decade ago is now a tree. I would like to obtain a twig from it to be transplanted on the island. Maybe we could add a moonstone or a pebble from Mars so as not to shut out the universe. The invitation is open.

'Copies of this note will be sent to Mayor Koch, who has been a major inspiration behind the designation of

Strawberry Fields, and to heads of state throughout the world. Let me take you to Strawberry Fields.

'Love, Yoko Ono, New York City, 19 August 1981.

'It is requested that all offers of plant material, rocks and stones be presented first in writing accompanied by a colour photograph and mailed to: Strawberry Fields, c/o Studio One, 1 West 72 Street, New York City, NY 10023.'

Strawberry Fields A Salvation Army children's home situated in Beaconsfield Road, Liverpool 25, near to where John lived in Menlove Avenue. There was originally a large Victorian mansion on the site, but that was knocked down and replaced by a modern building. Together with his mates, Pete Shotton and Nigel Whalley, John used to visit the annual fétes which took place in the grounds of Strawberry Fields each summer.

The several acres of ground were well wooded and ideal for John and his mates to play in. The garden fetes enabled them to sell lemonade bottles for a penny each. They later admitted to a habit of stealing items from stalls during those bittersweet days, which resounded to the throb of the Salvation Army Band.

The memories were to take strong

Tittenhurst Park.

root in John's mind and emerged as the haunting 'Strawberry Fields Forever', one of his greatest compositions, which was issued as a double A side with Paul's 'Penny Lane' in February 1967. He was later to name a boat after the place, and New York City has renamed three acres of Central Park Strawberry Fields.

Tittenhurst Park Huge, white Georgian mansion in London Road, Ascot, which John bought in May 1969 for approximately £150,000. The vast eighteenth century building boasted seven bedrooms, four bathrooms, three reception rooms, a lodge, staff apartments, cottages, a pavilion and swimming pool in 70 acres of parkland.

John and Yoko lived there until 1972 when they moved permanently to America. John had built an 8-track studio in the house and recorded his album *Imagine* there in 1971.

Ringo Starr later decided to make it his home, eventually moving in with his second wife Barbara Bach. It was reported at the time that he paid two million pounds for the property.

Trinity Road Parish Church Church in Hoylake, Cheshire where John's first child was christened John Charles Julian Lennon in November 1963. John was unable to attend the ceremony.

The Troubadour Club in Los Angeles. It was the scene of an infamous incident in March 1974 which hit the headlines throughout the world when John and Harry Nilsson were evicted from the premises.

It was during John's 'eight-month-long-weekend' and The Smothers Brothers were attempting a revival of their act at the club.

John was drinking brandy Alexanders for the first time and both John and Harry, who were drunk, began singing 'Can't Stand The Rain', prior to The Brothers appearing on stage.

Other people began clapping to the song. Once The Smothers Brothers appeared, John began to make some remarks, which didn't go down too well with the audience.

He went to the toilet and whilst there he picked up a Kotex and stuck it on his head.

He reportedly said to a waitress, 'Do you know who I am?' and she was quoted as replying, 'Yeah, you're an asshole with a Kotex on.'

They apparently began throwing punches at The Smothers Brothers manager and a waitress called Naomi, and were thrown out of the club. Naomi said afterwards: 'It's not the pain that hurts, it's finding out that one of your idols is a real asshole.'

University of California In 1982 the university instigated a special John Lennon Award. A sum of 1,000 dollars was to be awarded annually to a music student. The Dean of the Fine Arts Department, Robert Gray, commented: 'The award is to encourage the continuation of the creative process which John Lennon's work embodied.' Geraldine Keeling, a classical music student, was the first recipient of the award.

Valley View Farm One of the four farms which John bought from Dreamstreet Farms. A 316-acre spread near Franklin, Pennsylvania, it had a white farmhouse which John and Yoko enjoyed visiting.

All you need is Peace.

'Sie Liebt Dich . . .'

Oh boy, those were the days.

Performances

'Alchemical Wedding' Name of an event at the Royal Albert Hall on 18 December 1968. London's 'underground' scene held their special Christmas party at the hall and John and Yoko first introduced bagism to the world. The two of them appeared on stage moving about inside a large white bag.

BMI Awards Annual American awards from the music industry which presents citations of achievement from Broadcast Music Inc. for the most performed songs of the year. In 1981 John Lennon received three posthumous citations for 'Just Like Starting Over', 'Watching The Wheels' and 'Woman'. He was also awarded a cumulative citation pin acknowledging a total of 62 awards over the years. George Harrison also received an award at the same time for 'All Those Years Ago'.

'Built Around' Title of a piece of sculpture made by John which was on display at the Arts Laboratory in Drury Lane, London, early in 1968. It was his first sculpture to go on public display and was described by the *Observer* newspaper as 'a long low white plinth with two slats of wood angled upon it, encrusted with white, broken, plastic beakers and two porcelain doorknobs.'

The David Frost Show Frost, a British TV host/interviewer/investigator, first came to fame in the early 'sixties in the satirical series *That Was The Week That Was*. His career continued to thrive when he began to host his own shows on both sides of the Atlantic.

John and George appeared with the Maharishi on 30 September 1967 and the two Beatles returned the following week for a further appearance on 4 October. The Beatles performed 'Hey Jude' before a studio audience of 300 on *Frost On Sunday* on 4 September 1968 and John appeared on the 7 June and 14 June programmes of *The David Frost Show* in 1969. John and Yoko appeared together on 13 January 1972.

The Day They Shot Lennon Play written by James McLure, presented at the NJ Theatre, Princeton, USA, from 19 January until 6 February 1983.

The Destruction Of Art Symposium held in London in September 1966. Yoko Ono left New York to travel to England for the event.

The Dick Cavett Show John and Yoko appeared on this American ABC TV talk show on 22 September 1970, together with Dr Arthur Janov. They discussed Primal Scream therapy. Almost exactly a year later, on 21 September 1971, the pair were the only guests on the 90-minute late night show. In between their lengthy chat, excerpts from four of the John and Yoko films, *Imagine*, *Fly*, *Mrs Lennon* and *Erection* were screened.

An Evening With John & Yoko Event at the New Cinema Club, London in mid-September 1969, at which four of the couple's films were presented. The movies were the 15-minute *Two Virgins*, *Smile*, the Amsterdam film *Honeymoon* and the world première of *Self-Portrait*. John and Yoko fooled the press by sending along a surrogate couple enclosed in a large bag who, when arriving in John's white Rolls-Royce, were assumed to be John and Yoko. The pair were taken on stage where they chanted 'Hare Krishna' throughout the show.

The Filmmakers' Fortnight Festival

Major international annual film festival in Cannes, France. John and Yoko were invited to present two of their films, *Apotheosis (Balloon)* and *Fly* at the Festival on 15 May 1971. *Apotheosis (Balloon)* was booed by the audience.

The Foyles Literary Luncheon

Prestigious annual event in London. When it was announced on 23 March 1964 that John had won the Foyle's literary prize for his first book *In His Own Write*, he was naturally happy to accept the invitation to appear at the literary luncheon at the Dorchester Hotel the following month.

John and Cynthia spent the previous evening at the Ad Lib club and arrived at the Dorchester feeling a trifle under the weather, horrified to discover that it was a formal affair and that, as guest of honour, John was supposed to make a speech.

Cynthia sat between the Earl of Arran and singer Marty Wilde, John had to face a battery of TV cameras and press photographers when, following the toast he was required to stand and make his speech. He said: 'Ladies and gentlemen. Thank you very much: it's been a pleasure' (or, as some reports would have it: 'Thank you all very much. You've got a lucky face.') and sat down.

There was some displeasure at this break from tradition, but Brian Epstein came to the rescue with a speech.

The Grammy Awards

Prestigious American music industry annual awards show. John appeared as a guest presenter on 1 March 1975.

Half Wind Show

A Yoko Ono exhibition presented at London's Lisson Gallery in September 1967. John sponsored the exhibition, although he wanted it kept secret at the time and didn't even go to see it.

Yoko subtitled it *Yoko Plus Me* in reference to John's support. The exhibition consisted of numerous everyday objects cut in half, painted white and displayed in their usual settings: objects such as chairs, washbasins and a toothbrush.

'Iced Tea'

One of the exhibits at the Yoko Ono exhibition in Syracuse University, New York in October 1971, in which John participated. It was a gigantic block of ice in the shape of the letter T, which was allowed to melt.

Imagine

A musical review based on John's life which opened at the Colonial Tavern, Toronto, Canada on 18 May 1981. The performers called themselves Abbey Road Productions.

In His Own Write

One act play based on John's two books *In His Own Write* and *A Spaniard In The Works*.

It was directed by Victor Spinetti, who also co-wrote it for the stage with American playwright Adrienne Kennedy, and acted in the production. The play was originally performed for one night only on a bill with two other one-act plays *A Covent Garden Tragedy* and *An Unwarranted Intrusion*.

It was entitled *Scene Three, Act One*. Sir Laurence Olivier was impressed and approved its inclusion as part of the National Theatre's repertoire. It then opened at the Old Vic on 18 June 1968 and John, Yoko and Neil Aspinall attended the premiere.

In His Own Write One act play which opened at the Old Vic on 18 June 1968. Directed by Victor Spinetti, the play had been staged for a single performance in December 1967 as *Scene Three Act One*. It was based on John's two books and the idea of turning them into a play came from American writer Adrienne Kennedy. She contacted Victor Spinetti, who not only directed, but worked on the script with her. Jonathan Cape, John's British publishers, issued a book of the play in 1968 called *The Lennon Play: In His Own Write*. *John Lennon, Adrienne Kennedy, Victor Spinetti*. It was published in the US in the same year by Simon & Schuster.

During that time, John had begun his association with Yoko although still married to Cynthia. It was one of the first public events to which Yoko accompanied him. When they arrived at the theatre with Neil Aspinall, the waiting press were slightly hostile towards the couple and cried out, 'Where's your wife?'

In His Own Write One-man show starring Gareth Williams which ran for a short season at the Lyric Studio, Hammersmith, London in January 1982. Based on the books *In His Own Write* and *A Spaniard In The Works*, the show featured Williams reciting poems from the books, acting out sketches and singing John Lennon songs.

Interview With A Legend: John Lennon With Tom Snyder Of The Tomorrow Show A video-cassette issued by the Karl Video Corporation in the US in 1981, priced at 59 dollars and 95 cents. The main section of the video is a lengthy interview with John by Tom Snyder, first screened in 1975. Added, is the bulk of the *Tomorrow Show* first screened on 9 December 1980 with interviews by rock music journalist Lisa Robinson, who discusses John's years as a househusband and Jack Douglas, the producer of the *Double Fantasy* album.

Jesus Christ Religious musical scheduled to make its début at St Paul's Cathedral, London in 1970. John was offered the role of Jesus and suggested that he'd accept the part if Yoko could appear as Mary Magdalene. Negotiations must have fallen through because neither of them appeared in the production.

John Lennon — The Beatle Years Title of a stage show which Bill Sargent intended to present in America in 1981. Sargent, a Hollywood producer who had once made a proposal for a Beatles get-together, had hoped to feature the cast of *Beatlemania* in his planned production.

John Lennon — The Man The Memory A three-hour programme dedicated to John Lennon broadcast on the American RKO Radio network on Sunday 14 December 1980. The programme contained excerpts from John's last interview conducted scarcely six hours before he was shot. RKO had arranged an interview which was originally to have been broadcast on St Valentine's Day. Their team arrived at John's Dakota Buildings apartment at 2 pm on Monday 8 December 1980 and the interview lasted for three hours with

Yoko Ono also taking part. The interviewer was Dave Sholin. Also present at the apartments during the interview were scriptwriter Laurie Kaye, Bert Keane, a promotions director for Warner Brothers' Records and Ron Hummel, an engineer for the San Francisco radio station KFRC.

John Lennon: Rock 'N' Roll Never Forgets American radio special produced by a company called Westwood One. It was syndicated to a number of radio stations in the US between 17 and 19 September 1982. The programme featured an interview with Elliot Mintz.

Juke Box Jury Popular early-Saturday-evening BBC television show of the early 'sixties, hosted by David Jacobs. *JBJ* usually featured four celebrities who would sit in judgement on the latest pop record releases. The artists would sit next to each other behind a counter-like structure opposite to Jacobs. The only other prominent item on the set was a jukebox. There was an All-Beatles edition recorded at the Empire Theatre, Liverpool. Individual members of the group appeared on the show and actress Jane Asher was featured on the panel on several occasions. John appeared on *Juke Box Jury* on 29 June 1963.

Lennon Musical play devised by Bob Eaton, which had its world premiere at the Everyman Theatre, Hope Street, Liverpool on Wednesday 28 October 1981. Eaton interviewed numerous people who had known or been associated with John including Arthur Ballard, Victor Spinetti, Bob Wooler, Clive Epstein, Gerry Marsden, Joe

What step should we take next?

Flannery and Hunter Davies. The show's designer was Sue Mayes, who added a series of slides to the visual effects.

The printed programme for the show, which ran for several weeks, stated that it was presented 'with the permission and personal best wishes of Yoko Ono'.

The nine members of the cast each took on several roles. Jonathan Barlow appeared as John later in his life, and also as former drummer Pete Best and Ringo Starr. Carl Chase appeared as

George Harrison and TV producer Muriel Young, Graham Fellows was Bertrand Russell and Paul McCartney, John McCardle portrayed George Martin and Larry Parnes, Mark McGann appeared as the young Lennon and as George Harrison, Mia Soteriou acted the roles of Julia Lennon and Yoko Ono, Chris Walton appeared as Stu Sutcliffe and Brian Epstein, and Phil Whitchurch portrayed Pete Shotton, Allan Williams, Arthur Janov and Tony Barrow.

London Art Spectrum Event at the Alexandra Palace, London on 5 September 1971 which featured five films by John and Yoko: *Cold Turkey*, *The Ballad of John And Yoko*, *Give Peace A Chance*, *Instant Karma* and *Up Your Legs*.

The Mike Douglas Show American TV show which John and Yoko were to co-host for a week, appearing on five consecutive nights from 14 to 18 February 1972. One of their guests was Chuck Berry, and John performed 'Johnny B. Goode' and 'Memphis' with him, backed by Elephant's Memory, the New York Band, who provided backing for all the numbers on the show.

The other songs John performed were: 'Attica State', 'Imagine', 'It's So Hard', 'John Sinclair', 'The Luck Of The Irish', 'Sakura', 'Shake It', 'Sisters Oh Sisters', 'We're All Water', and 'Woman Is The Nigger Of The World'.

The Music Of Lennon & McCartney A spectacular 50-minute tribute to the song writing talents of John and Paul. Produced by Johnny Hamp it was directed by Phil Casson for Granada Television and first networked throughout Britain on 17 December 1965.

Henry Mancini, John and Johnny Hamp.

The programme highlighted the various treatments that had been applied to the Lennon/McCartney compositions by various artists throughout the world. French singer Dick Rivers sang in French, organist Alan Haven produced his jazz interpretation of 'A Hard Day's Night' and Peter Sellers gave an hilarious cod Shakespearean rendition of the same number, togged out in Richard III costume.

George Martin conducted a three-piece orchestra with his arrangement of 'I Feel Fine' and American pianist Henry Mancini gave a solo performance of the same number.

The Beatles played 'Day Tripper' and 'We Can Work It Out' and Paul began the song 'Yesterday', which was completed by Marianne Faithful.

The other performances included

Esther Phillips with 'And I Love Him', Peter and Gordon with 'World Without Love', Lulu with 'I Saw Him Standing There', Fritz Speigel's Barock And Roll Ensemble with 'She Loves You', Billy J. Kramer and The Dakotas with 'Bad To Me' and 'Do You Want To Know A Secret' and Cilla Black with 'It's For You'.

National Sculpture Exhibition

Major event in the British contemporary sculpture calendar in 1968. The organizers included Fabio Barraclough and Anthony Fawcett. Yoko asked Fawcett if she and John could contribute to the exhibition.

He in turn asked Barraclough who raised the matter at a committee meeting.

Yoko described their sculpture to Fawcett as, 'Two acorns planted in the ground, one facing to the east, the other to the west. The acorns will symbolise our meeting and love for each other and also the uniting and growth of our two cultures.'

John and Yoko had a special catalogue designed and printed which described their work, together with a silver plaque containing the engraved words: 'John by Yoko Ono. Yoko by John Lennon, Sometime in May 1968.'

The event was to take place at Coventry Cathedral with a preview on 15 June 1968.

However, when the Lennons arrived with their sculpture, the Canon of the cathedral refused to allow their exhibit to be brought inside the cathedral.

Eventually, a compromise was reached and John and Yoko planted their acorns in the ground outside the cathedral and had a wrought iron seat placed over them.

A week later the acorns were dug up and stolen. The pair sent two more acorns, together with a security guard to look after them until the exhibition ended.

Nationwide Britain's most popular, lightweight current affairs programme, televised by the BBC five nights a week. On 21 December 1982 the programme featured an interview with Yoko recorded inside the Dakota apartments. She was with Sean and the basic interview was on the theme of Christmas and the many happy Christmases they had spent together in the apartment. Yoko recalled a time when John bought 40 separate presents for Sean and how much he enjoyed watching Sean open each one.

Oh! Calcutta Notorious stage play by Kenneth Tynan featuring full-frontal nudity by both sexes and sexually explicit dialogue. Tynan, who was born in 1927, was one of Britain's most influential theatre critics and at one time was the literary manager of the National Theatre. His name became associated with controversy in the sixties when he became the first person ever to use the word 'fuck' live on British television.

Oh! Calcutta proved just as shocking to the public who considered it another example of the permissive sixties. Tynan asked a number of celebrities including John to contribute a small sketch. John wrote an item about masturbation based on a time in his boyhood when he'd masturbate in the company of friends, during which they'd call out the names of movie actresses.

Tynan died in 1980.

The Old Grey Whistle Test Long-running British rock music show on the TV channel BBC 2. In 1975 Bob Harris, who was then the show's main interviewer, telerecorded a lengthy interview with John in New York. The show was first broadcast on 18 April 1975 and has been screened on at least two subsequent occasions. John performed 'Slippin' And Slidin'' and 'Stand By Me' which have since appeared on several bootleg recordings.

One To One Name given to a special project of gathering funds for a number of small homes for retarded children in New York in order to provide them with more individual attention, hence the name 'One to One'. John and Yoko, ever conscious of aiding charities (at one time it was suggested that John was tithing out one tenth of his income to charitable trusts), agreed to give a special performance for the One To One organization.

The concert took place at Madison Square Garden on 30 August 1972. Stevie Wonder, Roberta Flack and Sha Na Na were also on the bill. John and Yoko appeared on stage after midnight and performed 16 numbers: 'New York City', 'It's So Hard', 'Sisters O Sisters', 'Woman Is The Nigger Of The World', 'Now Or Never', 'Well Well Well', 'Instant Karma', 'Mother', 'Open Your Box', 'Cold Turkey', 'Hound Dog', and 'Give Peace A Chance'.

The couple, who were backed by Elephant's Memory, received a five-minute standing ovation. The charities involved in the One To One venture, including

---

On stage at Madison Square Gardens.

the Willowbrook Handicapped Children's Home in New York, received over a million dollars for the event. Half a million dollars raised by the concert itself, including the TV rights, was matched by an equal amount presented by the government.

ABC Television screened the event on 15 December 1972.

Peace For Christmas Charity concert held at London's Lyceum Ballroom on 15 December 1969. The concert was to launch the John and Yoko 'War Is Over' campaign and was in aid of the United Nations Children's Fund. John and Yoko were joined on stage by George Harrison, Eric Clapton, Keith Moon, Billy Preston, Klaus Voorman, Alan White and the Delaney & Bonnie Band to whom John was to refer later as The Plastic Ono Supergroup.

In a pensive pose.

Ready, Steady, Go! Former Friday night live rock show by the London television company, Rediffusion. The Beatles made several appearances on *Ready, Steady, Go!*, a show with the tag 'The weekend starts here', which was hosted by Cathy McGowan. John and George were interviewed on the show on 16 April 1965.

Release BBC 2 television programme. John appeared on the show on 22 June 1968 to discuss the stage presentation of *In His Own Write*, an adaptation for the theatre of his two best-selling books, which had opened a few days previously.

Rock And Roll Circus A Rolling Stones television special, directed by Michael Lindsay Hogg, who was to work on the *Let It Be* films.

John made a special appearance on the show on 11 December 1968, performing 'Yer Blues', backed by Keith Richards of The Rolling Stones, Eric Clapton and Mitch Mitchell, drummer with The Jimi Hendrix Experience. The special also featured The Who and Jethro Tull. For some reason it has never been shown.

The Royal Variety Performance The Beatles were selected to appear on their first Royal Variety Performance at the Prince of Wales Theatre, Leicester Square before the Queen Mother, Princess Margaret and Lord Snowdon on 4 November 1963. Announcing their last number, 'Twist And Shout', John said, 'Will the people in the cheaper seats clap their hands? All the rest of you, just rattle your jewellery. . .' John found himself widely quoted in the following days papers.

The *Daily Mirror* used the term 'Beatlemania' for the first time, followed by stories of John's witty remark. This did much to consolidate his reputation as a wit.

It has been said that a comedian suggested to John that he should make a humorous remark at the royal performance.

There have been various versions of the quote, including: 'Those of you in the cheaper seats clap your hands, and those in the more expensive seats just rattle your jewellery.'

Salute To Sir Lew Grade Television tribute to Britain's famous TV mogul Sir Lew Grade, screened on 13 June 1975. Despite the fact that Sir Lew's company, ATV defeated John and Paul in their attempt to gain control of Northern Songs, the genial cigar-smoking impres-

sario was able to talk Paul into filming a TV special for him. *James Paul McCartney* was screened in 1973. Sir Lew also secured John for his own television special.

However, John produced a sardonic stunt by having the members of Etc, his backing group, wear masks with the image of a face on the back of their heads. This gave them the visual effect of having two faces. Was this John's way of saying Sir Lew was two-faced?

John and his band performed two numbers on the show: 'Slippin' And Slidin'' and 'Imagine'.

This Is Not Here Exhibition of the works of Yoko Ono presented at the Everson Museum of Art in Syracuse, New York, 9 to 27 October 1971. John was a guest artist. The exhibition was taped and later screened as *John and*

Power to the people.

You Are Here.

Yoko In Syracuse, NY on American television on 11 May 1972.

Today Current affairs programme on the British ITV network. John was interviewed on the programme on 24 June 1966 when his second book *A Spaniard In The Works* was published.

Tonight BBC television current affairs programme on which John appeared on 18 June 1966 to discuss *A Spaniard In The Works*.

Tonight American TV show on which John appeared with Paul on 15 May 1968. It was hosted by Joe Garagiola and among the topics discussed by the two Beatles were Apple and the Maharishi.

Trafalgar Square Wrapping Event One of Yoko's 1966 happenings conducted soon after she arrived in Britain from New York. Together with some helpers she covered one of the giant stone lions with white tarpaulin.

Unfinised Paintings And Objects By Yoko Ono Exhibition of Yoko's which was presented at the Indica Gallery in London from 9 to 12 November 1966. John Lennon turned up at the gallery on preview night before the official opening.

One of the first things he noticed was an apple on display which people were invited to watch as it decomposed. It had a price tag of £200.

John remarked 'I thought it was fantastic. I got the humour of her work immediately.'

He noticed that there was a pair of stepladders which enabled a spectator to get nearer to a large black canvas attached to the ceiling. There was a chain supporting a spyglass and when you looked through it you could see the word 'Yes' on the canvas.

John was then introduced to Yoko who later said that the only Beatle she really remembered by name at the time was Ringo. She was reluctant to grant his request when he asked if he could hammer a nail into one of the exhibits marked 'Hammer A Nail In'.

She didn't like the idea of it being done before the exhibition's opening. But because gallery co-owner John Dunbar kept on insisting that John was a millionaire and might buy the work she agreed on condition that he paid her five shillings.

When he said he'd pay her an imaginary five shillings for hammering in an imaginary nail, it was apparent to both of them that they were kindred spirits. That moment must have been when the 'Ballad of John & Yoko' really began.

Where It's At BBC Radio One programme which previewed *The Magical Mystery Tour* EP on 2 December 1967. On the same show, John was interviewed by disc jockey Kenny Everett.

World Of Books BBC radio programme. John's interview in which he discussed his new book *A Spaniard In The Works* was broadcast on the show on 3 July 1965.

The World This Weekend BBC radio programme which featured an interview with Yoko conducted by Chrissy Smith. Broadcast on 22 February 1981, the interview had been recorded two days previously in New York.

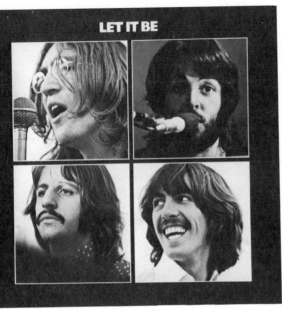

Records

'Across The Universe' The inspiration for the song came when John woke up at 7 o'clock one morning with the words 'pools of sorrow, waves of joy' spinning around in his head. He couldn't get back to sleep and began writing the song.

Evidence of the influence of the Maharishi Mahesh Yoga is contained in the chorus phrase 'Jai Guru De Va Om' which refers to the Maharishi's teacher, Guru Deva. The first version of the song was produced by George Martin on 4 February 1968.

During the session it was decided that some female voices were needed to sing the line 'Nothing's going to change my world.'

Paul found two girls outside the studio and brought them in on the session. Thus Gaylenn Pease and Lizzie Bravo found their own piece of immortality. The number was originally considered as the A side of a Beatles' single, but 'Lady Madonna' was chosen instead and the number lay on the shelf for some time.

Comedian Spike Milligan had suggested to the World Wildlife Fund that they issue an album, with the proceeds going to their charity, and 'Across The Universe' was donated by The Beatles.

The album was called *No One's Gonna Change Our World*, and was issued on EMI Star Line SRS 5013 (LP) on 12 December 1969. Other artists featured on the album included Cilla Black, Rolf Harris, The Hollies, Spike Milligan, The Bee Gees, Lulu, Dave Dee, Dozy, Beaky, Mick & Tich, Cliff Richard And The Shadows, Bruce Forsyth and Harry Seacombe.

When Phil Spector was called in to work on a number of Beatles tapes, he completely altered 'Across The Uni-

verse', removing the vocals by Paul and the two girls and introducing his 'wall of sound' and the famous 'Spector over-kill'. This version wound up on the *Let It Be* album.

The number also appeared on *The Beatles 1967-1970* LP issued in April 1973, and in the boxed set of albums *The Beatles Collection*, issued in December 1978 on the album *Rarities*.

Rarities itself was issued as a separate album in October 1979.

David Bowie featured the number on his *Young Americans* album and John played on the track with him. The song was also performed by The Beatles in the film *Let It Be*.

'Ain't She Sweet' The only track of The Beatles' original recordings in Hamburg on which John is lead vocalist. When The Beatles backed Tony Sheridan on the recordings produced by Bert Kaempfert for Polydor, they did a couple of tracks without Sheridan and 'Ain't She Sweet' was one of them. Apart from being lead singer, John played rhythm guitar, George Harrison played lead guitar, Stu Sutcliffe, bass guitar, Pete Best, drums and Paul McCartney played rhythm guitar and provided back-up vocals.

This occasion in 1960 was John's first visit to a recording studio and the number he sang was an 'oldie', like one or two of the others they recorded at that time. The number was penned by Jack Yellen and Milton Ager in the nine-teen-twenties. 'Ain't She Sweet' was issued on various Polydor albums and singles. At one stage in May 1964 it was a minor chart hit in Britain when issued as a single with 'If You Love Me, Baby' on the flip.

'Ain't That A Shame' Song which Julia Lennon taught John to play on a banjo and which he later said was the first rock and roll number he played. It was written by Antoine Domino and Dave Bartholomew and John performed the number on his *Rock 'N' Roll* album.

'Aisumasen (I'm Sorry)' A track on the *Mind Games* album. John wrote the song for Yoko. *Aisumasen* means 'I'm sorry' in Japanese.

'AOS' Number by Yoko which she performed at the Royal Albert Hall on 29 February 1968. John accompanied her on guitar and the appearance was recorded. The number, over seven minutes in length, appeared on the *Yoko Ono/Plastic Ono Band* album issued at the end of the following year.

Approximately Infinite Universe Yoko's own double album produced by John and Yoko. Yoko wrote every song on the LP on which she was backed by Elephant's Memory, The Endless Strings and Choir Boys. It was issued in America on Apple SVBB on 8 January 1973 and in Britain on Apple SAPDO 1001 on 16 February.

The album sleeve is a very slight variation of the cover of John's *Mind Games* album, which featured Yoko's profile jutting horizontally from the horizon like a range of mountains. This time John's face replaces hers.

The numbers on side one are: 'Yang Yang', 'Death Of Samantha', 'I Want My Love To Rest Tonight', 'What Did I Do!' and 'Have You Seen A Horizon Lately?'.

Side two features 'Approximately Infinite Universe', 'Peter The Dealer', 'Song For John', 'Catman (The Rosies

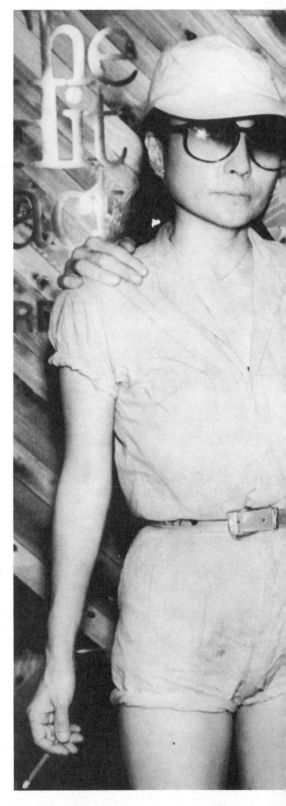

Are Coming)', 'What A Barstard The World Is' and 'Waiting For The Sunrise'.

Tracks on side three are: 'I Felt Like Smashing My Face In A Clear Glass Window', 'Winter Song', 'Kite Song', 'What A Mess', 'Shirankatta (I Didn't Know)' and 'Air Talk'.

Side four features: 'I Have A Woman Inside My Soul', 'Move On Fast', 'Now Or Never', 'Is Winter Here To Stay?' and 'Looking Over From My Hotel Window'.

'The Ballad Of John & Yoko'

The euphoria of marriage, bed-ins and the creative adventures he shared with Yoko caused John to rush to London to record this number. George and Ringo were unavailable at the time and only John and Paul perform on the record.

John's mention of Christ caused the record to be banned on a number of American radio stations, which may explain why it didn't top the charts in the US. Issued in Britain on Apple R 5786 on 30 May 1969 it remained at No 1 for three weeks and was in the charts for a total of 14 weeks. In America it was issued on Apple 2351 on 14 June and reached position No 8, and remained in the charts for nine weeks. The flipside was a George Harrison composition 'Old Brown Shoe'.

The Beatles Tapes From The David Wigg Interviews

Double-album issued in Britain on Polydor 2683 068 on 30 July 1976. The entire side one of the first album is devoted to interviews with John and Yoko which Wigg conducted with the couple at the Apple offices in June 1969 and at the San Regis Hotel, New York in October 1979. The album contained a booklet of photographs including one of Wigg, a *Daily Express* music journalist, with John and Yoko.

Bootlegs There are literally hundreds of bootleg recordings of The Beatles available, mainly in America, and a growing number of John Lennon bootlegs. These illegal recordings are rare in Britain, due to an Act of Parliament which effectively killed a growing bootleg trade. *A Guitar's All Right John, But You'll Never Earn Your Living By It* is the title of a bootleg issued on Audifon R6015 and is, of course, the famous Aunt Mimi quote. The cover sports the early Hamburg picture of a leather-clad John in the foreground and a full-length out-of-focus Stuart Sutcliffe in the background. The 10-inch album contains the tracks: 'Whatever Gets You Thru The Night', 'Lucy In The Sky With Diamonds', 'I Saw Her Standing There', 'Slippin' And Slidin'', 'Stand By Me', 'Oh My Love', 'Lady Marmalade', 'Working Class Hero' and 'Day Tripper'.

A Hard Road was a bootleg album issued in America in 1981 on Moriphon L05972. There is a colour cover of John playing piano. Side one features a message from John: '1970 Xmas Message', followed by four tracks from the One-To-One Concert at Madison Square Garden on 30 August 1972: 'Mother', 'Come Together', 'Give Peace A Chance' and 'Imagine'. Side two comprises mainly excerpts from the BBC interview conducted by Andy Peebles with John on 6 December 1980.

Come Back Johnny is another American bootleg album, this time issued in 1980 on Melvin MM09. Side one features John with Yoko, The Plastic Ono Band and Elephant's Memory on tracks such as 'New York City', 'It's So

Hard', 'Woman Is The Nigger Of The World', 'Well, Well, Well' and 'Instant Karma'. There is also a radio commercial for the *Walls and Bridges* album. Side two opens with an interview John conducted with Howard Cossell in 1974 followed by four numbers from the One-To-One Show: 'Mother', 'Come Together', 'Cold Turkey' and 'Hound Dog'. Also on the album is the Lennon/Chuck Berry duet on 'Johnny B. Goode' from the *Mike Douglas Show* and *Imagine*.

Listen To This Record is a bootleg picture disc, issued in America in 1981. It features a photograph of John from the *Walls and Bridges* album and excerpts from an interview of John by a New York radio station in 1974.

Working Class Hero is an American bootleg double album issued by Chet Mar Records in 1981. Side one contains 'Be My Baby' and 'Angel Baby' from the *Roots* album and 'Yer Blues' from the Rolling Stones' unreleased *Rock & Roll Circus*. Side two opens with a version of 'Imagine' which John performed on *The Mike Douglas Show* in February 1972. The following three tracks, 'Mother', 'Come Together' and 'Give Peace A Chance' are from the One-To-One concert at Madison Square Garden on 30 August 1972. Side three features 'Slippin' and Slidin'' and 'Stand By Me' from BBC2's *The Old Grey Whistle Test* of 18 April 1975, and 'Whatever Gets You Thru The Night', 'Lucy In The Sky With Diamonds' and 'I Saw Her Standing There', three tracks from the live recording of John with Elton John at Madison Square Garden in 1974. Side four opens with 'Lady Marmalade' which John recorded in the Dakota Building in 1975, followed by two songs he recorded with Chuck Berry on the *Mike Douglas Show* in 1972 —

'Memphis' and 'Johnny B. Goode'. 'Oh My Love' was recorded in Weybridge in 1975, 'Working Class Hero' was recorded at a party in 1972, 'Day Tripper' is taken from Radio One's *Top Gear* of October 1967 when John performed with Jimi Hendrix, and the final track is John's recording of 'Do The Oz'.

There are various lists of bootleg collections, the most detailed probably being Charles Reinhart's *You Can't Do That*, published by Pierian Press. This lists approximately fifty John Lennon bootlegs, with titles such as *Day Trippin' With Hendrix*, *Dr. Winston O'Boogie On The Tomorrow Show*, *John Lennon and Elvis Presley*, *Lennon vs. The World* and *Man Of The Decade*.

'Born In A Prison' Number penned by Yoko and included on the *Sometime In New York City* album. John and Yoko performed the number on stage at the One-To-One concert in 1972.

'Cold Turkey' Plastic Ono Band single which John recorded on 30 September 1969 with Eric Clapton on lead guitar, Klaus Vormann on bass and Ringo Starr on drums. John also began his policy of putting Yoko on the B side of his singles with 'Don't Worry Kyoko (Mummy's Only Looking For A Hand In The Snow)'.

The disc was issued in America on Apple 1813 on 20 October 1969 and in Britain on Apple 1001 on 24 October. The number which he'd originally offered to The Beatles wasn't a spectacular hit, reaching 14 in some British charts.

John then made his controversial movie of sending a messenger to Aunt

Who is the shy lady on your tie?

Mimi's house to retrieve his MBE from the top of the television set.

He then had it wrapped in brown paper and sent to the Queen at Buckingham Palace with the message, 'I am returning this MBE in protest against Britain's involvement in the Nigeria-Biafra thing, against our support of America in Vietnam and against *Cold Turkey* slipping down the charts. With love John Lennon'.

He also sent an identical letter to the Prime Minister and to the Secretary of the Central Chancery.

'Come Together' Another of John's personal favourites and one he wrote when he was originally asked by Timothy Leary's wife to pen a campaign song for Leary's proposed idea of running for Governor of California. Leary changed his mind and John adapted the song for The Beatles to record.

This is the number which sparked off the dispute involving Maurice Levy who claimed that both the melody and lyrics at the beginning of the song were taken from an early Chuck Berry composition.

John maintained that it was not plagiarism, merely a tribute, and agreed to settle the matter by recording two Chuck Berry songs, which led to further complications.

Another controversial aspect of the number was the fact that Coca Cola was mentioned. This caused the BBC to ban the number because it included a brand name and therefore broke their code regarding advertising.

It was the last track recorded for the *Abbey Road* album and also the first track on the LP issued in 1969. The number was also used as the 'B' side of the single 'Something'. The American

band Aerosmith had a hit with the number in 1978.

'The Continuing Story Of Bungalow Bill' One of John's songs featured on *The Beatles* double album. John sings lead vocal, and plays an acoustic guitar and organ while Yoko Ono sings one of the lines in the song. Maureen Starkey also sings on the chorus with Yoko, and the engineer Chris Thomas comes in on mellotron at the end of the track.

'Cookin'' John Lennon song on Ringo Starr's sixth album *Rotogravure*. Ringo commented: 'I asked John especially to write me a song . . . and John came down to LA especially to work with me, 'cause he does that on all the records: he comes down, writes a song and plays.'

'Crazy John' Song about John Lennon written and recorded by Tom Paxton and issued in the States on Elektra 45667 in 1969.

'Cry For A Shadow' A number recorded in Hamburg during The Beatles' sessions with Bert Kaempfert. Liverpool fans found out about the Hamburg recordings from the front cover story on issue No 2 of *Mersey Beat*, dated 20 July 1961.

Under the headline 'Beatles Sign Recording Contract!' the entire background to their Polydor session is given.

Part of the story read: 'The Beatles recorded two further numbers for Kaempfert on their own. One side, an instrumental written by George Harrison, has not yet been named — probable titles include "Cry For A Shadow" and "Beatle Bop".'

The other side, "Ain't She Sweet", featured a vocal by John Lennon. The boys weren't quite so satisfied with these two numbers, so they sold the rights to Polydor. Thus, in fact, under the contract, The Beatles still have four more records to make this year.'

In fact, 'Cry For A Shadow', the Beatles' first instrumental, although originally conceived by George, received some aid from John and was credited to both of them.

'Dear Prudence' Track on The Beatles' *White Album*. It is one of the numerous songs which John composed during his period at Rishikesh. When film actress Mia Farrow arrived there was some excitement in the camp at the eminence of celebrities gathered to study transcendental meditation under the master himself.

Mia brought along her younger sister Prudence. The girl seemed to spend almost all of her time meditating, hardly ever venturing out of her hut. She was an intense young thing who 'didn't come out to play'. John tried to persuade her to mix more with people, but she preferred to spend long hours in meditation. This inspired John to write the number.

'Death Of Samantha' Single written by Yoko Ono with performers' credits announced as Yoko Ono Plastic Ono Band with Elephant's Memory, The Endless Strings and Choir Boys.

Produced by John and Yoko, it featured another Yoko number 'Yang Yang' on the flip. The single was issued in America on 26 February 1973 on Apple 1859 and in Britain on Apple 47 on 4 May.

'Do You Want To Know A Secret?' John claimed that the inspiration for this number came from the memory of his mother singing a song to him from a Walt Disney film, either 'Fantasia' or 'Cinderella'. He decided to give the number to George Harrison and thus provide him with his first solo vocal with The Beatles.

The recording was featured on the *Please, Please Me* album (PCS 3042) and was also contained on the *Twist & Shout* EP, which rose to No 2 in the singles chart in Britain.

It was issued in the US by Vee Jay as the B side of 'Thank You Girl' in 1964, reached No 2 and was eleven weeks in the best sellers.

The number was given to Billy J. Kramer And The Dakotas, who had a No 1 single in Britain when it was issued on Parlophone R 5023 in April 1963. Kramer's version was also issued in the States later that year in September on Liberty 55586.

'Double Fantasy' Ironically this was to become the launching pad for John's return to the world of music after a five-year absence. His first record of the 'eighties — and his last.

After some years looking after his son Sean, John decided to take the boy on a holiday to Bermuda in the spring of 1969. Yoko remained in New York to carry on with the supervision of their various business enterprises.

It was while he was in a club listening to records that the inspiration came to him to take up music again. He was listening to the number 'Rock Lobster' by the B.52's and suddenly thought that the record sounded just like one of Yoko's.

John said that he thought, 'It's time to

Every man has a woman who loves him.

get out the old axe and wake the wife up.'

Inspiration began almost immediately and during the next three weeks he wrote two dozen numbers and had decided on the title of the planned album.

He commented, 'I was walking in the Botanical Gardens in Bermuda, taking Sean and the Nanny and the household, my little kitchen *entourage*. We all went to lunch and I looked down and there was this flower that said, 'Double Fantasy'. The flower was an orchid.

In August, John was at New York's Hit Factory studios recording the new album with Jack Douglas, who was to share the production credits with John and Yoko. John had made a deal with David Geffen, who had launched his own record label Geffen Records. The album, which had been subtitled *A Heart Play*, was issued in America on 17 November 1980 on Geffen GHS-2001 and in Britain on 21 November on Warner/Geffen Records K99131.

There were 14 numbers on the album, seven written by John and seven by Yoko, the songs alternating on the record.

Titles were, side one: '(Just Like) Starting Over', 'Kiss Kiss Kiss', 'Clean-Up Time', 'Give Me Something', 'I'm Losing You', 'I'm Moving On', 'Beautiful Boy (Darling Boy)'. Side two: 'Watching The Wheels', 'I'm Your Angel', 'Woman', 'Beautiful Boys', 'Dear Yoko', 'Every Man Has A Woman Who Loves Him' and 'Hard Times Are Over'.

'Dr Robert' Song included on the *Revolver* album with John singing lead vocals which have been double-tracked. John also plays maracas and harmonium. The number is about an American doctor who supplied drugs to his patients. Paul helped John to write part of the middle section of the song. John commented: 'There's some fellow in New York, and in the States we'd hear people say, "You can get anything you want off him; any pills you want." It was a big racket, but a joke, too, about this fellow who cured everyone of everything with all these pills, tranquillizers and injections for this and that; he just kept New York high. That's what "Dr. Robert" is all about, just a pill doctor who sees you're all right.'

'Fame' Number which John wrote in collaboration with David Bowie and guitarist Carlos Alomar whilst Bowie was recording his *Young Americans* album in New York early in 1975.

Bowie had completed his sessions in the Sigma Sound Studios and his producer, Tony Visconti, had returned to Britain when David got together with John at the Electric Lady studios.

Bowie had told John he'd like to include 'Across The Universe' on the album and John expressed his desire to play at the session. It was while they were in the studios that they decided to pen 'Fame' together.

Musicians on both tracks were David Bowie (vocal/guitar), John Lennon (vocal/guitar), Carlos Alomar, Earl Slick (guitars), Emir Kadasan (bass), Dennis Davis (drums), Ralph McDonald, Pablo Rosario (percussion), Jean Fineberg, Jean Millington (backing vocals).

Young Americans was issued on RCA RS 1006 on 7 March 1975. The single 'Fame' on RCA 2579 was issued in Britain in July and reached No 17 in the charts. It was released in America the following month where it reached the No 1 position, remaining there for two weeks with a chart life-span of 27 weeks.

Commenting on the number in his *Playboy* interview, John said, "Fame" was an incredible bluff that worked. I'm really knocked out that people actually dance to my records, but let's be honest, my rhythm and blues are thoroughly plastic.'

Producer Visconti, who had missed the recording sessions, said during interviews for the book *The Record Producers*: 'The first I heard of "Fame" and "Across The Universe" was when the record was released . . . so I never heard "Fame" until the public heard it, and I really wanted to record it. I'd met John Lennon the very same night that David had met him, and the three of us stayed up until about ten o'clock in the morning and had a great time together. I wish I'd been in the studio with them, but David wasn't elbowing me — it really was spontaneous. I was in England and David was in New York with John, and that's exactly the way it happened.'

'Get Back John' Song about John Lennon by Inner City Mission, released in America on Kama Sutra 510 in 1970.

'Glass Onion' Bemused by the number of people seeking significant messages in Beatles songs John decided, tongue-in-cheek, to pen a song which would contain some baffling lyrics. He even sings, 'Here's a clue for you all.'

The song also gave name-checks to 'Lady Madonna', 'Fixing A Hole', 'Strawberry Fields Forever', 'Fool On The Hill' and 'I Am The Walrus'. The number was featured on *The Beatles* double album.

Although it was John's song, Paul did help and commented: '(John) wrote it mainly, but I helped him on it, and when we were writing it we were thinking specifically of this whole idea of all these kind of people who write in and say "Who was the walrus, John? Were you the walrus?" or "Is Paul the walrus?"

'So eventually he said, "Let's do this joke tune 'Glass Onion' where all kinds of answers to the universe are."

'But we thought it was a joke. Now someone . . . told me he'd met this feller who chartered a yacht and was going out into the middle of the ocean because he knew the spot where he could go through the glass onion. Now this feller hasn't been seen since!'

'God Save Us' Number written by John and Yoko to raise money for the Oz defence fund. Oz was a British 'underground' magazine edited by an Australian, Richard Neville. Its owners had been taken to court in the famous 'Oz Obscenity Trial'. John testified on behalf of the magazine. The number was produced jointly by John, Yoko, Phil Spector and Mal Evans, and the lead vocalist, Bill Elliot, came from Newcastle. The A side was credited to Bill Elliot & The Elastic Oz Band, while the B side 'Do The Oz' was credited simply to The Elastic Oz Band who were, in fact, The Plastic Ono Band. This side was produced by John and Mal, and John was the lead vocalist on the track. The single was issued in America on 7 July 1971 on Apple 1835 and in Britain on 16 July 1971 on Apple 36.

'Going Down On Love' Composition by John included on his *Walls And Bridges* album.

'Good Morning, Good Morning'
A track on the *Sgt. Pepper* album. The number was inspired by a cornflakes commercial. John explained, 'I often sit at the piano working at songs with the telly on low in the background. If I'm a bit low and not getting much done, then the words on the telly come through. That's when I heard, "Good Morning, Good Morning." It was a cornflakes advertisement.'

The track opens with the sound of a crowing cock and closes with the clucking of a chicken, with several cow and sheep sounds provided by courtesy of George Martin's recording expertise. John supplies the lead vocals, Paul has a guitar solo and the brass section is provided by Sounds Incorporated.

'Goodnight Vienna' Song which John wrote specially for Ringo Starr which became the title track of the album issued on Apple PCS 7169. John sang and played guitar on the track, the title of which is reputed to be from a Liverpool expression meaning, 'Let's get out of here'. The cover featured a still of the alien Klaatu and his robot Gort emerging from their flying saucer in the film *The Day The Earth Stood Still*, with

Ringo's head replacing that of actor Michael Rennie's, the Klaatu character.

'Happiness Is A Warm Gun' One of John's favourite songs. The number had obvious sexual overtones, although some critics mistakenly thought that the happiness referred to was heroin.

The track was featured on *The Beatles* white album and John commented, 'George Martin had a book on guns which he told me about, I can't remember, or I think he showed me a cover of a magazine that said, "Happiness is a warm gun". I thought it was a fantastic, insane thing to say. A warm gun means that you've just shot something.'

'Happy Xmas (War Is Over)' Having spent two years on his peace campaign, with 'War Is Over' posters displayed on prominent billboards, John decided he'd like to attempt writing a Christmas hit in which he could include his message about Christmas being the season of good will to all men and peace on Earth.

He recorded the song in November 1971 with Yoko, the Plastic Ono Band and The Harlem Community Choir. The B side was Yoko's 'Listen, The Snow Is Falling'.

It was issued in America on Apple 1842 on 1 December 1971, but barely scraped into the top 30. There were legal problems surrounding its release in Britain which were finally resolved. Nearly 12 months had passed by the time the single was issued in the UK on Apple R 5970 on 24 November 1972 where it reached No 4 in the charts.

At the beginning of the number, John and Yoko can be heard whispering the names of their respective children, Julian and Kyoko.

Hear The Beatles Tell All Interview album originally issued to radio stations in America in September 1964 when it was issued as a promotional LP by Vee Jay Records on VJPRO 202. The complete A side of the album is devoted to an interview with John conducted by Jim Steck. The background music to the interview was composed by Lou Adler.

'Heartbreak Hotel' Famous hit for Elvis Presley and one of John's earliest influences. He said, 'It was Elvis who really got me interested in pop music and started me buying records. I thought that early stuff of his was great. The Bill Haley era passed me by in a way.

'When his records came on the wireless my mother would start dancing around, she thought they were so good. I used to hear them, but they didn't do anything for me. It was Elvis who got me hooked on beat music. When I heard "Heartbreak Hotel", I thought, "This is it", and I started to grow sideboards and all that gear.'

'Hello Little Girl' Number penned by John when he was 18. Although it was never issued as a Beatles single, the group recorded it during their Decca audition on 1 January 1962 and it has since appeared on a number of bootleg albums such as *The Decca Tapes*. The number was given to a Liverpool band, The Fourmost, to record and their version was issued on Parlophone R5056 in August 1963 and reached No 9 in the British charts.

The Fourmost recording was also contained on the album *The Songs Lennon & McCartney Gave Away*, issued in Britain on April 1979 on EMI NUT 18.

'Help!' Title number of The Beatles' second film. Recorded on 13 April 1965 it was issued on 23 July on Parlophone R5305 and went straight to No 1 in Britain. Several years later John said: 'The lyric is as good now as it was then. It is no different and it makes me feel secure to know that I was aware of myself then. I was just singing "help" and I meant it!'

Homenaje A John Lennon Argentinian album of tribute songs recorded by various artists.

'How Do You Sleep?' A rather malicious track on the *Imagine* album issued in October 1971. It seemed as if all of John's resentment of Paul's legal action in dissolving The Beatles' partnership had found substance in a song.

Although Paul isn't mentioned by name, the attack is obviously aimed at John's former long-term songwriting partner and, as if to blatantly confirm this, John enclosed a postcard size photograph in the album of himself fondling a pig in parody of Paul's *Ram* album cover.

The track begins with sounds of audience noises and the tuning of violins. Then it launches into the attack, dismissing Paul as a creator of muzak, of being under Linda's thumb and of having become a washed-out artist.

George Harrison performed a guitar solo on the track. John explained: 'You know, I wasn't really feeling that vicious at the time. But I was using my resentment toward Paul to create a song, let's put it that way. He saw that it pointedly refers to him, and people kept hounding him about it. But, you know, there were a few digs on *his* album before mine.

'They are so obscure, other people don't notice them, but I heard them. I thought, "Well, I'm not obscure, I just get down to the nitty-gritty." So he'd done it his way and I did it mine. But as to the line he quoted, yeah, I think Paul died creatively in a way.'

'How I Won The War' Single issued in Britain on United Artists UP 1196 on 13 October 1967 with 'Aftermath' as the flip. Credited to Musketeer Gripweed and The Third Troop, it obviously had many fans thinking it was a special release from John, as he portrayed Musketeer Gripweed in the film.

In fact, John repeats one line from the film soundtrack on the A side of the record and the B side is an instrumental by the Ken Thorne Orchestra.

This little piggie . . .

The moptop reaches down to the shoulders.

'I Am The Walrus' Regarded as one of John's classics, a surrealistic mind trip written under the influence of LSD over two weekends in September 1967. It is John's only contribution to the *Magical Mystery Tour* television film, and one of its inspirations was the *Walrus And The Carpenter* piece from Lewis Carroll's *Alice In Wonderland*. John said: 'We saw the movie in LA. The walrus was a big capitalist that ate all the oysters; if you must know, that was it.

'I always had this image of the walrus in the garden and I loved it, and so I didn't even check what the walrus was. I didn't go round saying "I'm the walrus, is it something?" But the way it's written, everybody assumes that it means something.

'I mean, even I did, we all just presumed just 'cause I said "I am the walrus", that it must mean "I am God" or something, but it's just poetry. But it became symbolic of me.'

In addition to the contributions of the four Beatles, George Martin provided three horns and a string selection comprising eight violins and four cellos.

John began by playing the Mellotron. A strange crackling radio sound at the end of the record turns out to be excerpts from Shakespeare's *King Lear*, which was being broadcast at the time.

A two-note wail repeated regularly was inspired by the sound of a police car siren which John heard. Many people sought to discover hidden meanings in the unusual lyrics. The BBC objected to a reference to a naughty girl with her knickers down, and in a subsequent number, 'Glass Onion', John wrote that the walrus was Paul.

The number was issued on 24 November 1967 on Parlophone R5655 as the flipside of 'Hello Goodbye' and it reached No 1 in the British charts.

'I Call Your Name' Number which John wrote in Liverpool when he was 16. He completed the middle eight in 1963 to enable Billy J. Kramer to record the song. It was used as the flipside of Kramer's hit 'Bad To Me' which John also wrote. The Beatles also recorded the number and it was included on their fifth British EP *Long Tall Sally* issued in June 1964.

'I Want You (She's So Heavy)' Really the merging together of two songs John wrote about Yoko, 'I Want You' and 'She's So Heavy'. The number was included on the *Abbey Road* album and at over seven minutes in length it was the longest track on the album.

'I'll Be Back' Number which John penned. It is said to have been inspired by his meeting his father again after a period of almost 20 years. It was recorded in 1964 with John on lead vocals and was the final track on the *A Hard Day's Night* album. It was also included on the *Beatles '65* and *Love Songs* compilations.

Imagine By John Lennon and The Plastic Ono Band with the FluzFiddlers. John's fifth album, recorded in July 1971 and issued in America on 9 September of that year on Apple SW 3379, and in Britain on 2 October on Apple PAS 10004. The album topped both the American and British charts for three weeks, was 30 weeks in the American charts and 57 weeks in the British charts. It was awarded a gold disc on 1 October 1971.

The ten songs were all written by John and recorded in his own studios in the Tittenhurst Park mansion in Ascot, England. The album is noted for the classic song 'Imagine', his song dedicated to Yoko 'Jealous Guy', and his savage attack on Paul McCartney 'How Do You Sleep?'

There was also a postcard in the packaging of the original release depicting John grappling with a pig in a pose similar to the one of Paul with a ram on Paul's *Ram* album.

The titles on the LP were: 'Imagine', 'Crippled Inside', 'Jealous Guy', 'It's So Hard', 'I Don't Want To Be A Soldier Mama, I Don't Want To Die', 'Give Me Some Truth', 'Oh My Love', 'How Do You Sleep?', 'How?' and 'Oh, Yoko'.

'I'm Happy Just To Dance With You' Song which John wrote specially for George Harrison. It was included in the film and album of *Help!*.

'I'm Only Sleeping' Composition by John for which he sings lead vocals. Recorded in 1966, it first appeared on the *Revolver* album and was also included on *The Beatles Rarities* compilation.

'I'm So Tired' Written by John when he had become bewitched by Yoko although he was still married to Cynthia. He completed the song on his 28th birthday and it was included on *The Beatles* double album in 1968.

'I'm The Greatest' Number which John wrote specially for Ringo Starr, featured on the album *Ringo*, issued on December 1973 on Apple PCTC 252. John, George and Ringo all played together on the track, with Klaus Voorman and Billy Preston. These two musicians had been considered as replacements for Paul when the group had toyed with the idea of continuing playing together after Paul's legal action had brought about the official break-up of The Beatles. The number was also included on Ringo's *Blast From Your Past* album, issued on Apple PCS 7170 in December 1975.

'In My Life' One of John's favourite songs, which was originally inspired by his memories of Liverpool. He wrote it in 1965 when he was living at Kenwood and commented, 'I used to write upstairs where I had about ten Brunell tape recorders all linked up. I could never make a rock and roll record, but I could make some far-out stuff on it. I wrote it upstairs. That was one where I wrote the lyrics first and then sang it. That was usually the case with things like "In My Life" and "Universe" and some of the ones that stand out a bit.'

The number was recorded the same year and originally appeared on the *Rubber Soul* album. It was later included on the compilations *The Beatles 1962-1966* and *Love Songs*.

George Harrison also liked the song very much and rearranged it for his own interpretive performance on his 1974 Dark Horse tour.

'Instant Karma!' John Lennon woke up one morning in 1970 with the words of a tune in his head. He immediately set about writing a song and, during his drive to Apple, stopped at a shop to buy a grand piano and request its immediate shipment to Apple.

Arriving in Savile Row, he asked for EMI's No 1 studio to be booked from six o'clock that evening and set his assistants to work contacting producer Phil Spector and a number of musicians.

Work on the record started at seven that same evening and during the early hours of the morning, John sent two 'roadies' up to the Speakeasy Club in Margaret Street to gather a number of people to act as a 'choir' on the number.

The record was issued the following week. An amazingly rapid creation; written and recorded within one day, mixed and released by the following week.

Musicians on the record were Alan White (drums), George Harrison (guitar), Klaus Voorman (bass), Billy Preston (organ), John and Klaus on electric piano and Alan and George on grand piano, with Mal Evans on percussion.

'Instant Karma! (We All Shine On)' was recorded on 26 January 1970 and issued in Britain on Apple 1003 on 6 February. It reached No 5 in the charts with a chart life-span of nine weeks. It was issued in America on 20 February on Apple 1818 and reached the position of No 3 in the charts.

The number was produced by Phil Spector but the B side was produced by John himself. This was a number by Yoko Ono called 'Who Has Seen The Wind'. 'Instant Karma!' was included on the *Shaved Fish* album collection and John was filmed performing the number during the One-To-One concert in August 1972.

'It Won't Be Long' In addition to writing the song, John took over on lead vocals which were double-tracked when the number was featured on the first track on the *With The Beatles* album issued in November 1963.

It's Alright Yoko Ono's 1982 album, her first issued by Polydor Records on Polydor Deluxe Pold 5073, written and produced by herself and recorded at the

Hit Factory in New York. The titles are: side one: 'My Man', 'Never Say Good-bye', 'Speck Of Dust', 'Loneliness', 'Tomorrow May Never Come'. Side two: 'It's Alright', 'Wake Up', 'Let The Tears Dry', 'Dream Love' and 'I See Rainbows'. The photographs for the sleeve were taken by Bob Gruen. Some controversy was aroused by the picture on the back of the sleeve which featured Yoko and Sean in Central Park with the ghost of John standing next to them.

'It's Johnny's Birthday' Number written by George Harrison to celebrate John's 30th birthday. It was included on the *All Things Must Pass* triple album issued in November 1970.

'Je Suis Le Plus Mieux: The Last Reunion' Bootleg 12 inch maxi-single. Taken from the *Ringo* album sessions, the disc features two versions of John performing his 'I'm The Greatest'. John sings lead vocals and plays piano and is accompanied by Ringo on drums, George Harrison on lead guitar, Billy Preston on organ and Klaus Voorman on bass guitar. It was issued in 1982.

'Jealous Guy' One of the highlights of the 1971 *Imagine* album. Once again, John's inspiration was Yoko who also helped him to write the song. He admitted that he was an extremely jealous person and Yoko has recounted how he once made her write out a list for him of all the men she'd slept with before she'd met him.

One of the many groups of musicians to be deeply affected by the news of John's death were Roxy Music. They were performing in Germany at the time and decided to include one of John's songs in their act as a tribute. Their lead singer Brian Ferry chose 'Jealous Guy', which was so well received by the audience that they decided to record it as a single when they returned to England. It was issued on Polydor Roxy 2 in February 1981 and reached the top of the British charts in March, where it remained for two weeks.

John Lennon Set of albums in a silver box, issued in England by EMI, following similar packages released earlier in the year in West Germany and Italy. The albums in the box are *Live Peace In Toronto 1969*, *John Lennon/Plastic Ono Band*, *Imagine*, *Some Time In New York City*, *Mind Games*, *Walls And Bridges*, *Rock 'n' Roll* and *Shaved Fish*. A special souvenir bonus was the addition of *Lennon — The Liverpool Echo's Tribute To John Lennon*, a 20-page magazine with 30 photographs containing the various articles about John featured over the years in the *Liverpool Echo*.

The John Lennon Collection EMI compilation issued in 1982 on EMTV 37 and heavily promoted by a campaign of television advertising. The album reached number one in the charts and the tracks were: 'Give Peace A Chance', 'Instant Karma!', 'Power To The People', 'Whatever Gets You Thru The Night', 'No. 9 Dream', 'Mind Games', 'Love', 'Happy Xmas (War Is Over)', 'Imagine', 'Jealous Guy', 'Stand By Me', '(Just Like) Starting Over', 'Woman', 'I'm Losing You', 'Beautiful Boy (Darling Boy)', 'Watching The Wheels' and 'Dear Yoko'. The packaging contained some finely reproduced Annie Leibovitz shots of John and the lyrics to all the songs on the album.

John Lennon For President
Album by David Peel And The Super Apple Band, issued in the US on Orange Records ORA-005 in 1980. Tracks were: side one: 'John Lennon For President Speech', 'The Yoko Ono Interview', 'Amerika'. Side two: 'The Rock 'n' Roll Preamble', 'John Lennon For President Speech', 'John Lennon For President', 'Imagine', 'The John And Yoko Interview' and 'Imagine'. The last 'Imagine' track is a 25-second one with Tiny Tim whispering lyrics.

'John Lennon Interview' 7 inch picture-disc released by Orange Records in 1981. The colour photograph is of John, Yoko and David Peel (who runs Orange Records) and the A side is the interview which originally appeared on David Peel's album *Bring Back The Beatles*. The B side is a tribute to John by Peel called 'In My Life'.

'John Lennon On Ronnie Hawkins' Special promotional single which was issued as a limited edition to radio stations to promote a new Ronnie Hawkins release. John was indebted to Hawkins for having him as a guest at his farm in Canada and he recorded a spoken introduction to the number 'Down In The Alley'.

John Lennon/Plastic Ono Band
Often called *The Primal Album* because most of the songs were written while John was undergoing a four-month treatment of primal therapy with Arthur Janov. The songs indicate this, most of them being autobiographical and providing John with an opportunity to rid himself of many of the feelings he'd previously kept under wraps: songs about his mother Julia, such as 'Mother'

and 'Mummy's Dead', his disillusionment with the belief in a supreme being in 'God'. John sometimes called this album his 'Sgt. Pepper'. It was produced jointly by John, Yoko and Phil Spector and issued in both Britain and the US on the same day: 11 December 1970. In Britain it was released on Apple 7124 and in America on Apple SW 3372.

The tracks were: side one: 'Mother', 'Hold One', 'I Found Out', 'Working Class Hero', 'Isolation'. Side two: 'Remember', 'Love', 'Well Well Well', 'Look At Me', 'God', 'My Mummy's Dead'.

The album reached the No 6 position in the States with a chart life of 22 weeks.

'John Lennon Remembered' Unusual tribute single issued on Marigold MP 705 in the States. It consisted of a completely blank A side, lasting for ten minutes. The flipside was 'Lookin' Back' by Rich Dodson.

John Lennon Telecasts Bootleg album comprising material from various TV appearances John made in 1972 on shows hosted by Mike Douglas, David Frost and Dick Cavett.

'John You Went Too Far This Time' American single criticizing John Lennon for his full frontal nude display on the cover of the *Two Virgins* album, recorded by Rainbo on Roulette 7030 in 1969. It was later revealed that Rainbo was the actress Sissy Spacek.

'Julia' John's poignant, haunting ode to his late mother, one of two songs in which he attempted to voice his feelings about her. He was aided in some small

Yoko gathers musicians to become a recording artist in her own right.

part by Yoko, who is referred to in the song by the phrase 'Oceanchild', the Japanese for Yoko. Paul, George and Ringo weren't present at the recording of this track on 13 October 1968 and John sang his solo vocals accompanied by himself on acoustic guitars, at times double-tracked.

The number was included on *The Beatles* double album set, sometimes called *The White Album* which was released on 22 November 1968. The track was also issued as the flipside of the single 'Ob-La-Di Ob-La-Da' which was issued in America on 8 November 1976.

'(Just Like) Starting Over' After John's five-year absence from the music world, the title was appropriate. John was aware that many fans were frustrated at the five years he spent rearing

Sean and neglecting his musical career. In the interviews to promote the new single, John commented: 'Why were people angry at me for not working? You know, if I was dead, they wouldn't be angry at me. If I'd conveniently died in the mid-seventies, after my *Rock And Roll* album or *Walls And Bridges*, they'd all be writing this worshipful stuff about what a great guy I was and all. But I didn't die, and it just infuriated people that I would live and just do what I wanted.'

It was the last single issued before John's death. The B side was Yoko's 'Kiss Kiss Kiss' and the record was issued on both sides of the Atlantic on 31 October 1980. In America it was issued on Geffen Records GEF 49604 and in Britain on WEA/Geffen Records K 79186.

The record had reached No 8 in

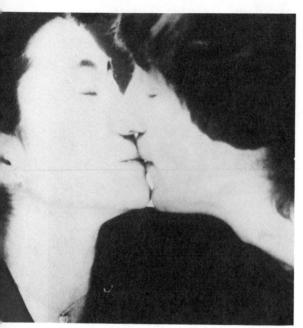

With a loving kiss.

Britain and was dropping. Dave Geffen said: 'John was very anxious to have a number one hit in England. That would have been a real kick for him and it had nothing to do with money ... he wanted this record to be a hit in England for Yoko — and himself.'

As soon as news of John's death was issued, the record began to climb and it topped the charts in England the following week.

John had said: 'It's called "Starting Over" because that's exactly what I'm doing. It took me 40 years finally to grow up. I see things now that I never knew existed before.'

The musicians who backed him on the record were the same sessionmen who performed on his album. They all hailed from New York: Tony Levin (bass), Andy Newmark (drums), Hugh McCracken (guitar); Earl Slick (guitar), George Small (piano) and Arthur Jenkins (percussion).

'Leave My Kitten Alone' Composition penned by Little Willie John in 1959. A London disc jockey discovered a version of the song in which John Lennon was lead vocalist in the EMI vaults in London. The number was recorded by John in the mid-sixties, but never released.

'Let John & Yoko Stay In The USA' American single. Penned by Artie Resnick and Paul Nauman, it was recorded by Justice Department and issued on New Design 1008 in 1972.

'The LS Bumble Bee' Single issued in Britain on Decca F12551 on 27 January 1967 with 'Bee Side' as the B side! It was a release that was to gain the stature of a mystery disc for some years as the word on the grapevine was that John Lennon was involved in the number either as writer or one of the vocalists.

This was due to some fans saying that they recognized John's voice on the record. There was also the suspicion by some record collectors that John was attempting to make a comment about LSD on the disc. The rumour gained momentum because the number was included on some Beatles· bootleg releases, thus confusing fans still further.

In fact, the song was written and recorded by Peter Cook and Dudley Moore who were friends of John. He had appeared on their television show 'Not Only ... But Also' and had dined at Cook's home.

'Luck Of The Irish' A single planned by John and Yoko which was to be issued on Apple 1846 with 'Attica State' on the B side. The record wasn't issued as it was felt that it would conflict with

Paul's 'Give Ireland Back To The Irish'.

'Many Rivers To Cross' Number arranged and produced by John for Harry Nilsson. This appeared on the *Pussy Cats* album, but was also issued as a single. The Jimmy-Cliff-penned song was released in the US as a single on 8 July 1974 on RCA PB 10001 with Nilsson's song, 'Don't Forget Me' on the flip. It was issued in Britain on RCA 2459 on 13 September 1974.

Mind Games Album release which followed the heavily slated *Some Time In New York City*. The title was obviously inspired by the Masters and Houston book of the same name which had made a great impression on John. The cover featured a small, full-length figure of John, with Yoko's profile lying across the horizon like a mountain range. The packaging contained a small booklet of information concerning John and Yoko's conceptual utopia: Nutopia. The couple declared that their imaginary kingdom should have its flag displayed at the United Nations. The flag was a plain white one, and the 'Nutopian International Anthem' on the album consisted of several seconds of silence.

The album was issued in America on 2 November 1973 on Apple SW 3414 and in Britain on 16 November on Apple PCS 7165. It entered the American charts on 24 November 1973 where it reached the position of No 9, with a chart life of 18 weeks.

The tracks were: 'Mind Games', 'Tight AS', 'Aisumasen (I'm Sorry)', 'One Day (At A Time)', 'Bring On The Lucie (Freda Peeple)', 'The Nutopian International Anthem', 'Invitation', 'Out Of The Blue', 'Only People', 'I Know', 'You Are Here' and 'Meet City'.

'Mind Games' coupled with 'Meat City'. Single by John issued in America on Apple 1868 on 29 October 1973 and in Britain on Apple R5994 on 16 November. It reached 26 in the British charts with a chart life of nine weeks and 18 in the States with a chart life of 13 weeks.

'No Bed For Beatle John' Composition penned by Yoko and performed by her on stage at the Lady Mitchell Hall, Cambridge on 2 March 1969 with backing from John on guitar, John Tchikai on sax and John Stevens on percussion. The number was one of the tracks featured on the *Unfinished Music No.2/Life With The Lions* album.

'Norwegian Wood (This Bird Has Flown)' Track on the *Rubber Soul* album, a number penned by John about an affair he'd had. He wrote the song while living at Kenwood and the number featured George Harrison on sitar, an Indian instrument given prominence for the first time on a Western pop record. John explained: 'I was trying to write about an affair without letting my wife know I was writing about an affair, so it was very gobbledygook. I was sort of writing from my experiences, girls, flats, things like that.'

'Not A Second Time' Number penned by John and included as the last number on the *With The Beatles* album, with John's lead vocal double-tracked. This interesting song was highlighted by critic William Mann in his famous analysis of The Beatles' music in *The Times* in 1963. His comment about this particular number read: '. . . harmonic interest is typical of their quicker songs too, and one gets the impression that they think simultaneously of harmony and melody, so firmly are the major tonic sevenths and ninths built into their tunes, and the flat submediant key switches, so natural in the Aeolian cadence at the end of "Not A Second Time" (The chord progression that ends Mahler's "Song Of The Earth") . . .'

An incredulous John when asked to comment on the review remarked, 'Really, it was chords, just like any other chords.'

'Number 9 Dream' The second track from the *Walls And Bridges* album to be issued as a single. It was also featured on the *Shaved Fish* compilation.

It was issued in America on Apple 1878 on 16 December 1974 where it reached appropriately 9 in the charts. The British release on Apple R6003 on 31 January 1975 reached 23.

The song was another of John's poetic commentaries on his love for Yoko and 9 was their favourite number at the time. The flipside was entitled 'What You Got'.

'Old Dirt Road' A number which John wrote with Harry Nilsson in 1974. The song was included on the *Walls And Bridges* album. Harry himself recorded the number at a later date and it is featured on his album *Flash Harry* (Mercury 6302 022).

'One After 909' One of the first songs John composed. He wrote it in the late 'fifties, but it did not appear on a recording until the close of The Beatles' career, when it was used on the *Let It Be* album. It was one of five numbers recorded on the roof of the Apple building and the vocal was sung by Paul.

Up on the roof.

'One Day At A Time' Number by John which was included on his 1973 album *Mind Games* and also used as the B side of Elton John's 1975 hit single 'Lucy In The Sky With Diamonds'.

John played guitar on the track, although he used the pseudonym Dr. Winston O'Boogie. Anthony Fawcett also used the name as the title of his book about John.

The Plastic Ono Band — Live Peace In Toronto 1969 The break-up of The Beatles was more or less in the air when John received an invitation to appear at the Toronto Rock 'n' Roll Revival. He hurriedly gathered together a group and they flew over to Canada for the performance.

John took the stage to announce, 'We're going to do numbers we know because we've never played together before. But here goes and good luck.'

The musicians were Eric Clapton on lead guitar, Klaus Voorman (whom John, George and Ringo had considered as a replacement for Paul) on bass and drummer Alan White. Yoko was also part of the group and she performed some numbers covered in a sheet.

The album was recorded live at the

Varsity Stadium at the Toronto Rock 'n' Roll Revival on 13 September 1969. It was released in both America and Britain on 12 December 1969, in the US on Apple SW 3362 and in the UK on Apple 2001.

It entered the American charts on 10 January 1970 where it reached the position of No 10 with a chart life of 32 weeks. Side one had John and the band performing some of his favourite rock and roll numbers whilst side two was mainly a showcase for Yoko.

The side one tracks opened with an introduction of the band. Then came a version of Carl Perkins' 'Blue Suede Shoes', followed by 'Money, That's What I Want', which had been penned by Berry Gordy and Janie Bradford, and the Larry Williams' classic 'Dizzie Miss Lizzie'.

There were then three of John's com-positions, 'Yer Blues', 'Cold Turkey' and 'Give Peace A Chance'. Side two began with Yoko and John's 'Don't Worry Kyoko (Mummy's Only Looking For Her Hand In The Snow)' and Yoko's 'John, John (Let's Hope For Peace)'.

Rockin' in Toronto.

157

'Polythene Pam' Short number included on the *Abbey Road* album and one of the many songs John composed while at Rishikesh. Explaining why he sang the song in a pronounced Liverpool accent, he remarked that is because the number was supposed to be about a mythical Liverpool scrubber dressed in her jackboots and kilt.

'Power To The People' Written soon after John's interview with Tariq Ali. John was becoming politically aware and radical viewpoints intrigued him. He began to wear military garb which gave him and Yoko the appearance of revolutionaries: berets and army jackets with sergeant's stripes.

An American release of the single pictured him giving a clenched fist salute whilst wearing a tin helmet with a Japanese slogan painted on it. The single was issued in Britain on Apple R5892 on 12 March 1971 with 'Open Your Box' as the flip.

This number penned by Yoko and recorded by Yoko Ono and The Plastic Ono Band originally proved too hot for the record company executives who regarded some of the lyrics as being suggestive. They insisted on John and Yoko changing various words, and they did this.

The American release on 22 March on Apple 1830 featured 'Touch Me' as the flip.

The single reached 7 in the British charts and 8 in the US charts.

The number was included on the *Shaved Fish* album and John and Yoko performed the song on stage at the John Sinclair benefit in 1971.

Pussy Cats Album which John produced for Harry Nilsson in 1974 on which he also performed. It was recorded in New York and Los Angeles between March and May of that year and issued a few months later in America on RCA CPL I-0570 on 19 August, and in Britain on RCA APL 100570 on 30 August. Tracks were: side one: 'Many Rivers To Cross', 'Subterranean Homesick Blues', 'Don't Forget Me', 'All My Life', 'Old Forgotten Soldier'. Side two: 'Save The Last Dance For Me', Medley, 'Mucho Mungo', 'Loop De Loop', 'Black Sails', and 'Rock Around The Clock'. 'Mucho Mungo' was penned by John. Among the musicians featured on the sessions were Jesse Ed Davis (guitar), Danny Kootch (guitar), Sneaky Pete (pedal steel guitar), Bobby Keys (sax), Ken Ascher (piano), Ringo Starr (drums), Jim Keltner (drums) and Keith Moon (Chinese wood blocks!).

'Rain' When John penned this number he couldn't have predicted how it would eventually come out. He returned home one evening with a copy of the master tape. He was still under the effect of drugs and accidentally played it backwards. He liked the sound so much that he arranged for a line of his vocals to be played backwards on the finished recording, which was issued as the flipside of 'Paperback Writer' on Parlophone R5452 on 10 June 1966. It was also issued on the *Hey Jude* album, released in Britain in May 1979. The number has been recorded by over a dozen artists including Todd Rundgren, Petula Clark and Keith Carradine.

John explained: 'I got home about five in the morning, stoned out of my head. I staggered up to my tape recorder and I put it on, but it came out backwards, and I was in a trance on the earphones. What is it? What is it? It's too much you know, and I really wanted the whole song backwards almost, and that was it. So we tagged it on the end. I just happened to have the tape the wrong way round, it just came out backwards, it just blew my mind. The voice sounds like an old Indian.'

'Ram You Hard' Single by John Lennon And The Bleechers. Despite the name, it wasn't the John we are thinking of. The record was issued on Punch PH23 and the flipside was 'Soul Stew' by The Mediators.

'Remember Love' First Yoko song to be featured on a John Lennon single. It was issued as the flipside of 'Give Peace A Chance' in April 1969.

'Revolution' One of the many songs John penned when he was meditating at the Maharishi's ashram in Rishikesh. Originally a ten-minute number, it was clipped to three minutes, 22 seconds when it was issued as the B side of 'Hey Jude!', Apple's first Beatles single release.

In all, there were four different versions of the number, a slower version of which was included on *The Beatles* white album. A third version of the number was called 'Revolution No 9', although this was one of John's experimental tapes with various sounds mixed together, ranging from pieces of conversation to laughter.

Lasting eight minutes and 15 seconds, the number features no lyrics or vocals. It was also included on the double album.

John said: 'There was a third version that was just abstract *musique concrete*, kinds of loops and that, people scream-

ing. I thought I was painting in sound a picture of revolution — but I made a mistake, you know. The mistake was that it was anti-revolution.

'On the version released as a single I said "When you talk about destruction you can count me out". I didn't want to get killed. I didn't really know that much about the Maoists, but I just knew that they seemed to be so few and yet they painted themselves green and stood in front of the police waiting to get picked off.

'I just thought it was unsubtle, you know. I thought the original Communist revolutionaries co-ordinated themselves a bit better and didn't go around shouting about it.

'That was how I felt. I was really asking a question. As someone from the working class, I was always interested in Russia and China and everything that related to the working class, even though I was playing the capitalist game.'

'Rock And Roll People' Composition by John recorded by Johnny Winter and featured on his *John Dawson Winter III* album issued in the US in 1974 and in Britain the following year.

'Rock Around The Clock' The number, first used on the soundtrack of the film *The Blackboard Jungle*, helped to launch rock 'n' roll around the world. As a result an entire film based on the number was rush-released. It starred Bill Haley And The Comets whose version of the song first made an impact on the British charts in 1955. The screening of the film in Britain caused riots in the cinemas and headlines in the press.

To the young John Lennon, it was a movie he couldn't miss. 'I went to see it and was most surprised; nobody was screaming, nobody was dancing. I mean, I had read that everybody danced in the aisles. It must have all been done before I went. I was all set to tear up the seats too but nobody joined in.'

'Rock Peace' An instrumental by the Plastic Ono Band announced as a follow-up to 'Give Peace A Chance' in August 1969. The single never appeared and the second Plastic Ono disc 'Cold Turkey' was issued several weeks later in October.

Roots Album issued by mail order following a television campaign. This LP was released on Adam VIII 801 in January 1975 by Morris Levy following a complex story involving John's recordings of songs which were similar to Chuck Berry material.

Levy was Berry's publisher and a deal was struck in which John agreed to record some Berry songs. John sent some rough tapes of his recordings to Levy who issued the Roots album which featured a photograph of a long-haired bespectacled John on the cover with the title 'John Lennon Sings The Great Rock And Roll Hits'.

This was the material John had been recording for his Rock 'n' Roll album. John began a lawsuit against the release of the record and only 3,000 copies were issued. The case was never resolved.

The tracks were: 'Be Bop-A-Lula', 'Ain't That A Shame', 'Stand By Me', 'Sweet Little Sixteen', 'Rip It Up', 'Angel Baby', 'Do You Want To Dance', 'You Can't Catch Me', 'Bony Moronie', 'Peggy Sue', 'Bring It On Home To Me', 'Slippin' And Slidin', 'Be My Baby', 'Ya Ya' and 'Just Because'.

Two of the tracks, 'Angel Baby' and 'Be My Baby', were not included on the Rock 'n' Roll album.

'Scumbag' Number written by John, Yoko and Frank Zappa. When John and Yoko appeared on stage with Zappa at the Fillmore East in June 1971 Yoko wailed 'Scumbag' from inside a bag. The number was included on the album Some Time In New York City.

'Season of Glass' Yoko's first album following the death of John. Issued on Geffen 2004, it caused a great deal of controversy as the cover featured John's blood-stained spectacles and one of the tracks opened with the sound of four gunshots followed by a scream.

Many of the tracks concerned Yoko's love for John and her sorrow and loneliness following his death. Tracks on the album, all written by Yoko, included 'Goodbye Sadness', 'Turn Of The Wheel', 'Mindweaver', 'I Don't Know Why', 'No, No, No', 'Dogtown' and 'Mother Of The Universe'.

'Sexy Sadie' Originally written as a rebuke to the Maharishi Mahesh Yoga who had allegedly offended actress Mia Farrow. The original title was to have been 'Maharishi What Have You Done, You Made A Fool Of Everyone', but John was advised not to refer to the Maharishi by name. The track was featured on The Beatles white album. Discussing the episode when he confronted the Maharishi, John said: 'When George started thinking it might be true, I thought, well, it must be true because if George is doubting him, there must be something in it. So we went to see the Maharishi. The whole gang of us the next day charged down to his hut, his bungalow, his very rich-looking bungalow in the mountains.

'I was the spokesman and as usual when the dirty work came I actually had to be the leader. Wherever the scene was, when it came to the nitty gritty I had to do the speaking. And I said, "We're leaving." He asked why and all that shit and I said, "Well, if you're so cosmic, you'll know why," because he was always intimating that he did miracles, you know.'

Shaved Fish (Collectable Lennon) Compilation album of previously released recordings produced by John and Phil Spector which John had issued to celebrate the birth of his son Sean earlier in the month. It was to be his last release for some years as he intended to devote the rest of the decade to rearing Sean personally. The album was issued on Apple PCS 7173 on 24 October 1975 and the tracks were: 'Give Peace A Chance', 'Cold Turkey', 'Instant Karma', 'Power To The People', 'Mother', 'Woman Is The Nigger Of The World', 'Imagine', 'Whatever Gets You Thru The Night', 'Mind Games', 'No 9 Dream' 'Happy Xmas (War Is Over)', and Reprise: 'Give Peace A Chance'.

'She Said, She Said' Song on which John sings vocal and plays acoustic guitars, with some vocal backing from Paul and George. The track, which was included on the 1966 *Revolver* album, was inspired by incidents which occurred during John's second LSD trip whilst at a party in California. It followed the group's appearance at the Hollywood Bowl when actor Peter Fonda kept repeating, 'I know what it's like to be dead, man.'

Some Time In New York City Album which was a great disappointment to critics and fans alike who realized that John's creativity had been stifled by the influence of such American radicals as Jerry Rubin and Abbie Hoffman. They involved him in a number of causes such as the case of Angela Davis, an imprisoned black radical, John Sinclair, imprisoned leader of the White Panthers, a protest at the shooting of prisoners during the Attica prison riots, opinions on Northern Ireland, comments on women's lib and suchlike.

Issued as a double album with tracks recorded at the Lyceum Ballroom, London in 1969 and at a Fillmore East concert in New York with Frank Zappa, *Some Time In New York City* was issued in America on 12 June 1972 on Apple SVBB 3392 and in Britain on 15 September on Apple PCSP 716. This album rose no higher than 48 in the American charts, although it had a chart life of 17 weeks.

The cover was styled on the *New York Times*, and the lyrics to the various songs were presented beneath headlines, illustrated with photographs. 'We're All Water', for instance, was illustrated by a trick photograph showing a naked Richard Nixon and Chairman Mao dancing together.

The tracks recorded at the Lyceum featured Eric Clapton, Klaus Voorman, George Harrison, Billy Preston, Nicky Hopkins, Keith Moon, Alan White, Jim Gordon, Bobby Keyes and Delaney, Bonnie & Friends under the collective name of The Plastic Ono Band.

Titles of the tracks were: 'Woman Is The Nigger Of The World', 'Sisters O Sisters', 'Attica State', 'Born In A Prison', 'New York City', 'Sunday Bloody Sunday', 'The Luck Of The Irish', 'John Sinclair', 'Angela', 'We're All Water', 'Cold Turkey', 'Don't Worry Kyoko', 'Well (Baby Please Don't Go)', 'Jamrag', 'Scumbag' and 'Aii'.

Yoko penned 'Sisters O Sisters', 'Born In A Prison', 'We're All Water', 'Don't Worry Kyoko' and 'Aii' and co-wrote 'Jamrag' and 'Scumbag' with John.

'Song For John' Unreleased number recorded by John and Yoko in March 1969.

'Stand By Me' Number written by Ben E. King, Jerry Leiber, Mike Stoller and Ollie Jones which King first issued as a single in April 1961.

The song went on to become something of a standard in Soul and C & W circles. John recorded it for his *Rock And Roll* album and issued it as a single in America on Apple 1881 on 10 March 1975. The record was issued in Britain on Apple R6005 on 18 April.

The B side was a number which John had written for Keith Moon's debut album *Two Sides Of The Moon*, which was also issued in America in March 1975 and in Britain in May. John's number 'Move Over Mr. L' was featured on the first track of side two. Mal Evans was one of the album's producers.

'Strawberry Fields' A haunting song which John wrote over a six week period in Almeria, Spain during the filming of *How I Won The War*. Inspiration came from an old Victorian house close to Aunt Mimi's Mendips in Liverpool, a former home for Salvation Army orphans where John used to attend garden parties.

When The Beatles recorded it in 1966 there were two versions of the song and John liked half of one and half of the other and asked George Martin if he could join the two halves together for a single.

This was difficult as the two versions were in different keys, but he managed it and the result was a surreal but distinctive sound. At the end of the track John mutters, 'Cranberry sauce'. Many people in America seeking clues in the 'Paul is dead' period claim that the words were really, 'I buried Paul'.

The single was not issued until 17 February 1967 when it was released on

A few steps which were to turn Abbey Road into the most famous crossing in the world.

Parlophone R5570 as a double A side with Paul's bright and breezy 'Penny Lane', another Liverpool spot quite close to Strawberry Fields.

Despite almost half a million sales during the first week of its release, the single became the first Beatles release since 'Love Me Do' not to make the top of the British charts. It reached No 2.

'That'll Be The Day' Buddy Holly number. It was the first song John could play to his own satisfaction.

Timeless Picture-disc issued by a Brooklyn company called Silhouette Music early in 1981. Side one features a montage of five colour photographs of John including a picture of him with Yoko and the cartoon rendition from *Yellow Submarine*. The track features 'Imagine' and 'Let It Be' and also has an 'Imagine' studio outtake and an excerpt from a Chicago press conference in 1966 concerning John.

There was a limited pressing of 10,000 copies of the disc and the B side presented a colour photo of The Beatles dressed as Matadors, excerpts from a 1964 press conference in Vancouver and the song 'We Love You Beatles'.

'Tomorrow Never Knows' Last track on the *Revolver* album. John was inspired in his writing of the lyrics by the *Tibetan Book Of The Dead* and had originally called the number 'The Void'. He said, 'With "Tomorrow Never Knows" I had imagined in my head that in the background you would hear thousands of monks chanting.

'It was impractical of course and we did something different. I should have tried to get nearer to my original idea because that was what I really wanted.'

The first title was dropped and it was Ringo who suggested the phrase 'Tomorrow Never Knows'. John sings solo vocal on the number and was involved in ideas of experimental recording at the time. He used tape machines playing at different speeds, tape loops and backward-running tapes to produce an unusual and slightly psychedelic sound.

Tribute Discs There have been quite a number of records dedicated to John following his death and various fanzines have collated lists of such tributes. Charles Reinhart, author of *You Can't Do That* (a discography of Beatles bootlegs and novelty discs) has compiled several tribute disc lists. Recordings have been made by a wide range of artists, from the fan to the Superstar. Some of the main tribute records include:

'All Those Years Ago' George Harrison's own tribute to John, a unique record as it also features Paul McCartney and Ringo Starr. The three got together to record the track, which is also included on George's *Somewhere in England* album. It was the only tribute record to hit the Top Ten and reached No 2 in some American charts. It was issued on Dark Horse DRC 49725 on 11 May 1981.

'The Dream Is Over' Written and sung by David Faircloth and produced by Robby Robertson, the single was issued in the States on Nugget Records NST 8005.

'Elegy For The Walrus' This song by Sid Bradley was a limited-edition acetate sent to American radio stations.

'Empty Garden (Hey Hey Johnny)' Elton John's own tribute to his friend and featured on his *Jump Up* album,

issued in 1982 on Rocket Records (HISPD 127). The song was composed by Elton and Bernie Taupin. It was later issued as a single on Rocket XPRES 77.

'For The Walrus (Tribute to JL)' Single by Sando, issued on the first anniversary of John's death.

'I Did It For You' Recorded by the band Full Circle on Mother Records in the States.

'Imagine, A Tribute To John' American record by Glass Onion, issued on Onion Records UR 2317A/B. Originally recorded on 9 December 1980 by a group of fans comprising Charles F. Rosenay III (vocals), Mike Streeto (drums), Dean Falcone (bass), Steve Harris (keyboards) and Miles Standish (additional instruments).

'It Was Nice To Know You, John' Issued on Tapestry TR005, this tribute single was produced and sung by fifties' singles idol Bobby Vinton and written by Vinton and his son Robbie.

'John' Recorded within 24 hours of John's murder, a tribute disc issued in America on Sun 1160 by Baxter, Baxter & Baxter (brothers Rick, Mark and Duncan). Produced by Shelby Singleton Jr and written by Stephen Kilgore, Virginia Fielder and B. Castleman. 'A Hard Day's Night', 'Yesterday', 'I'll Follow The Sun', 'Ticket To Ride', 'Can't Buy Me Love', 'Imagine' and 'Tell Me Why' are mentioned in the lyrics.

'John Lennon Pt. 1/Pt. 2' Sponsored by an American Presbyterian organization, this record of interviews and songs, with a spiritual slant, was issued by a radio station on MA 1869. Each side contains five minutes of music and dialogue taken from a radio series called What's It All About. The single, by Bill Huie, was originally issued to radio stations.

'John Would Agree' American tribute single written and sung by Bob Farnsworth.

'The Late Great Johnny Ace' Paul Simon's tribute to John Lennon which Simon & Garfunkel performed in Central Park, New York on 19 September 1981 before half a million people. The song is one of the tracks on their double-album Concert At The Park. Michael Lindsay-Hogg, producer of Let It Be, filmed a video of the concert.

'The Legend Of Lennon (In Memory Of John Lennon)' Written, sung and produced by John Gill and issued in the US on Sunlite Records 81001.

'Life Is Real (Song For Lennon)' Tribute song by the British group Queen, written by their lead singer Freddie Mercury and included on their spring 1982 album Hot Space (EMI EMA 797).

'Live With Love' American single dedicated 'to the living spirit of John Lennon' and issued by Crescent Records on the first anniversary of John's death. The A side 'Live With Love' was penned by Ross and Holly Hoffman and sung by a 16-year-old girl Daphne Latham. The B side was John's self-penned song from the Revolver album 'Tomorrow Never Knows', sung by Dawn Thompson.

'Much Missed Man' Single issued in Britain on the Mayfield Records label (MA 103) on 29 January 1982. Joe Flannery, a Liverpudlian who was active as a group manager in the Mersey Beat years was in contact with John by phone a few weeks before the murder. When he heard the tragic news he wrote a poem, which was put to music by fellow Liverpudlian Peter Wynne and sung on the record by local singer Phil Boardman.

'Nobody Knows' Sung by Billy Squire

and featured on his album *Don't Say No*, issued on Capitol 12146.

'Rest In Peace' American single by Juan Hernandez.

'To You Yoko: A Tribute To John' Issued on the Rota Doi label by A Tint Of Darkness, this American single was written by F.L. Pittman, L.C. Coney and C. Rupert.

'Voices In The Sky (A Tribute To John)' A track taken from the album *I Remember Love (And Rock & Roll)* by Joey Welz. Welz was formerly keyboards player with Bill Haley & The Comets and in the sleeve notes he mentions that he once jammed with The Beatles at Hamburg's Star Club. The single was issued in America on Music City Records 5008.

'We Won't Say Goodbye, John' American single written, produced and sung by Irene Koster. One of the many backing singers in the chorus of the record is Peter Noone, former leader of Herman's Hermits. The proceeds of the record were donated to the Spirit Foundation.

Unfinished Music No 1: Two Virgins John and Yoko's first collaboration on record and more familiarly known as *Two Virgins*. The experimental sounds range from a pub piano tinkling to the recording of birds outside the window.

John said: 'We started the album at midnight and finished it at dawn. Then we made love.' It was originally released on 29 November 1968 on Apple SAPCOR 2, although EMI refused to have anything to do with issuing the album.

If critics were to hammer the musical content and what they considered 'a load of rubbish', the actual album sleeve itself was to create a furore. It comprised a full frontal shot of both John and Yoko, stark naked and the back cover was a rear view of the same subject. John had coaxed Paul into writing a brief caption for the cover: 'When two great saints meet it is a humble experience. The long battles to prove he was a saint.'

The reaction from both press and public was furiously hostile. A small British label Track Records agreed to handle the album, but they wrapped it in a brown paper bag to escape being prosecuted under the Obscene Publications Act and it was issued on the Tetragammaton label in the US.

Answering criticism, John commented: 'If people can't face up to the fact of other people being naked or smoking pot, or whatever they want to do, then we're never going to get anywhere. People have got to become aware that it's none of their business, and that being nude is not obscene. Being ourselves is what's important.'

He also added: 'We were both a bit embarrassed when we peeled off for the picture, so I took it myself with a delayed action shutter. The picture was to prove that we are not a couple of demented freaks, that we are not deformed in any way and that our minds are healthy. If we can make society accept these kind of things without offence, without sniggering, then we shall be achieving our purpose.'

The tracks comprised: 'Two Virgins No 1', 'Together', 'Two Virgins No 2', 'Two Virgins No 3', 'Two Virgins No 4', 'Two Virgins No 5', 'Two Virgins No 6', 'Hushabye, Hushabye', 'Two Virgins No 7', 'Two Virgins No 8', 'Two Virgins No 9', 'Two Virgins No 10'.

The album was issued in America in

January 1969 and entered the charts on 8 February. It was eight weeks in the charts but the highest position it reached was 124.

Unfinished Music No 2: Life With The Lions John and Yoko's second album and the first release on a new experimental label from Apple called Zapple (this was one of only two released on Zapple). Produced by John and Yoko, it was issued on Zapple 01 in Britain on 2 May 1969. The cover displayed a photograph of John and Yoko looking despondent at Queen Charlotte's Hospital, London following the miscarriage of their child, with Yoko propped up in bed and John crouching on the floor on which he'd slept during Yoko's term at the hospital.

The reverse side of the sleeve featured a contrasting picture also portraying their torment at the time. It showed John protecting Yoko amid a crowd of policemen following their marijuana drug bust.

Side One of the album was recorded live at Lady Mitchell Hall in Cambridge on 2 March 1969. In addition to John and Yoko there are musicians John Tchikai on saxophone and John Stevens on percussion. The side runs for 26.30 minutes and is entitled 'Cambridge 1969' and contains the tracks 'Song For John', 'Cambridge 1969', 'Let's Go On Flying', 'Snow Is Falling All The Time' and 'Mummy's Only Looking For Her Hand In The Snow'.

Side Two comprises 'No Bed For Beatle', 'Baby's Heartbeat', 'Two Minutes Silence' and 'Radio Play'. 'Two Minute's Silence' is exactly what the title describes and 'Baby's Heartbeat' was the recording of the heartbeat of their unborn baby.

The album was issued in America on Zapple ST 3357 on 26 May 1969 and entered the US charts on 28 June 1969. It reached No 174 on the Top 200 chart, remaining in the charts for eight weeks.

Commenting on the LP, John said: '. . .the album was part of a series that will go on for the rest of our lives. We'd like to be able to produce them as quickly as newspapers and television can. It will be a constant autobiography of our life together.'

Unfinished Music No 4 Another projected Zapple album from John and Yoko. At the time it was announced John commented: 'One side is laughing, the other side is whispering.' The album was never released.

Walls And Bridges Recorded in August 1974 *Walls and Bridges* was issued in America on 26 September on Apple SW 3416 and in Britain on 4 October on Apple PCTC 253. The cover displayed some of John's childhood paintings with the written message: 'John Lennon. June 1952. Age 11'.

John took the album's title from a commercial he'd seen on television and explained: 'Walls keep you in either

166

protectively or otherwise and bridges get you somewhere else.'

The package contained a further booklet with reproductions of paintings he'd done when he was 11 years old. He also had a surfeit of pseudonyms on this album including Rev Thumbs Ghurkin, Dr Winston O'Boogie and Dwarf McDougal.

The record entered the American charts on 12 October and reached the No 1 position, with a chart life of 27 weeks. The tracks were: 'Going Down On Love', 'Whatever Gets You Thru The Night', 'Old Dirt Road', 'What You Got', 'Bless You', 'Scared', 'No 9 Dream', 'Surprise, Surprise', 'Sweet Bird Of Paradox', 'Steel And Glass', 'Beef Jerky', 'Nobody Loves You When You're Down And Out' and 'Ya Ya'.

He wrote ten of the songs in a single week in New York that summer. 'Bless You' is dedicated to Yoko, while 'Steel And Glass' is reputed to be about Allen Klein. Elton John backed him on piano and organ with vocal harmony on the track 'Whatever Gets You Thru The Night'. John's promise to return the favour resulted in his participation in Elton's version of 'Lucy In The Sky With Diamonds' and his famous appearance at Elton's Madison Square Gardens performance.

'We Love You' Rolling Stones single, issued on Decca F 12654 in Britain on 18 August 1967 and on London 905 on 28 August in the States, with 'Dandelion' as the flip. John and Paul McCartney provided backing vocals on the record and John can clearly be heard singing 'We Love You'.

Wedding Album Third album by John and Yoko in their autobiographical

series of experimental records produced in March and April 1969. The cover featured them smartly dressed in white, holding hands. The back cover-photograph portrayed them during their bed-in in Amsterdam. The album was a boxed set containing various items (such as a piece of plastic wedding cake, a postcard, a facsimile of the wedding certificate and a small booklet of press clippings) whose introduction caused the album to be delayed for some months. It was eventually released in America on Apple SMAX 3361 on 20 October 1969 and in Britain on Apple SAPCOR 11 on 7 November of the same year. The LP entered the American charts on 13 December 1969 where its highest position was 178. It remained in the Top 200 album charts for three weeks.

Side One was entitled, simply 'John And Yoko' and ran for 22.23 minutes. Side Two, entitled 'Amsterdam' was 24.52 minutes in length.

'What's The News Mary Jane?' Number which John penned with Alexis (Magic Alex) Mardas which was slated for the *White Album*. It was eventually dropped from the album and announced as a Plastic Ono Band release the following year, but it never materialized. However, two bootleg versions of the song have been available for a number of years, one six minutes and 35 seconds in length, the other seven minutes, seven seconds and both under the title, 'What A Shame Mary Jane Had A Pain At The Party.'

'Winston's Walk' One of John Winston Lennon's earliest compositions recorded by The Beatles in 1962 but never released. John sings lead vocals on the number.

'Woman' Haunting, evocative love song obviously inspired by Yoko which was originally featured on the *Double Fantasy* album. Following John's death, it was issued in January 1981 on Geffen K 79195 and became a chart topper on both sides of the Atlantic first entering the British charts at 3 and reaching 1 the following week on 7 February. Simultaneously with the LP *Double Fantasy*, it

reached the top of the album charts.

It was among the shoal of releases in the wake of the tragedy and there was a blitz of John's material on the charts, since the initial impact of The Beatles in America in 1964.

His hit singles in a short period of time included three number ones: '(Just Like) Startin' Over', 'Woman' and 'Imagine' in addition to hits with 'Give Peace A Chance', 'Happy Christmas (War Is Over)' and three top 20 albums.

There were also two Beatle albums in the chart at that time, as well as the single featuring John's duet with Elton John on 'I Saw Her Standing There'.

The single went on to win several awards including a Grammy and an Ivor Novello Award.

The backing musicians were session men from New York and included Tony Levin on bass, Arthur Jenkins on percussion, George Small on piano, Earl Slick and Hugh McCracken on guitars and Andy Newmark on drums.

Incidentally, Paul McCartney had

written a song called 'Woman' some years previously, which was recorded by Peter And Gordon.

'Woman Power' A side of a Yoko Ono single issued in America on Apple 1867 on 24 September 1973. The single produced by Yoko also featured her singing another of her compositions 'Men, Men, Men' on the flipside. John played guitar on 'Woman Power'.

'Working Class Hero' American bootleg double-album issued by Chet Mar Records in 1981. Side one contains 'Be My Baby' and 'Angel Baby' from the *Roots* album and 'Yer Blues' from the Rolling Stones' unreleased *Rock & Roll Circus*. Side two opens with a version of 'Imagine' which John performed on *The Mike Douglas Show* in February 1972. The following three tracks: 'Mother', 'Come Together' and 'Give Peace A Chance' are from the *One-To-One* concert at Madison Square Garden on 30 August 1972. Side three features 'Slippin' and Slidin'' and 'Stand By Me' from BBC 2 TV's *The Old Grey Whistle Test* of 18 April 1975 and 'Whatever Gets You Thru The Night', 'Lucy In The Sky With Diamonds' and 'I Saw Her Standing There', three tracks from the live recording of John with Elton John at Madison Square Garden in 1974.

Side four opens with 'Lady Marmalade' which John recorded in the Dakota building in 1975, followed by two songs he recorded with Chuck Berry on *The Mike Douglas Show* in 1972 — 'Memphis' and 'Johnny B. Goode'

'Oh My Love' was recorded in Weybridge in 1975, 'Working Class Hero' was recorded at a party in 1972, 'Day Tripper' is taken from Radio One's *Top Gear* of October 1967 when John per-

formed with Jimi Hendrix, and the final track is John's recording of 'Do The Oz'.

'Yer Blues' A tongue-in-cheek tribute to the British blues boom of the time. It was written by John in 1968 during his period at the Maharishi's ashram in Rishikesh. He sings lead vocal on the track which was featured on The Beatles' *White Album* and on the *Live Peace In Toronto* album, which he performed at the Toronto Rock 'n' Roll Revival Concert in 1969. John also performed the number on the unshown 'Rock 'n' Roll Circus' TV special.

'You've Got To Hide Your Love Away' The Bob Dylan influence was apparent in this number, as John explained: 'This was written in my Dylan days for the film *Help!* When I was a teenager I used to write poetry, but was always trying to hide my real feelings.'

The track was featured on the *Help!* album and was also given to The Silkie to record as a single. The Silkie were a folk group from Hull University, comprising Sylvia Tatler (vocals), Mike Ramsden (guitar/vocals), Ivor Aylesbury (guitar/vocals) and Kevin Cunningham (double bass). They had been signed by Brian Epstein. Since The Silkie were part of the same Nems stable, John and Paul decided to co-produce the single for the group, with Paul playing guitar and George Harrison making an appearance on tambourine. The song was issued in the UK on 10 September 1965 on Fontana TF 600 and in the States on Fontana 1525 on 20 September.

The flipside was entitled 'City Winds'. It was a minor hit in Britain, entering the *New Musical Express* charts at No 29 for a single week.

Taking a dive.

How I won the war.

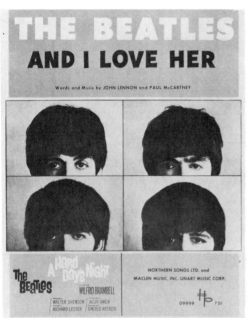

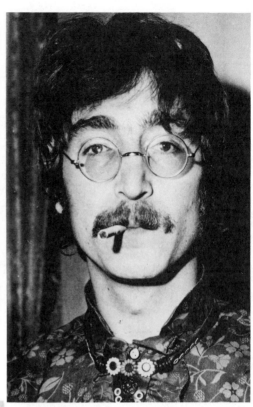

Films

Apotheosis (Balloon) First of John and Yoko's films in which John took charge, investigating the possibilities of a feature-length colour film, although the finished movie is actually 18 minutes in length.

Filming first began in the English countryside on a foggy September day in 1969. A balloonist was hired and together with cameraman Nick Knowland, John and Yoko set the project rolling at a deserted airfield near Basingstoke.

The movie starts with a slow motion exploration of John and Yoko, moving from their feet to above their heads into the sky. With Nick and the balloonist filming aerial scenes, John wanted to capture the sensation of flying as the camera was exploring the air in a hot-air balloon.

The actual title of the film was suggested by Derek Hill of the Institute of Contemporary Arts in London where the film was premiered in October 1969. John was unhappy with the results of the initial filming and began work on *Apotheosis No 2* at the village of Lavenham in Sussex.

Clock An hour-long John and Yoko film shot in the St Regis Hotel, New York in 1971 consisting of a view of a French clock in the hotel's lobby.

Eat The Document Film of Bob Dylan's European tour of 1966 which includes a scene in which John and Bob Dylan are pictured sitting in a taxicab. John makes some comments about Dylan in a strong Liverpool accent. The film was premiered in New York in February 1967.

Erection 19-minute John/Yoko film made in London during 1970 and 1971.

It depicts the construction of the International Hotel. A stills camera filmed the erection of the building from a fixed position for a period of eighteen months, photographer Iain MacMillan taking the stills and Yoko Ono and Joe Jones composing the soundtrack.

Film No 4 (Bottoms) Controversial film which first brought Yoko Ono's name to the headlines in Britain. Whilst in London, she filmed 365 bare buttocks belonging to a number of 'Swinging London' people, including celebrities of both sexes. This 80-minute film, made during the spring of 1967, was a fuller version of her 1965 *Number 4* film made in New York and featuring twelve bare bottoms.

It was not given a certificate by the British Board of Film Censors but was licensed to be shown by the Greater London Council. It received its world premiere at the Jacey Tatler cinema in the West End in August 1967. The movie was also shown at the 1967 Knokke-Le-Zoute *avant-garde* film festival held in Belgium.

Although she did not enter *Film No 4* in the actual competition Yoko, conscious of the value of attracting publicity, lay in the foyer of the cinema in a black bag for eight hours surrounded by signs stating 'Yoko Ono Is Not Here'.

In an interview with the *Sunday Times*, she said: 'It's a social protest. It's signing a petition with your behind instead of your signature. We haven't just gone out in the street and snatched people's bottoms and given them a quick pound. All the people, most of them artists, writers and actors, have volunteered to do it for nothing.'

John called the film *Many Happy Endings*.

Portrait of two movie moguls.

Fly A 19-minute film co-directed by John and Yoko in New York in 1971. The movie featured a housefly walking across the naked body of a young woman, Virginia Lust. Over 200 house-flies were used during the two days of filming.

Freedom Films Two 60-second shorts, specially produced by John and Yoko for the Chicago Film Festival in 1971. John's contribution was simply the scratching of the word 'Freedom' on to the film so that the word had an animated jerk. Yoko's effort consisted of a slow motion shot of a girl pulling off her bra and tossing it away.

Give Peace A Chance A John/Yoko film short edited down to three minutes of one of their bed-ins-for-peace.

A Hard Day's Night The Beatles' first movie. The title came from a line in

Starring in a movie.

'Sad Michael', one of John's stories in the book *In His Own Write*. Scriptwriter Alun Owen attempted to capture something of the personality of each of the Fab Four. In one scene John is taking a bubble bath and he disappears beneath the foam. The plug is pulled out and the bath empties, with no indication as to where he has gone.

This is a touch of surreal humour in the Lennon mould. When asked by a reporter at the press conference: 'What's your philosophy of life?' he retorts: 'I'm torn between Zen and I'm-all-right-Jack!'

The dialogue seems to suit John, although he later said, 'We were a bit infuriated by the glibness and silliness of the dialogue and we were always trying to get it more realistic, but they wouldn't have it. It ended up OK, but the next one

was just bullshit because it really had *nothing* to do with The Beatles.'

Strangely enough there were solo scenes written for Paul, George and Ringo, but not for John. George had his own little piece set in an advertising studio. Ringo took a stroll by a canal bank, wandered into a pub and ended up in clink. And Paul had a scene with a girl but this was edited out of the final print.

How I Won The War Film in which John made his first appearance minus his fellow Beatles in the role of Private Gripweed of the Third Troop of the Fourth Musketeers. The part was specially written for John. It was an anti-war movie set in the Western desert, Dunkirk, Dieppe, El Alamein and Arnhem with newsreel shots linking parts of the film.

How I Won The War was based on a novel by Patrick Ryan and the screenplay was written by Charles Wood. John once again teamed up with Richard Lester, director of *A Hard Day's Night* and *Help!*. Lester produced and directed this film for United Artists, who also distributed and directed The Beatles' films. Location work in Germany and Almeria, Spain, began in 1966.

John's wife Cynthia said: 'When he was doing *How I Won The War* he was petrified. It was the first thing he'd done on his own, and it was like leaving the family nest. He went through hell.'

John explained: 'I did the film because I believed in it. There never has been a war film which showed war as it really is. A man fighting in a battle doesn't see the whole thing. He never meets the enemy until the day a man comes round the corner and sticks a bayonet in him and he can't quite

Why do you call her Priceless Margarine?

believe it is happening.'

The film was premièred at the London Pavilion on 18 October 1967 and part of the *Sunday Times* review read: 'John Lennon dies the death in Dick Lester's film *How I Won The War*. A shell from a German tank catches him just below his ribs and he expires in a welter of well-photographed gore.'

Although the part of Gripweed was only a supporting role, the Press dubbed it the film 'starring a Beatle' and 'John Lennon's film'. Headlines were created at the premiere which was attended by The Beatles and their wives because of demonstrations by the right wing political group the National Front.

They believed it was an insult to the British war dead of the Second World War and 100 of them mingled with the 1,200 members of the Pavilion audience and began to throw stink bombs and cause chaos. Eventually, 50 policemen had to be called in to control the situation.

The United Artists synopsis of the plot issued on the film's release read:

'Lieutenant Ernest Goodbody (Michael Crawford) had a trying war. So did his men; mostly as a result of his trying.

He was young, inexperienced. The Third Troop of the Fourth Musketeers was his first command. He was keen, and saw war as a game, nobler even than his favourite sport of cricket.

'He loved his men and cared for them, and the more he loved and cared for them, the more they hated him. It was no coincidence that his regimental number was 131313.

'His Troop Sergeant Transom (Lee Montague), the regular soldier, the anchor man of the outfit, foresaw trouble the first time he clapped eyes on him. He was right . . .

'But somehow they staggered from campaign to campaign, until destiny led them to the Western desert and their Finest Hour . . .

'In the end (which is the beginning) Goodbody was bound to get himself captured . . . it was inevitable. Ostensibly leading his platoon on a night attack across the Rhine towards the end of the war, Goodbody finds himself alone in his rubber boat in the middle of the river. His men are nowhere to be seen. This does not surprise him unduly. It has happened before.

'He bumps ashore by a bridge, the last intact across the Rhine. In the first few frightened minutes of capture he begins to remember how it all started.

'His training as an officer, his meeting with that veteran of veterans, Lt Col Grapple (Michael Hordern), who impresses him immensely, and who keeps turning up throughout his career to re-inspire him with the rousing cry of ''Bum on, young fella! Bum on!'' — to the next place along the line . . . Rome . . . Paris . . . Berlin . . . Moscow.

It's not the Ritz, but the grub's OK.

'And then Egypt, and the days the jolly general puts an arm on his shoulder and murmurs smoothly, "Would you like to do something for me? Get away from here? See some action, eh?"

'"I would like you," said the general, "to nip 300 miles behind the enemy lines and set up an advance cricket pitch . . . so that when the battle is over and the Very Important Person drives through, he will see the men, straight from battle, happy, relaxed, enjoying themselves . . . you do that for me? Good show!"

'Goodbody makes the landing, but somehow, his men, including Gripweed (John Lennon) and Clapper (Roy Kinnear) do not . . . and he wanders disconsolately round the desert, complaining that he is much too young to win the war on his own.

'All these memories flood through Goodbody's mind in those first few moments of capture. He is taken before Odlebog, the Bridge Commandant (Karl Michael Vogler), and finds he can relax.

'Odlebog has guarded the bridge throughout the war, and loves it. Now the retiring German army is going to blow it up, and he is sad.

'Goodbody finds Odlebog is the first person he can talk to about the war, his men and why he is a soldier. They get on famously and Goodbody helps the German with his demolition charges.

'They discuss their mutual experiences . . . Goodbody remembers the desert, how he eventually found his men, the difficulty with morale, how he struggled through, had their cricket pitch roller stolen by Italians, how they failed to capture a German dump for much needed petrol and the triumphant moment when they shot down their first plane. The fact that it was British took the edge off that moment slightly . . .

Musketeer Gripweed.

'He remembers the death of Corporal Dooley (Ewan Hooper), of Private Drogue (James Cossins) and Private Spool (Ronald Lacey). And old soldier Juniper (Jack MacGowran) who raised morale by "entertaining the troops" in the most unlikely way and most unlikely places . . . and how he was going to recommend him for promotion . . . until he found Juniper was going mad . . . and how, after all their labours, the Very Important Person drives through with barely a glance at their cricket pitch . . .

'Goodbody and Odlebog get very friendly . . . Odlebog decides he cannot blow his bridge up . . . he'll give it to Goodbody . . .

'Goodbody says he could not possibly accept . . . but he will buy it. As the last remnants of the German Army hurry past, they haggle over the price. . . .

'Goodbody writes the cheque and buys the bridge, and Lt. Col. Grapple roars through in the leading British tank.

'"By courtesy of the Fourth Musketeers,'' says Goodbody, with a graceful wave of the hand. ''Bum on, young fella,'' roars Grapple. ''Bum on to Moscow.''

'Many years later, in his little suburban semi-detached house, Goodbody attempts to hold a reunion. Only one man sits with empty chairs around him ... the last of the Musketeers, the melancholy Musketeer (Jack Hedley) who was a coward.

'''I wanted to fight. I knew we had to fight. I really wanted to ... but I couldn't.''

'''I know you did, I know you did, says Goodbody soothingly, ''but I won the war.''

Imagine 81-minute colour film directed and produced by John and Yoko featuring the tracks from the album *Imagine*. Released in 1972, the music from John, Yoko and The Plastic Ono Band provided a soundtrack for numerous scenes filmed at Ascot and New York, with guest appearances by George Harrison, Fred Astaire, Jack Palance, Phil Spector, Dick Cavett and Andy Warhol. The film was premiered on American television on 23 December 1972.

Imagine — The Story Of John Lennon And Yoko Ono A three-hour TV film tracing the John/Yoko relationship from November 1966 until December 1980. Johnny Carson Productions acquired rights to the film from Yoko in 1983.

The Irish Tapes Documentary produced and directed by John Reilly and Stefan Moore. A video film with a pro IRA slant, it was supported financially by John and Yoko, and John also contributed some music for the soundtrack.

John Lennon's Killer: The Nowhere Man Title of a projected film based on an article on Mark Chapman by Craig Unger, first published on 22 June 1981. Unger also penned the first draft of the script.

Number I Yoko Ono's first movie short. A five-minute film in slow motion of a match being struck.

Self-Portrait Controversial 42-minute film from John and Yoko. The entire film was centred on John's penis arising from a flaccid to an erect state in slow motion. Its world premiere took place in September 1969 with showings at the Institute of Contemporary Arts and the New Cinema Club, London.

Shades Of A Personality Title of one of the projects for The Beatles' third film. Scripted by Owen Holder, it concerned one central character with four personalities, enabling all four Beatles to portray the same person. The group were originally to begin filming with director Michelangelo Antonioni in Spain in September 1967, but the project fell through. The *New Musical Express* had reported earlier, 'John Lennon will play the part of the man himself, while the three other Beatles will portray each of the facets of his split personality: the dreamer, the humanbeing and the man as perceived by the outside world.'

Smile Early John and Yoko film collaboration. The idea was originally Yoko's, the initial concept being almost a facial version of her *Bottoms* film as she said she wanted to make a film

Two Virgins.

Ten For Two Film owned by Yoko Ono of John's concert in 1971 in aid of John Sinclair, a political activist.

Two Virgins Filmed at Kenwood, *Two Virgins*, a 19-minute film, was the first joint movie venture together with *Smile* for John and Yoko. The film superimposed their faces and ended with these separating and the couple settling into an embrace. John remarked, 'The idea of the film won't really be dug for another fifty or a hundred years probably.'

'which included a smiling face snap of every single human in the world. But that had obvious technical difficulties.' She finally decided on a film of John's face smiling and said it would be available 'for people who'd like to have the film on their wall as a light-portrait.' It was shot with a high-speed camera able to take 20,000 frames per minute, in the garden of Kenwood. Originally a three-minute film, it was slowed down for public screening to last for 52 minutes. The film was premiered at the Chicago Film Festival in 1968, together with *Two Virgins* and was one of the films shown during the 'An Evening With John and Yoko' film event at the New Cinema Club, London in September 1969.

Sweet Toronto Film of the 9th September 1969 Toronto Rock And Roll Revival Concert. John and Yoko's appearance with Eric Clapton, Klaus Voorman and Alan White was cut from the movie as the producers felt that audiences of rock and roll enthusiasts might object to the John and Yoko performance.

Up Your Legs Forever Film which John and Yoko made in New York in 1970. They decided to ask a few hundred people, including a number of celebrities, to donate their legs for peace. Among the participants who allowed Yoko to aim the camera at their bare legs was film producer D A Pennebaker, film star George Segal, *Rolling Stone Magazine* proprietor Jann Wenner and artist Larry Rivers. The completed film was first screened in New York in December 1970, together with *Fly*.

Walking On Thin Ice Promotional film of the album depicting John and Yoko's naked bodies pictured from the waist up making love. The film was screened at the Ritz Disco in New York in 1981 and was also available on a local pay TV station in New York City.

Working Class Hero Unreleased film of John recording the *Imagine* album at Tittenhurst Park, Ascot with Phil Spector. Director Mike Knowland shot 35 hours of colour film which was edited by Franco Rosso, but Allen Klein wanted the movie shelved as he proposed something slicker for use on American TV.

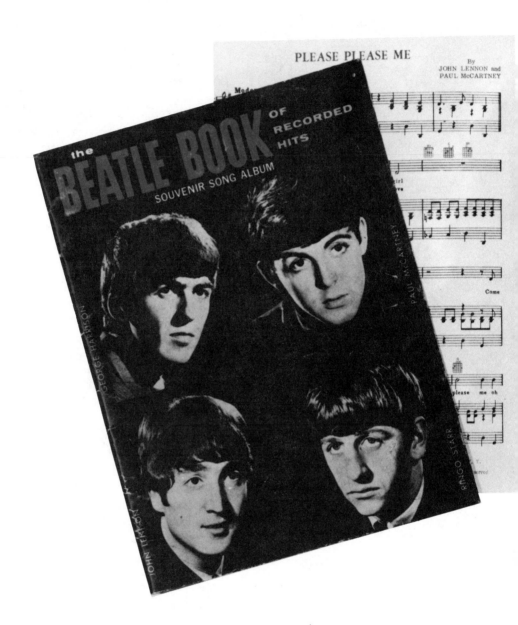

Publications

Club Sandwich Giant sized official magazine of the Paul McCartney Fan Club printed on coated paper and published by MPL Communications. Issue No. 23 was devoted entirely to John and comprised a selection of large photographs by Linda McCartney. There were 41 shots, 26 of them in colour. The only text, apart from the cover title 'John', was a brief tribute, penned by Paul, which began: 'I met John a long time ago at Woolton Village Fete and in all the years I knew him I saw a man of many faces, sometimes aggressive, sometimes warm and gentle.'

Datebook American 'teen magazine of the 'sixties which, on the eve of The Beatles' final US tour in August 1966, reprinted an article which had originally appeared a few month's previously in London's *Evening Standard*.

In the feature written by Maureen Cleave, John said, 'Christianity will go. It will go. It will vanish and shrink. I needn't argue about that. I'm right and I will be proved right. We are more popular than Jesus now. I don't know which will go first — rock 'n' roll or Christianity. Jesus was all right, but his disciples were thick and ordinary.'

The American magazine's printing of this feature released a flood of anti-Beatle feeling in various parts of the States.

The Fab Four Publication Glossy magazine produced by Le Club Des 4 De Liverpool, a French fan club. Their special issue in tribute to John contained many large-size photographs. The cover was a pic taken at Central Park and interior illustrations include John and Paul as The Nurk Twins; Hamburg photographs by Jurgen Vollmer; a visit to the London fan club in 1963; at Abbey Road studios with Neil Aspinall; shots from *A Hard Day's Night*; at the George V Hotel in 1965; John and Cynthia; John singing 'You've Got To Hide Your Love Away'; John with Roy Kinnear; in Hamburg in 1966; filming at Strawberry Fields; with Yoko at the Robert Fraser Gallery and dozens of others in a chronological pictorial history ending with shots of John at the Hit Factory on 4 September 1980.

Fairy Tales Title of a projected book by Cynthia Lennon, a collection of her drawings of The Beatles.

The First Sex Book by Elizabeth Gould Davis which Yoko encouraged John to read to help him to understand the slavery to which women have been subjected for thousands of years. He said the book made him cry.

The Gay Liberation Book Publication which featured a specially written limerick by John.

Grapefruit Yoko's book of short, conceptual ideas. It was first published by Wanternaum Press in 1964. Yoko promoted it when she arrived in Britain and even sent copies to reviewers wrapped in a pair of panties.

Shortly after her first meeting with John she sent him a copy by post and he placed the book by his bedside, occasionally dipping into the seemingly bizarre, often single-word instructions and poems.

He commented, 'I used to read it sometimes and I'd get very annoyed by it. It would say things like "paint until you drop dead" and "bleed", and then sometimes I'd be very enlightened by it.'

Grapefruit was reprinted by the major American publishers Simon & Schuster in 1970 and John penned a two-line introduction for it.

Harmony Magazine devoted to information concerning microbiotic food and diets. John was asked to review the magazine and his contribution consisted of a few drawings. A sketch of himself reading *Harmony* and the caption 'So I read this' was followed by a sketch of a naked John and Yoko residing on a cloud above a bright sun with them both commenting, 'Hi Greg!' The greeting was a reference to Greg's, a microbiotic food store in London.

I Am Also A You Title of a book by American writer Jay Thompson. John wrote the introduction to it.

I.Me.Mine George Harrison's autobiographical analysis of his songs, with a brief guide down his personal lifelines by Derek Taylor. Originally published in a limited edition of 2,000 copies at a staggering £184 per book, it was later issued in a more reasonably priced hardbound edition.

When it was first published in 1980 it hurt John quite deeply because, after the years of intense closeness experienced by the members of The Beatles, George turned up with a book in which there was no mention of John.

In his *Playboy* interview John said, 'By my glaring omission from the book, my influence on his life is absolutely zilch and nil. Not mentioned . . . he remembers every two-bit sax player or guitarist he met in subsequent years. I'm not in the book.'

John went on to detail the help he'd given George in writing a number of

Where was I in I.Me.Mine?

songs, only to find there was no credit whatsoever in George's book. George was to hear of John's statement and decided to write a song for him as a gesture of apology. Before he'd finished it, John was murdered. George later rewrote the number, which became 'All Those Years Ago'.

Imagine Title of songbook published by Wise Publications featuring the music and lyrics of all the songs contained on the Imagine album. The book also reproduces three dozen photographs of John and Yoko by Tom Hanley with captions by Mike Hennessy.

In His Own Write John's first book. It was published in Britain by Jonathan Cape on 23 March 1963 and in America by Simon & Schuster the following month; it became an immediate best seller. It was issued in France in translation under the title En Flagrante Delire.

John later commented: 'I first began to write when I was fourteen. Just private stuff for myself and my friends. Then when the group started going on the road, I used to take my typewriter just to tap away as the fancy took me. Then a friend of mine took some of the material to Cape, the publishers, and the man said: "This is brilliant. I'd like to do this." and that was before he even knew who I was.'

The book was designed by Robert Freeman with illustrations by John. An introduction by Paul McCartney was penned in a similar style to that of John. In His Own Write provided John with the opportunity of publishing the surrealist writings he first began to pen at Quarry Bank High School for Pete Shotton's eyes with The Daily Howl and continued in Mersey Beat with Beatcomber.

Several of the Mersey Beat stories are included: 'Liddypool', 'On Safairy With Whide Hunter' and 'I Remember Arnold.'

The rest of the contents are: 'Partly Dave', 'No Flies On Frank', 'Good Dog Nigel', 'At The Denis', 'The Fat Growth Of Eric Hearble', 'The Wrestling Dog', 'Randolph's Party', 'The Famous Five Through Woenow Abbet', 'Sad Michael', 'I Wandered', 'A Letter', 'Scene Three Act One', 'Treasure Ivan', 'All Abord Speeching', 'The Fingletoad Resort Of Teddiviscious', 'Alec Speaking!', 'You Might As Well Arsk', 'Nicely, Nicely Clive', 'Neville Club', 'The Moldy, Moldy Man', 'I Sat Belonely', 'Henry and Harry', 'Deaf Ted Danoota (and Me)', 'A Surprise For Little Bobby', 'Halbut Returb', 'Unhappy Frank', 'On This Churly Morn', 'Victor Triumphs Again' and 'Mrs Weatherby Learns A Lesson'.

Instant Karma American fan magazine launched in December 1981 by Marsha Ewing of Michigan. The bimonthly specialized in articles on John and Yoko.

International Times Alternative newspaper of London's 'underground' scene in the 'sixties. It was published on an erratic schedule, but generally fortnightly for several years with contributors such as Miles (who wrote several Beatle books, including John Lennon In His Own Words). The paper had a number of financial crises before it eventually went under. At one period John donated £1,000 to aid its continued publication.

Irish Families' Arms and Origins Book by Edward Maclysaght, published in 1957. John used an extract from the book in the booklet enclosed with his Walls And Bridges album. It read 'No one of the name of Lennon has distinguished himself in political, military or cultural life in Ireland (or for that matter in England either).' Beneath the quote,

John had written: 'Oh yeh? John Lennon.'

John 68-page magazine published in America by SMH Publications in 1964 and devoted entirely to John, with articles such as 'Where To See John In Person' and 'Win A Letter From John'. The publishers also issued separate one-shot magazines on George, Paul and Ringo.

John Lennon Book by Tadeu Gonzaga Martins published in Brazil by Sintese Books in 1982.

John Lennon: A Family Album Photo-book published in Japan in 1983 containing 100 colour shots by Nichi F. Saimaru taken during John and Yoko's trips to Japan between 1976 and 1980.

John Lennon: A Man Who Cared Magazine issued by Paradise Press in the US following John's death. It comprises material from the book *The Beatles, The Fabulous Story Of John, Paul, George and Ringo*, first published in 1975, with additional material updating the story by Chris Rowley.

John Lennon: A Melody Maker Tribute Well-produced magazine, one of several British productions issued within weeks of John's death. It contains 100 photographs, ten of them in colour. The main text comprised 'Life And Times of John Lennon' by Ray Coleman, *Melody Maker*'s editor-in-chief, a bibliography, 'I Remember John' by Tony Barrow, the Beatles' former PR, 'The Music' by Patrick Humphries, a discography, 'The Early Days' by Bill Harry and 'In His Own Write', a selection of quotes. An interesting innovation

is the reproduction of the original typewritten captions from the picture agencies, which accompanied certain shots.

Also reproduced are several of the messages John sent to the *Melody Maker* over the years, including a postcard to Ray Coleman. Typical of John's humour, it read: 'Dear Ted, Having a wonderful. The weather is quite. Wish you were. The food is. So are we. See you when we get. Ours truly. Them Beatles.'

John Lennon: A Real Live Fairytale Book written and illustrated by Marica Huyette between 1975 and 1976 containing 50 surrealistic drawings, together with background text on the story behind the illustrations. Produced in a limited edition as a large paperback with two colour plates by Hidden Studio.

John Lennon, All You Need Is Love American tribute magazine issued by Mar-Jam Publishing containing a history of John's life and The Beatles' career plus discography, quotes and lots of colour photographs.

John Lennon & The Beatles, A Loving Tribute American publication issued by *16 Magazine* and including a number of their Beatle articles originally published in the 'sixties, together with lots of photographs and a poster.

John Lennon & The Beatles: A Special Tribute American magazine published by Harris Publications at the beginning of 1981 shortly after John's killing. It contains over 100 black and white photographs and eleven colour pictures. There are several pages documenting the events surrounding John's death but the main section of the magazine is a basic story of The Beatles'

A time for some serious thinking.

career, simple, straightforward and lacking in any great detail. There are one or two minor mistakes such as the reference to Jim McCartney's band as 'a black ragtime band' and the attribution of George's activities in 1968 to Paul. Apart from that it offers nothing new and is more a tribute to The Beatles' career as a whole than to John's in particular.

John Lennon: Beatles Memory Book

Another tribute magazine from Harris Publications of New York early in 1981 and containing 11 colour pictures and 67 black and white photographs. Oddly different from its sister magazine, *John Lennon & The Beatles*, the *Memory Book* has a curious piece entitled 'Unforgettable Moments With John Lennon', which begins with a soliloquy with God in near-hysterical, emotional style eg: 'She's strong, my Yoko. But weak like I am weak. She needs me, God. Needs me near her. Sean needs me. Maybe, God . . . maybe even the world needs me. But you took me away. Why, God? Why, before I was ready? If only I could have said just one more time, ''I love you Yoko for now and for always and

The image and the music matures.

into all eternity. From everlasting to everlasting''.'

The article is coarse at times and then goes into a first person account with the author of the piece intimating that he was a close friend of John's. But there is no credit. In fact, none of the article-writers are named although several of the pieces are written in the first person. There is a lengthy piece by a fan 'We Will Canonize Him With Our Love'; 'One-Two-Three-Four!!!', a general article about the Fab Four, 'Beatlemania England 1962', a sketchy piece on their early career, 'Beatlemania USA' con-cerning their American success, 'The Break-Up Of The Beatles' and 'On His Own With Yoko Ono'.

John Lennon: Death Of A Dream

Paperback penned by George Carpozi Jr, published by Manor Books in America in 1980 and rushed to the new-stands scant weeks after John's death. Hurriedly cobbled together, it reveals shortcomings. Book 1 entitled *A Henious Crime* comprises six chapters dealing with the murder. Book 2, entitled *His Legacy* comprises the largest section of the work with eight chapters which include a filmography, discography, basic story of The Beatles career and an interview with DJ Murray Kaufman.

Book 3 is a short section containing some tributes and excerpts from newspapers concerning the shooting. There is a short photo insert of approximately two dozen pictures.

John Lennon Im Spiegel Der Weltpress Continental publication featuring 92 pages of newspaper cuttings from England, America, Switzerland, Germany, Austria, Belgium, France and Holland on John's death.

John Lennon In His Own Words One of a series of books published by Omnibus Press consisting of quotes. Others in the series include *Paul McCartney In His Own Words* and *The Beatles In Their Own Words*. This volume published in 1980 was compiled by Brian Miles, who also put together the book of Beatle quotes.

Much of the book consists of photographs: there are nearly 120 of them, a great number taken from newspaper clippings, causing the reproduction to be less than perfect.

There are no credits for the photographs, which come from a number of sources. Most of the quotes have been gathered from interviews John conducted with such people as Jann Wenner. The quotes have been assembled in chronological order in a year-by-year sequence.

John Lennon 1940-1980 Book published in French by Artefact of Paris in 1980. Compiled by Har van Fulpen with the help of The Beatles Fan Club of Amsterdam, it includes excerpts from the *Playboy* magazine interview, the lyrics of 'Strawberry Fields Forever', 'Lucy In The Sky With Diamonds', 'Across The Universe', 'Ballad of John And Yoko', 'Happy Christmas (War Is Over)' and 'Give Peace A Chance', a chronology and album discography. There are 36 black and white photographs, most covering a full page. Other illustrations include the covers of British popular papers *The Daily Mirror*, *Sun*, *Daily Star*, *Daily Mail* and *Daily Express* of Wednesday 10 December 1980. Headlines were: 'Death Of A Hero' *(Daily Mirror)*, 'They Loved Him, Yeah, Yeah, Yeah' *(Sun)*, 'The Man Who Shot Lennon' *(Daily Express)*, 'John Winston Lennon R.I.P.' *(Daily Star)*, and 'The Killer Autograph' *(Daily Mail)*. There is a 'War Is Over' leaflet, a 'War Is Over' American street sign and the reproduction of a letter John and Yoko wrote to the *Melody Maker* on 13 December 1971.

John Lennon. 1940-1980 Also called *The Front Page News Book*, published by ESE California in 1981. Compiled by Ernest E. Schworck, the large-size publication, printed in both paperback and hardbound editions, was a 90-page compilation selected from 100 newspapers from around the world on 9 and 10 December showing how they presented the news of John's death.

John Lennon 1940-1980: A Biography Book by Ray Connolly first published in Britain by Fontana Paperbacks in 1981. Priced at £2.50 it contained over 60 black and white photographs on coated paper, four small colour shots on the cover and a full page back cover colour shot of John in dark glasses signing his autograph. The picture researcher was John Spencer, who gathered a strong selection of pictures including one of John dancing with George Harrison's mother, John and Yoko at the *Magic Christian* premiere with a sign 'Britain Murdered Hanratty' and the pair donating their hair to Michael X.

It's a well-written, straightforward biography in three sections: Liverpool, The World and New York, with 12 separate chapters. In his foreword, Ray acknowledges that he had to draw 'upon the work of other journalists, and upon the memories of the principal characters and their accounts of their lives as told to me and to other writers.'

However, he was also able to draw on a number of the interviews he conducted personally with John for London's *Evening Standard* between the years 1967 and 1972. He was due to interview John and Yoko on Tuesday, 9 December 1980. Of the large number of books hurriedly published following John's death, this is one of the most valid and readable.

The John Lennon Story Earliest paperback biography of John Lennon, published in Britain by Futura Publications in 1976. Written by George Tremlett, it was one in a series of over a dozen books by him which also included *The Paul McCartney Story*. Tremlett was a highly active journalist in the 'sixties, specializing in pop music in partnership with his wife Jane. A meticulous researcher, Tremlett visited Liverpool in the early 'sixties where he bought various items of Beatles memorabilia including photographs and contracts. In 1982 he put his huge files of rock material up for sale, having become a full-time politician in London.

The book sports a cover by the popular artist Achilleos depicting John in three aspects of his life. The 16-page photo insert contains a selection of relatively rare photographs, which includes pictures of The Beatles performing at the *Mersey Beat* Poll awards and John and Yoko on stage at the Lyceum Ballroom, London.

The biographical section is 105 pages long, written in chronological order from interviews Tremlett had conducted over a 12-year period with numerous people including Mimi Smith, Yoko Ono, George Martin, Tony Sheridan, Mal Evans and Neil Aspinall. This is the main strength of the book, as the people interviewed add insight to the Lennon story and provide some excellent anecdotes. There is also a 55-page John Lennon Chronology which takes us up to February 1975.

The John Lennon Story Special newspaper compiled and produced by a Birmingham paper *The Evening Mail*, shortly after John's death. This was one of a series of one-shot issues produced by the newspaper. All contributions were written by its own staff rather than by friends or journalists who actually knew John, therefore, there are no new pieces of information or flashes of insight in the edition.

Nevertheless, it is an expertly produced issue with full colour photographs on the cover, back cover and centre pages. There are over 50 photographs. The contributing journalists are Stafford Hildred, Fred Norris, Mike Parry, Jackie Bailey, Arthur Steele, Martin Stote and Christopher Walker, plus New York writers Fred Wehner and Martin Dunn.

The first article, 'I Didn't Know What I Wanted — Apart From Being An Eccentric Millionaire', was a brief story of John's early years in Liverpool, mainly culled from the Hunter Davis book. 'Magic Will Live On' is a different journalist's view of the same period. 'On The Night Lennon And Co Joined The Boys In Blue' is a double-page feature detailing in full The Beatles' appearance at the Hippodrome, Birmingham on 9 November 1963. 'Thanks For The Memories' is a piece about Cynthia Lennon, much of the material inspired by her book A Twist Of Lennon.

'Bottoms Up — And Yoko Moves Into The World Of Pop' is a lightweight piece about Yoko.

'The Radio Scoop That Became An Obituary' gives details of Andy Peebles' BBC 1 radio interview with John. 'Rebel Who Escaped From The Backstreets To Luxury' is another journalist's reworking of the same material contained in the first two articles in the Special.

The headline is provocative. John never lived in the backstreets but came from a nice semi-detached house in a 'posh' part of Liverpool.

'Film Stars — And All They Had To Do Was Act Naturally' concerns their film career. 'The Man Who Put The Show On The Road' is a piece about Brian Epstein. Other features include items on the Maharishi, record sales, the Lennon/McCartney split, a discography, John's literary efforts, their American success and an update on George, Ringo and Paul.

John Lennon: Summer Of 1980
Collection of photographs of John, taken by eight photographers during 1980. Yoko Ono wrote the introduction to the book which contains eighty photographs by Bob Gruen, Annie Leibowitz, Allan Tannebaum and Jack Mitchell.

John Lennon: The Life & The Legend
Lavish colour magazine produced by the staff of the Sunday Times Magazine with over 100 photographs, most of them in colour and a number printed as large double-page spreads. 'The Dream Is Over' relates the events leading to John's death.

This is followed by a series of two-page photographs covering each year of The Beatles' career from 1962. 'Twist & Shout: The Early Days And The Beatles' Years' is a tribute penned by Beatles' official biographer Hunter Davis who also contributed John's obituary to The Times newspaper.

'In My Life . . . A Personal File' is a selection of photographs of the memorabilia Hunter picked up when he was writing the authorized biography.

They include a Polyfoto strip of John when he was five years old and John's handwritten lyrics to a number of his songs and several personal photographs from the Hamburg days.

'Sometime In New York City: Lennon After The Beatles' is a précis of his career mainly in America by Michael Watts. 'Gimme Some Truth: The Thoughts Of John Lennon' is a collection of quotes; 'Thank You Very Much and I Hope I've Passed The Audition' is a selection of 20 of John's best works, a personal choice by Paul Gambaccini, the American DJ working for Radio One. Gambaccini also wrote the book Paul McCartney In His Own Words. Also included is 'Some Days In The Life', a chronology by Mark Lewisohn, one of Britain's most fervent Beatle fans and columnist for The Beatles' Monthly.

John Lennon Tribute Magazine published by Woodhill Press, New York in 1980. It contains more than a dozen colour pictures, including reproductions of film posters, and more than 90 black and white photographs, among which are reproductions of album sleeves. There are a series of short, sketchy articles: 'The Beatles: The Early Years', 'The Birth of Beatlemania', 'The Beatles: The Golden Years' and 'The Break Up And Aftermath'. There is only one writer's credit. The last item in the book is 'The Final Melody' by George Carpozi jr, the story of John's death.

John Lennon: Working Class Hero Handsome British tribute magazine which does not have the publisher or printer credited. However, it is believed to have been produced by the *New Musical Express*, as Tony Tyler and Roy Carr (authors of *The Beatles: An Illustrated Record*) are the only contributors. Twelve large colour pictures and 70 black and white photographs are printed on good quality paper. The main feature 'John Lennon 1940-1980' has been penned by Tony Carr and the other contribution 'John Lennon: A Chronology' by Roy Carr. The contents are completed with the lyrics to 'Working Class Hero' and 'God'.

John Lennon's Secret Book penned by David Stuart Ryan and published by Kozmik Press in 1982. This is a straight-forward and readable account of John's life with an interesting selection of photographs, a poster and a cover illustration based on an Annie Leibowitz photograph. With this is a note which says, 'The front cover pictures John Lennon on the last day of his life.'

John became a man of many faces.

Also interesting is a Lennon family tree and a section, 'Origins Of The Favourite Song Lyrics Of John Lennon', with information about 22 songs. During his researches, Ryan spent some time in Liverpool interviewing people such as Bob Wooler and Allan Williams and visiting the Everyman Theatre to see the *Lennon* play.

Unfortunately, he takes some of Philip Norman's assumptions from *Shout! The True Story Of The Beatles* to be fact, rather than the speculation they really are. For example, there is the statement Norman makes that Brian Epstein fell in love with John the moment he saw him at the Cavern, and that this became the main reason for his signing the group. This is unsubstantiated, but the author seems to take Norman's speculation for granted.

Apart from that, the narrative is extremely well written and the book itself is well produced.

Just William Mischievous scamp created by author Richmal Crompton. The adventures of this boy and his friends became tremendously popular in Britain in a series of books. The character has also been filmed on several occasions and has spawned a number of TV series. John avidly read the *Just William* books when he was a boy and must have relished the adventures in which William Brown became involved.

The Legacy Of John Lennon: Charming Or Harming A Generation?

Book by David A. Noebel, published at the beginning of 1983 by Nashville publishers Thomas Nelson who commented, 'John Lennon's life and music typify an ongoing, conscious betrayal of biblical values. Young people are being encouraged by rock music to accept rebellious life-styles and immoral behaviour.'

The Reverend Noebel had already published two right-wing anti-Beatle tracts in 1968 entitled *The Beatles: A Study In Drugs, Sex And Revolution* and *Communism, Hypnotism and The Beatles*.

Lennon Songbook published in Britain by Wise Publications in 1980 subtitled *The big hits from The Beatles and the solo years*. Of the 20 songs, 16 are credited to Lennon and McCartney, four to John. There are over 20 black-and-white pictures, including a shot from *How I Won The War*, John and Yoko planting an acorn, John and Yoko crouching in the nude, some early Hamburg shots, The Beatles at the seaside wearing old-fashioned striped bathing suits, John lying prostrate under his psychedelic Rolls-Royce and John and Yoko in adjoining hospital beds.

The Lennon Factor American hardbound book of poetry by Paul Young, published by Stein & Day in 1972. This slim volume is much sought after by collectors and has a simple cover which features a sketch of a long-haired bearded John walking by in a white suit.

Lennon 1982 Color Calendar 34-page calendar of photographs released in the US by Sunshine Publications.

Lennon '69: Search For Liberation Published in 1981, this book was available from members of the Krishna Consciousness Society who were selling it on city streets in both Britain and America. Edited by Jeff Long for the Bhaktivedanta Book Trust, it features a lengthy conversation between John and A.C. Bhaktivedanta Swami Prabhupada which took place at Tittenhurst Park on 14 September 1969. Yoko Ono and George Harrison were also present.

Apart from the transcript and various items from the Guru about reincarnation and the Society of Krishna Consciousness, there is the reproduction of a letter which the Swami sent to George Harrison. In this he discusses a dream he says he had about John and his belief that John had been a wealthy Indian musician in a previous life.

Lennon Photo Special American picture magazine tribute including 16-page colour section issued by Sunshine Publications.

The Lennon Tapes Book issued by BBC Publications in 1981, comprising a verbatim transcript of the three-hour interview conducted by disc jockey Andy Peebles with John and Yoko on 6 December 1980. Intended to be a half hour discussion concerning the *Double Fantasy* album, it developed into a conversation that touched on many subjects. The interview itself adds nothing new by way of information or insight to existing knowledge and is not as incisive as, say, the Jann Wenner *Rolling Stone* interviews or the *Playboy* interviews.

The Radio One interviews were first

broadcast over five Sundays, commencing 18 January 1981. All royalties from the book were donated to charities nominated by Yoko and Andy Peebles.

L'Expresse French magazine which in April 1970 reported an interview with John Lennon. In this he said The Beatles were high on pot when they received their MBE from the Queen, having smoked a joint in the toilets at Buckingham Palace.

The episode was untrue, being an example of John's sometimes odd sense of humour. But the French journalist had believed him and his magazine went ahead and printed the story. Although John said he'd made the story up, it has continued to appear in various articles and books.

The Literary Lennon This is a major analysis of John's published writing, the major part of the book being concerned with *In His Own Write* and *A Spaniard In The Works*. Also contained is an analysis of his *Mersey Beat* writings and his contribution to the fan club records. It was issued by Pierian Press in 1983.

The Little Prince Enchanting, mystical story by the French writer Antoine de Saint-Exupery. It became a cult classic in the 'fifties, influencing a variety of actors including James Dean. John and Yoko appreciated the innocence, love and wisdom shown by the Little Prince as he arrived on Earth from another world. They claimed that a phrase from the book: 'The essential is invisible to the eye', led them to create Bagism.

The Little Prince has since been made into a big-budget film, but much has been lost in the transition from a slim volume, with a simple message and much charm to a brash, full-colour motion picture.

Look Magazine Prominent American news magazine which featured a colour photograph of John by Richard Avedon on its cover on 9 January 1967. On the 18 March 1969 issue it sported a colour cover of John and Yoko and the caption, 'John and Yoko Inc. Beatle John and his girl friend join forces and pow! This issue John and Yoko'.

Another publication of the same name but published in Iowa used a colour cover of John on its 13 December 1966 issue. This *Look* magazine featured a shot of John besides his Rolls Royce, with the caption, 'John Lennon, A shorn Beatle tries it on his own.' And the magazine included a large feature with colour shots from the set of *How I Won The War*.

Mersey Beat: The Beginnings Of The Beatles Book featuring replica pages of the *Mersey Beat* newspaper. It was originally published in Britain in 1977 by Omnibus Press and included numerous items by and about John, including his 'Dubious origins of The Beatles' piece, his 'Classified Advertisements'; some Beatcomber columns, the two poems 'The Tales Of Hermit Fred' and 'The Land Of The Lunapots', stories about the *Daily Howl*, reviews of John's books and several separate features about him, together with over a dozen photographs of John, to be found only in this book.

Mind Games An instruction book of exercises to enlarge consciousness, written by Robert Masters and Jean Houston. John Lennon read it and commented: 'I have read three important and revolutionary books in the last three years: Yoko Ono's *Grapefruit*, Arthur Janov's *Primal Scream* and now *Mind Games*. I suggest you read and experience them.'

More Irish Families Book by Edward Maclysacht published by the Irish Academia Press. A sequel to the *Irish Families* book, it contains a seven-line entry on John.

The 1975 John Lennon Interview Slim 16-page book edited by Lavinia Van Driver which contains a transcript of *The Old Grey Whistle Test* interview by Bob Harris, first televised on BBC in February 1975.

One Day At A Time Lavishly illustrated book by Anthony Fawcett, an English-born ex-art critic, covering the years he acted as John and Yoko's assistant. First published in America in 1976 by Grove Press and in Britain in 1977 by New English Library, it was reprinted in 1980 with an epilogue on the last four years of John's life.

Fawcett, who completed his book in New York, brings an insider's view to the years he acted as personal assistant to the duo. Part one entitled 'The Man' comprises the main bulk of the book and documents John's activities since his early days with Yoko until his eventual settling in New York, with lots of fascinating detail of the events in between. Part two is a short section entitled 'The Magic', which is an analysis of John's creative talents as a musician, poet and painter. The book also contains a chronology and a discography.

There are over 200 photographs taken by various photographers including David Gahr, Bob Gruen, Brian Hamill, Annie Leibovitz, Keith McMillan, David Nutter, Chuck Pulin, Ethan Russell and Ann Yorke.

Intriguing pictures include the collage on the wall of Stephen Saunder's house, the erotic lithograph of a naked Yoko, John's handwritten introduction to his 'Bag One' set, a gathering on a glass-roofed train in Canada, the bag at the alchemical wedding and the acorn-planting ceremony at Coventry.

The One Who Writes The Lyrics For Elton John Book of Bernie Taupin's lyrics illustrated by guest artists in the style of *The Beatles Illustrated Lyrics*. John contributed a collage illustrating the song 'Bennie & The Jets'. Among the many images in the picture are girls' legs, the head of Andy Warhol, two naked girls in stockings and suspenders and a pair of motorbikes.

The Penguin John Lennon *In His Own Write* and *A Spaniard In The Works* collected in one volume and published by the British paperback firm Penguin Books in 1966. Signet Books in America also published the two works in one volume in 1967 as *The Writing Beatle — John Lennon In His Own Write And A Spaniard In The Works*.

People's Almanack American book published in the mid-seventies and compiled by writer Irving Wallace and his son David Wallechinsky. John completed a questionnaire from the authors concerning his ideas of a utopia. It was included in the book.

The Playboy Interviews With John Lennon And Yoko Ono Conducted by David Sheff. A paperback book published in America by Playboy Press in 1982 and in the UK by New English Library during the same year.

This was the most important printed interview since Jann Wenner's, complementing the former by bringing John's story in his own words up through the seventies. The original interview for *Playboy* magazine was set to be a major exclusive: John's first interview for almost five years.

A *Newsweek* reporter, Barbara Graustark, pre-empted *Playboy* and rushed her interview into print first. The *Playboy* interview itself was a 20,000 word piece, printed in the January 1981 issue (coincidentally, with Ringo Starr's wife Barbara Bach gracing the cover). This was published in December and read by John and Yoko on 7 December, the eve of his killing.

Sheff conducted several interviews with John and Yoko and his tapes ran to almost 20 hours. There was such an abundance of material that over 60,000 words were gathered to be presented in book form.

There is a discussion on exactly who wrote the various songs published under the Lennon & McCartney credit, John's relationship with Sean and Julian, John's films, women's rights, his 'long weekend', Tony Cox and Kyoko, and George Harrison's book *I, Me, Mine*. John unburdens himself of much of the guilt he felt over the years regarding his son Julian, Yoko's daughter Kyoko and his idiocy at the Troubadour club.

Rolling Stone American rock magazine launched in November 1967 by Jann Wenner and featuring a photograph of John on the cover of its premier issue. The publication took a particular interest in John's career and he became the recipient of the first-ever award presented by the paper to a prominent rock star for his contribution to music.

The first major interview with John was conducted by Jonathan Cott and appeared in the 23 November 1968 issue. The most famous interview was the lengthy 'Working Class Hero' which ran in two issues dated 7 January and 4 February 1971 and were later issued in book form as *Lennon Remembers*.

His final *Rolling Stone* interview was conducted on 5 December 1980 and the photographic session to tie-in with the proposed cover story was taken on the morning of his death, 8 December. Due to the tragedy, a special issue was put together which was published on 22 January 1981.

Rolling Stone has published a series of books of collected items from the magazine, several of them featuring Lennon interviews or articles about him. *The Ballad of John And Yoko* is a book which contains a large portion of the material from the special issue of January 1981.

The Shining Best-selling horror novel by Stephen King which was filmed by Stanley Kubrick. King said that the inspiration for the title came from the John Lennon/Plastic Ono Band single 'Instant Karma'. The author was impressed by the line 'We all shine on' and decided to call the novel *The Shine*. However, he changed it to *The Shining* when he discovered that the word 'shine' was a derogatory word for negro in America.

Sky Writing By Word Of Mouth Unpublished book written by John during his years at the Dakota Building. It was among a number of items stolen from the apartment after his death.

Songs Of John Lennon Title of

When the Beatles were in bloom.

songbook published in Britain by Wise Publications featuring the music and lyrics of 16 John Lennon compositions. The book also contains 20 photographs by Ethan Russell, Richard Di Lello and Annie Leibovitz and a 33 page John Lennon interview which originally appeared in *Rolling Stone* magazine in 1970.

A Spaniard In The Works John's second book, first published by Jonathan Cape in 1965. Designed by Robert Freeman it had drawings by John.

The book continued in the vein of *In His Own Write* and the contents were: 'A Spaniard In The Works', 'The Fat Budgie', 'Snore Wife And Some Several Dwarfs', 'The Singularge Experience Of Miss Anne Duffield', 'The Faulty Bagnose', 'We Must Not Forget The General Erection', 'Benjamin Distasteful', 'The Wumberlog (Of The Magic Dog)', 'Arminta Ditch', 'Cassandle', 'The National Health Cow', 'Readers Lettuce', 'Silly Norman', 'Mr. Borris Morris', 'Bernice's Sheep', 'Last Will And Testicle', 'Our Dad' and 'I Belief, Boof'.

Sport, Speed And Illustrated From the age of seven, John began to work on a series of books with this title adding 'Edited and Illustrated by J. W. Lennon.' The books contained pictures of soccer players and film stars which he'd pasted in among the various poems, cartoons, short stories and serials which he had composed.

Strawberry Fields Forever: John Lennon Remembered One of the first paperbacks on the market following John's death. A Delilah/Bantam book with 30 interior photographs, it was written by Vic Garbarini and Brian Cullman with Barbara Graustark. There is an introduction by David Marsh, a short item 'The Dream Is Over', 'Seven Days In December', an article on the events surrounding John's death, 'Sometime In NYC' a feature on John and Yoko becoming residents of New York, 'All The Lonely People: The Early Years', a piece on The Beatles' early career, 'Strawberry Fields', The Beatles career until 1970. 'The Plastic Ono Band', John's post-Beatles career, 'Two Virgins', the complete interview which Barbara Graustark conducted with John and Yoko in September, 1980 for *Newsweek* magazine and 'Chronology: Liverpool To New York, 1940-1980'.

Teen Bag's Tribute To John Lennon American tribute magazine, edited by Adrian B Lopez and published by Lopez Publications.

365 Days Of Sean When John was enjoying his period as a housemother, he was thoroughly engrossed in every aspect of the baby Sean's life. He began taking snaps of his son each day, almost from the moment of birth and both he and Yoko discussed the idea of publishing a book called *365 Days Of Sean* which would comprise a selection of photographs of Sean taken each day during the first 12 months of his life.

The Three Stigmata Of Palmer Eldritch Controversial science-fiction novel penned in 1964 by the brilliant sci-fi author Philip K. Dick who died in 1982. Members of an overcrowded Earth are forcibly transported as settlers to planets with hostile environments. Living within protective domes, they take drugs such as Can-D and Chew-Z which transport them to exotic dream-worlds. John Lennon was so impressed with the book that he intended to buy the film rights and make a movie of it.

Tribute To John Lennon Special edition of Britain's *Daily Mirror* newspaper published in December 1980 by Mirrorbooks, written by Pat Doncaster and containing 87 well-selected photographs and illustrations. The text is quite sparse and the design and layout allow for lots of large pictorial spreads.

The straightforward text outlines some of the highlights of John's life in chronological order, but it is the photographic material which creates the impact. 'The Many Faces Of A Genius', for instance, is a double page spread of photos of John from the early days to one taken shortly before his death. It presents in one visual feast the many guises in which John appeared over the years. The last photograph in the paper is especially poignant. It depicts John at the piano and the sheet music before him is *Thanks For The Memory*.

A Tribute To John Lennon, 1940-1980 A small, hardbound volume, published on both sides of the Atlantic by Proteus Books in 1981. This is a collection of tributes and editorials commenting on the Lennon tragedy from newspapers in Britain and America. There are almost 40 brief articles with such titles as: 'The Walrus Was John', 'Lennon Without Tears', 'The Dream Is Ended' and 'Minstrel Extraordinaire' by a variety of writers including Ray Connolly and Don Short.

The majority of the items are written in a highly emotive style, indicating the impact Lennon had on the lives of so many people of his generation. At times, the style begins to become over-powering, so it is probably advisable not to read the book at one sitting. A number of valid points are made including the fact that, as was the case with the death of Kennedy, most people remember where and what they were doing when they first heard the news of John's killing. Most writers also agree that because of his death, he will never grow old. There are 16 photographs and a jacket illustration by J P Tibbles. All royalties from the book were distributed equally between The Spirit Foundation and Handgun Control Inc.

A Twist Of Lennon Cynthia Lennon's biography, first published in Britain in a paperback version by Star Books in 1978. Although sub-titled *Her first-hand story of that incredible pheno-menon — The Beatles*, it's very much her own personal history. It shows little awareness of the drama of what life with The Beatles must have been like.

Cynthia had very little to do with the musical side of their career and betrays remarkable ignorance of the Mersey beat scene and how it arose, attributing it almost solely to the efforts of a small coffee bar owner. She also has the date of her own marriage wrong.

Judging by this book, Cynthia was an innocent tossed about by world events. We can always remember Cynthia as the one left on the railway platform as The Beatles chugged off to Bangor, or being refused entrance to hotels by policemen who didn't believe she was Mrs. Lennon. We remember the photo-graphs of her with tears in her eyes.

In some ways this is a courageous book because Cynthia is revealed as vulnerable and unworldly. It exposes her naivety and shows that whilst the experience of The Beatles' world stretched John it did nothing for her. Cynthia remained very much the middle class girl from the Wirral who found it almost impossible to break out of that shell.

One has the feeling that she was grateful all the time: grateful for her marriage in the first place, grateful for being allowed to tag along, and not complaining when she had to give birth to Julian with no moral support, and then having to spend the next critical months trying to evade the press and hide her own marriage.

A Twist Of Lennon reveals to us why John eventually turned to Yoko: not in the narration, but between the lines. John was seeking a partner to stretch him, stir his imagination, become a mother figure, an equal partner, even to occasionally dominate the relationship. Cynthia was incapable of any of these roles.

She remained the traditional northern housewife, subservient to her husband and aware of her maternal responsibili-ties. She'd try to look like Brigitte Bardot to please him, wither beneath his acerbic wit, yet end up feeling the guilty one.

After describing the terribly shoddy treatment she received, she ends the book with only sweetness and light in her attitude to John and Yoko. She gives us a 'thanks-for-the-memory' finish when we expected some human feeling to come to the surface: no rancour, no vitriol, no fury; only humiliation.

The book is illustrated with a series of

Sweet Cynthia, her autobiography has a tender touch.

her drawings which reveal no intrinsic artistic value. They are competent drawings executed by someone who was obviously a modest art student, but there is none of the individuality and sheer talent found in John's drawings. John and Yoko were artists, Cynthia was not.

Her vulnerability is also exposed in a series of twee poems which are almost embarrassing to read. One feels that such honest exposure of emotions is almost masochistic.

Everyone is 'nice' in the world of Cynthia Lennon because when the odd villain does appear, as in the case of Alexis Mardas, no real passion is evident. Cynthia merely taps people's wrists if they betray her.

Her descriptions of people are sugary: 'My great friend Phyllis', 'Dot was such a gentle soul', 'George was a perfect gentleman and Judy a perfect lady', 'his lovely wife Sybil Burton'.

Everyone's so nice and lovely, it's as if Cynthia is grateful for the scraps of friendship thrown her way and totally overawed by the opportunity of mixing with the famous such as Michael Crawford, Stanley Baker, Peter Cooke and Dudley Moore. She never gains the confidence of a Patti Boyd or Yoko Ono.

Ultimately, the book is sad. Cynthia was a spectator during the heyday of the world's greatest musical phenomenon when she could have been a participant. She remained a spectator, on the periphery, afraid to take her rightful place in the drama.

The Widow's Tale Tentative title for Yoko's projected book about her life with John for which she reputedly received the offer of a five million dollar advance.

Come in No 9, your time is up!

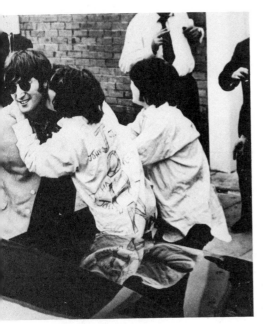

A touch of Johnmania.

Personal facts

John meets his long-lost cousins Down Under.

Action For The Crippled Child
Name of the charity for which John designed a Christmas card in 1966.

Advertisements John and Yoko were always conscious of the media and its power as a means of communication. Despite their access to the press, they occasionally paid for advertisements to convey a message they wished to get across. Their 'War Is Over' campaign, with its huge display posters, is an example of how they utilized advertising. Another example occurred on John's 40th birthday when Yoko hired a plane to fly past the Dakota building in New York with the message 'Sean and Yoko Love You'.

On 24 July 1967, Brian Epstein and The Beatles were among the signatories to a full page advertisement in *The Times* newspaper (London) in which they stated: 'The law against marijuana is immoral in principal and unworkable in practice'. They advocated the legalisation of this soft drug. On 8 November 1968 John and Yoko took out advertisements in the music press in support of the 'Peace Ship', an independent radio station aboard a ship in the Middle East which attempted to advocate peace between the Israelis and the Arabs.

One of their most famous advertisements appeared in Sunday newspapers in New York, London and Tokyo on 27 May 1979 under the headline:
A LOVE LETTER FROM JOHN AND YOKO TO PEOPLE WHO ASK US WHAT, WHEN AND WHY

The past ten years we noticed everything we wished came true in its own time, good or bad, one way or the other. We kept telling each other that, one of these days, we would have to get organized and wish for only good

things. Then our baby arrived! We were overjoyed and at the same time felt very responsible.

Now our wishes would also affect *him*. We felt it was time for us to stop discussing and do something about our wishing process: The Spring Cleaning of our minds! It was a lot of work. We kept finding things in those old closets in our minds that we hadn't realized were still there, things we wished we hadn't found. As we did our cleaning, we also started to notice many wrong things in our house: there was a shelf which should have never been there in the first place, a painting we grew to dislike, and there were the two dingy rooms which became light and breezy when we broke the walls between them.

We started to love the plants, which one of us originally thought were robbing the air from us! We began to enjoy the drum beat of the city which used to annoy us. We made a lot of mistakes and still do.

In the past we spent a lot of energy in trying to get something we thought we wanted, wondered why we didn't get it, only to find out that one or both of us didn't really want it.

One day, we received a sudden rain of chocolates from people around the world. 'Hey, what's this! We're not eating sugar stuff, are we? Who's wishing it?' We both laughed. We discovered that when two of us wished in unison, it happened faster. As the Good Book says — Where two are gathered together — It's true. Two is plenty. A Newclear Seed.

More and more we are starting to wish and pray. The things we have tried to achieve in the past by flashing a V sign, we try now through wishing. We are not doing this because it is simpler.

Two thousand posters in London announced John and Yoko's message of peace.

John gives a 'peace' of his mind.

Wishing is more effective than waving flags. It works. It's like magic. Magic is simple. Magic is real. The secret of it is to know that it is simple, and not kill it with an elaborate ritual which is a sign of insecurity.

When somebody is angry with us, we draw a halo around his or her head in our minds. Does the person stop being angry then? Well, we don't know! We know, though, that when we draw a halo around a person, suddenly the person starts to look like an angel to us. This helps us to feel warm toward the person, reminds us that everyone has goodness inside, and that all people who come to us are angels in disguise, carrying messages and gifts to use from the Universe. Magic is logical. Try it sometime.

We still have a long way to go. It seems the more we get into cleaning, the faster the wishing and receiving process gets. The house is getting very comfortable now. Sean is beautiful. The plants are growing. The cats are purring. The town is shining, sun, rain, or snow. We live in a beautiful universe. We are thankful every day for the plentifulness of our life. This is not a euphemism. We understand that we, the city, the country, the earth are facing very hard times, and there is panic in the air. Still the sun is shining and we are here together, and there is love between us, our city, the country, the earth. If two people like us can do what we are doing with our lives, any miracle is possible! It's true we can do with a few big miracles right now. The thing is to recognize

204

them when they come to you and be thankful. First they come in a small way, in everyday life, then they come in rivers, and in oceans. It's goin' to be all right! The future of the earth is up to all of us.

Many people are sending us vibes every day in letters, telegrams, taps on the gate, or just flowers and nice thoughts. We thank them all and appreciate them for respecting our quiet space, which we need. Thank you for all the love you send us. We feel it every day. We love you, too. We know you are concerned about us. That is nice. That's why you want to know what we are doing. That's why everybody is asking us What, When and Why. We understand. Well, this is what we've been doing. We hope that you have the same quiet space in your mind to make your own wishes come true.

If you think of us next time, remember, our silence is a silence of love and not of indifference. Remember, we are writing in the sky instead of on paper — that's our song. Lift your eyes and look up in the sky. There's our message. Lift your eyes again and look around you, and you will see that you are walking in the sky, which extends to the ground. We are all part of the sky, more so than of the ground. Remember, we love you. John and Yoko Ono.
May 27, 1979
New York City
P.S. We noticed that three angels were looking over our shoulders when we wrote this!

The Aesthetics Of John Lennon

A songwriting workshop launched at the College of Continuing Education at the University of Southern California in 1981.

Aunt Mimi Name given to one of the Lennon's pet cats when the family lived in Weybridge.

Bag One Name which John gave to his set of lithographs. John and Yoko ran a company called Bag One Productions which they had formed in order to market their creative product. The idea that John should attempt to express himself in lithographic drawings came from art critic Anthony Fawcett in 1968. Anthony, who became personal assistant to John and Yoko, continued to encourage John to produce work in this field. It is to his credit that the actual lithographs saw the light of day. A second set, based on the I Ching, was never completed.

From a large selection of sketches and drawings, John eventually chose a series of a dozen, half of which depicted scenes of his life with Yoko, such as their first Bed-In and wedding ceremony. The other half are quite explicit erotic scenes, including one of Yoko lying on her back with her legs apart and John making love to Yoko from the rear. In one lithograph there are two images of John, one engaged in the act of cunilingus, the other sucking her breast.

The finished work included a written sheet by John containing an A to Z of 'my story both humble and true'. Some of the items were:
A is for Parrot which we can plainly see
H is for England and (Heather)
M is for Venezuela where the oranges come from
T is for Tommy who won the war
S is for pancake or whole wheat bread
X is Easter — have one yourself
Y is a crooked letter and you can't straighten it.

Bag One comprised 14 separate

prints which were assembled into a limited edition of 300 sets. The lithographs were contained in a magnificent white leather bag designed by French clothes designer Ted Lapidus with the letters 'Bag One' and John's signature printed in black.

The prints were taken to Canada where John signed each one personally during his brief stay at Ronnie Hawkins' farm. Priced at £40 each or £550 per set, the lithographs were first exhibited at the London Art Gallery in January 1970 where eight of the prints were confiscated by the police as being obscene. The case was taken to court but was dismissed by the judge. The exhibition was moved on to the Lee Nordness Gallery in New York.

Beatcomber Humorous column which appeared in several issues of the newspaper *Mersey Beat*, comprising John's stories and poems. After Bill Harry had printed in the first issue 'In The Dubious Origins Of Beatles, Translated From The John Lennon', John was thrilled at seeing his work in print for the first time. He was also pleased that it had been uncensored. He gave Bill a huge bundle of virtually all his works, approximately 250 stories, cartoons and poems, together with permission for Harry to use them as he saw fit.

Bill commenced using the work by presenting the poem 'I Remember Arnold' in issue No 4, dated 17 August 1961. This was later used in John's book *In His Own Write*.

Bill then decided to present one item at a time, using the name 'Beatcomber'. He chose the name becase he was particularly fond of the *Daily Express*. The initial 'Beatcomber' column appeared in issue No 6 dated 14 September 1961

and was entitled 'Around and About'. This was a skit on the *Mersey Beat* 'Entertainments Guide' on page 3 of the paper, and the gossip column 'Mersey Roundabout', penned by Virginia Harry. It read:

AROUND & ABOUT

'Reviving the old tradition of Judro Bathing is slowly but slowly dancing in Liddypool once more. Had you remembering these owld custard of Boldy Street blowing? The Peer Hat is very popularce for sun eating and boots for nude brighter is handys when sailing. We are not happy with her Queen Victorious Monologue, but Walky Through Gallery is goodly when the rain, and Sit Georgie House is black (and white from the little pilgrims flying from Hellsy College). Talk Hall is very histerical with old things wot are fakes and King Anne never slept there I tell you. Shout Airborne is handly for planes if you like (no longer government patrolled) and the L.C.C.C. (Liddypool Cha Cha Cha) are doing a great thing. The *Mersey Boat* is selling another three copies to some go home foreigners who went home.

'A little guide to entertain may be of some helpless, so here it is:

'The Casbin — Stricktly no members only.

'The Sheates — The Bohernia of Liddypool.

'The Jackarandy — Membrains only.

'La Locantry — Next to La Grafty.

'La Matumba — for a cheap heal.

'The Pheolix — Also Bohumbert.

'El Camunal — Bald Stream.

'The Dodd Spot — Watch out for details.

'There are but to name a few of the few with so little for so many, we'll fight 'em in the streets, so to Speke. We've been engaged for 43 years and he still smokes. I am an unmurdered mother of 19 years, am I pensionable? My dog bites me when I bite it. There is a lot to do in Liddypool, but not all convenience.'

John was later to edit and adapt the item for use as 'Liddypool' in *In His Own Write*.

It wasn't until the following year that the next Beatcomber item appeared, entitled 'Small Stan'. It read:

SMALL STAN

'Once upon a Tom there was a small little Stan, who was very small.

'"You are very small Stan," they said.

'"I am only little," replied Stan answering, feeling very small. Who could blame him, for Stan was only small?

'"You must be small Stan," people were oft heard to cry, noticing how extremely very small Stan was in fact. But being small (Stan was small) had its condensations.

'Who else but Stan (the small) could wear all those small clothes?

'Stan was highly regarded by everyone (for Stan was small and little). However, one day Stan saw an adverse in the *Mersey Bean* for "Club you quickly grow you boots." So on that very day Small Stan (by name called) purchased a pair of the very same. So now when Stan passes by, folks say, "Is not that small Stan wearing a pair of those clubs you quickly grow you boots?"

'And it is.'

The next story to appear was 'On Safairy With Whide Hunter' and this, unfortunately, was the last Beatcomber piece.

Mersey Beat had by now become so successful locally, that the tiny top floor office, which seemed quite adequate when Bill and Virginia Harry were running the paper, seemed quite small after the addition of Pat Delaney to deliver copies, a secretary Pat Finn and an advertising man Raymond Caine. Larger offices had to be found and their landlord, David Land, a wine merchant, offered them a set of two offices on the floor below.

Virginia was left in charge of the move while Bill was out of the office most of the time collecting material for the paper.

Ensconced in the new offices, he then set out to write the next issue and couldn't trace the bundle of John's papers, from which he intended selecting the next Beatcomber item. He asked Virginia where the papers were and told her he'd left them in the top drawer of his desk.

It transpired that during the move she'd disposed of a pile of useless papers and, unfortunately mistaken the bundle of John's writings as old copy to be thrown out. This had occurred a few day's previously, so there was no point in turning over the dustbins.

They both had to give the very distressing news to John that evening in the Blue Angel club, and he was so choked at having lost so much of his work that he cried on Virginia's shoulder.

Although no one could be blamed for this unfortunate accident, Harry was aware of how deeply John felt about his poems and stories. So he decided to see if he could trace any of John's lost works. He discovered that John had written exercise books which had been confiscated by teachers. Harry tried unsuccessfully to contact the teachers concerned to see if the books existed.

However, two girls from Quarry Bank School came into the office one day while he was absent and left two poems which had been ripped from one of the *Daily Howl* books.

As they hadn't left either their names, addresses or phone numbers he was unable to investigate further. However, he was able to publish the two poems in *Mersey Beat* in February 1964. The first was entitled:

THE TALES OF HERMIT FRED
The wandering Hermit Fred am I
With candle stick bun
I nit spaghetti pie
And crum do I have fun
I peel old bagpipes for my wife
And cut all negroes' hair
As breathing is my very life
To stop I do not dare
     The other poem was called!
     THE LAND OF THE LUNAPOTS
'Twas custard time and as I
Snuffed at the haggis pie pie
The noodles ran about my plunk
Which rode my wrytle uncle drunk
'Twas Wilbur's graftiens graffen Bing
That makes black puddings want to sing
For them in music can be heard
Like the dying cough of a humming bird
The lowland chick astound agasted
Wonder how long it lasted
In this land of Lunapots
I who sail the earth in paper yachts.

Harry also traced a copy of the *Daily Howl* which had been left behind in the Gambier Terrace flat and it was returned to John. Bill was also able to give John a copy of the 'Small Stan' piece, although it never appeared in any of his books.

Biography The very first biography of The Beatles was written by John at the request of Bill Harry. During the months running up to the publication of the music paper *Mersey Beat* in July, 1961, Harry asked John if he would write a biography of the group in his own style.

Whilst at Liverpool Art College with John, Bill had been shown John's poems and felt that he would be capable of coming up with an interesting piece of prose. John presented him with the completed article on some scraps of paper one day at the Jacaranda Club. Bill decided to call it, *On The Dubious Origins Of Beatles. Translated From The John Lennon*, and used it unedited in the first issue of *Mersey Beat*.

It read:

'Once upon a time there were three little boys called John, George and Paul, by name christened. They decided to get together because they were the getting-together type. When they were together they wondered what for after all, what for? So all of a sudden they all grew guitars and formed a noise. Funnily enough, no one was interested, least of all the three little men.

'So-o-o-o on discovering a fourth little even littler man called Stuart Sutcliffe running about them they said, quote "Sonny get a bass guitar and you will be all right".

'And he did — but he wasn't all right because he couldn't play. Still there was no beat and a kindly old aged man said, quote "Thou hast no drums!" We had no drums! they coffed. So a series of drums came and went and came.

'Suddenly, in Scotland, touring with Johnny Gentle, the group (called The Beatles) discovered they had not a very nice sound because they had no ampli-fiers. They got some.

'Many people ask what are Beatles? Why Beatles? Ugh, Beatles! How did the name arrive? So we will tell you. It came

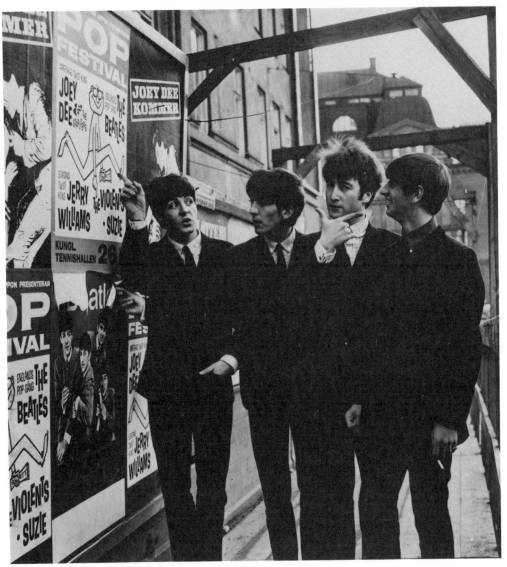

Have you heard of these chaps?

in a vision. A man appeared on a flaming pie and said unto them, 'From this day on you are Beatles with an 'A'.'

'''Thank you, Mister Man,'' they said.

'And then a man with a beard cut off said, ''Will you go to Germany (Hamburg) and play mighty rock for the peasants for money?'' And we said we would play mighty anything for money.

'But before we could go we had to grow a drummer, so we grew one in West Derby in a club called Some Casbah and his trouble was Pete Best.

'We called ''Hello, Pete, come off to Germany!'' ''Yes!''

'Z ooooom! After a few months, Peter and Paul (who is called McArtrey son of Jim McArtrey, his father) lit a Kino (cinema) and the German police said

209

"Bad Beatles, you must go home and light your English cinemas".

'Zooooom, half a group. But even before this, the Gestapo had taken my friend little George Harrison (of Speke) away because he was only twelve and too young to vote in Germany. But after two months in England he grew 18, and the Gestapos said, "You can come".

'So suddenly all back in Liverpool Village were many groups playing in grey suits and Jim said, "Why have you no grey suits?"

'"We don't like them, Jim", we said speaking to Jim.

'After playing in the clubs a bit, everyone said, "Go to Germany!" So we are. Zooooom! Stuart gone. Zoom zoom! John (of Woolton) George (of Speke) Peter and Paul zoom zoom. All of them gone.

'Thank you club members, from John and George (what are friends).'

Once 'Please, Please Me' had topped the charts, the boys were asked to provide biographical notes of a more conventional nature and the following is a synthesis of the biographical material John filled in for the press in 1963:

JOHN LENNON
Date of birth: 9th October 1940
Weight: 11½ stone
Height: 5 feet 11 inches
Colour of eyes: brown
Colour of hair: brown
First professional appearance: club in Liverpool
Likes: music, books, painting, television
Hates: thick heads and traditional jazz
Favourite food: steak and chips, curries and jelly
Favourite clothes: dark coloured in suede and leather
Favourite colour: black
Favourite games: ball games
Favourite singers: Carl Perkins, Chuck Berry, Kay Starr
Favourite actors: Marlon Brando, Peter Sellers
Favourite actress: Brigitte Bardot
Favourite companions: blonde, intelligent girls
Ambition: money and everything
Instruments played: rhythm guitar, harmonica
Educated: Quarry Bank Grammar and Liverpool College of Art
Hobbies: writing songs, poems and plays, girls, painting, TV, meeting people
Favourite drinks: whiskey and tea
Favourite band: Quincy Jones
Tastes in music: R&B, gospel
Personal ambition: to write a musical
Favourite instrumentalist: Sonny Terry
Favourite composer: Luther Dixon
Former occupation: art student
Brothers/sisters: none

There have been numerous biographical books written about John, but none of them with his co-operation. Since he did not pen an autobiography, the nearest we have to 'horses' mouth' versions of John's life are the various lengthy interviews he conducted with journalists such as Jann Wenner and David Sheff. Even here, they are short on details and John's own memory betrayed him when asked to recollect incidents from his past.

There was, of course, *The Beatles. The Authorised Biography* written by Hunter Davies in which each member of The Beatles put himself at Hunter's disposal during his researches.

However, it was a rather antiseptic

version of their story. The first paperback biography of John was written by George Tremlett and there have been other biographies by people who knew him at least, such as Ray Connolly.

The biography written by Cynthia Lennon gives some details of the couple's married life, although it is marred by inaccuracies. New works on his later life, such as *The Ballad Of John And Yoko* have appeared and Yoko Ono herself was reported as contemplating writing her own in-depth story of her life with John.

Carol Nickname given by Elton John to John Lennon.

CBS Records Major American record company which set up a fund to provide a scholarship in composition at the Julliard School of Music in New York as a tribute to John.

Centro John & Yoko Por La Paz Argentinian organization launched by Horacio Daniel Dubini to 'spread John and Yoko's work, artistic, cultural and humanitarian, and raise money for charitable foundations and institutions.'

Cincinnati Pops Orchestra Orchestra which performed at 'A Tribute To John Lennon/A Concert In His Memory 1940-1980' at the New Haven Veterans Memorial Coliseum on 9 December 1981. The concert was organized in four sections. The first 'A Symphonia Fantasia For Orchestra' arranged by Frank Proto, performed abstract variations of John's music. Roberta Flack next appeared singing songs from the *Double Fantasy* album and numbers such as 'A Hard Day's Night'. Dr James Westwater then presented a slide show of pictures

of John and Yoko with their music playing in the background. David Clayton-Thomas next appeared and the show ended with a 'singalong' featuring Flack, Thomas, the orchestra and a four-piece rock group.

Club Dakota Erstwhile private club launched by John in one of the spare rooms of his apartments in the Dakota Building on New Year's Eve, 1979. He told his mate Elliot Mintz that he'd like to turn the room into something similar to an old English club to which he could invite his close friends. He placed an old Wurlitzer jukebox, piano, couches and numerous second-hand items such as a cigarette machine in the room. He and Elliot dressed in black tie and tails for the New Year opening, to which Yoko had been invited. The Club Dakota lasted barely a couple of weeks.

Crying Lady Ghost Spectral figure which John claimed he once witnessed inside the Dakota building.

'Cut Piece' Title of a Yoko Ono conceptual happening performed at Carnegie Recital Hall in New York in March 1965. Yoko sat in a chair on stage and members of the audience came up and with scissors snipped off pieces of her clothing.

The Dissenters Name coined by Bill Harry for a loose-knit group of friends (Harry, Stuart Sutcliffe, John Lennon, Rod Murray) at Liverpool College of Art when America's beat generation was popular with British students.

Harry felt that instead of being inspired by poets in San Francisco, creative people in Liverpool should express their feelings about their own

A Roller picture gallery.

environment.

Liverpool had character, history and individuality. In music, verse and paintings it could convey as romantic an image as America's West Coast.

Harry first discussed this with Stuart Sutcliffe and the two intended preparing a book about Liverpool with Stu's illustrations and Harry's text.

Harry felt that they should form a group and attempt to portray what they felt was wrong with society in whatever form of creative work. Hence the term The Dissenters.

Discussions took place in Ye Cracke and in students' flats. Although the group didn't last very long, their ideals continued and they did achieve the aim of popularizing Liverpool: Harry with his newspaper *Mersey Beat*, John with his music and Stuart, in the short time he lived, with his paintings.

Doing Lennon Science-fiction short story by Gregory Benford first published in the April 1975 issue of *Analog* and included in the anthology *Best Science Fiction Of The Year 5* published by Victor Gollancz in 1976. A wealthy man obsessed by The Beatles and Lennon in particular plans to enter suspended animation and pretend that he is John

He later donated the hand-painted Phantom V to the Smithsonian Institute in Washington. This was the car which was said to have inspired *Magical Mystery Tour*.

In 1982 Britain's glossy Sunday magazines displayed a special advertisement from Rolls-Royce — a list of distinguished past owners, including John and Brian Epstein. Every person mentioned on the list was deceased.

Despite passing his test, John preferred to leave the driving wheel to the capable hands of others and had a number of chauffeurs, including Bill Corbett and Les Anthony. When John decided to handle the car on a driving holiday in Scotland with Yoko, Julian and Kyoko he lost control of the vehicle. Everyone was taken to hospital and the car was a write-off.

'Eulogy For A Dreamer' Title of poetic tribute to John written by Baltimore poet Scarlett Rose. The poem was published in several newspapers and recited on the radio station WIYY-98 and on WJZ-TV. There was such a positive reaction from the public that the artist, Daniel Yohe, used the poem for a commemorative poster, lettered by a calligraphist and printed on high quality art paper in a limited edition. The poster went on sale at a number of art galleries in Maryland.

The Fat Budgie Cartoon which John drew and allowed the charity, Oxfam, to use as a Christmas card in 1964. A half-million cards featuring the Fat Budgie were printed. The illustration came from page 16 of John's book *A Spaniard In The Works* in which the circular-shaped bird was the subject of one of John's intriguing poems. The Fat

when he is awakened in the twenty-second century. A charming story with several twists and a description of a revived Beatlemania in the far future.

Driving John first learned to drive at the age of 24 and after passing his test in 1966 he bought a black mini-Cooper, a black Rolls-Royce and a black Ferrari. He sold the Ferrari soon afterwards and it was with the Rolls-Royce that he became mainly associated. He had one Rolls painted in psychedelic patterns and in 1970 paid £50,000 for the Rolls-Royce Phantom which had been built specially for The Beatles in 1965.

Budgie was a yellow pet called Jeffrey who ate scrambled eggs on toast.

'The Feminization Of Society'

Article which Yoko wrote for the New York Times in 1971.

Frankenstein's Monster

Frankenstein's Monster Creature created by authoress Mary Shelley in the classic novel *Frankenstein*, which has become one of the most familiar of all monster stories. In *Yellow Submarine*, Ringo and Captain Fred enter a room where a giant Frankenstein monster awaits his revival on a table. Despite Fred's protests, Ringo sets the machinery in motion and amidst much crackling of electricity and flashing of lights, the creature is animated and arises, towering above them. Then, in a speedy transformation, the creature turns into John.

Friends Of Lennon A group of fans from Baltimore, Maryland, who in 1981, formed an association of followers who believed that John's soul was in danger from Satan and that his killer was Satan's agent.

They took out an advertisement in the American magazine *Beatlefan* in October 1981 which read:

'Mark Chapman voiced his hatred of John Lennon for a decade before he finally murdered him. The time he spent working with Vietnamese refugees has been called the most healthy, positive period of his life.

'His hatred for John became especially vocal during this time and when his work there was finished, the last thing he said to his friends and acquaintances was, "About five years from now, one of us will do something famous, and it will bring us all together."

'This was in December of 1975. Since then he allegedly tried to commit suicide twice.

'When sentenced, Chapman flaunted the mercy shown him by once again insisting that he was a protector of innocents, a policeman of righteousness. That this man did not get the maximum sentence is a mockery of justice. The whole treatment of John's murder has been an abomination to man and God himself.

'Our aim is to start an organization of Beatlefans who will reject the spirit of Satan, the Prince of Lies, wholeheartedly.

'Immediate goals include putting a Christmas message addressed to John's eternal spirit and his family and friends on Earth in a major US magazine and meeting in New York on the first anniversary of John's martyrdom.'

Gitane Brand of French cigarette to which John was partial.

Gollum Enchanted creature featured in J R R Tolkien's modern classic *Lord Of The Rings*. He is a pathetic creature whose mind has been warped by a magical elfin ring. When there were proposals that The Beatles should appear in a film adaptation of the book, it was mentioned that John would take the part of Gollum. The other members would be Frodo (Paul), Gandalf (George) and Sam (Ringo).

Green Card Documentary evidence of John's right to remain in the USA. On 2 March 1973 while in New York, John received notice that he had to leave the United States voluntarily within 60 days or be deported. He appealed and the Nixon government's Court of Appeal

A sign for peace.

overturned the appeal two years later in 1975.

Strong public opinion in favour of John led to a change of official opinion and news filtered down that the government no longer objected to his stay. Immigration judge Ira Fieldsteel finally approved John's application to remain as a resident. This came after a one-hour hearing in which Gloria Swanson, Norman Mailer, Geraldo Rivers and sculptor Isamu Nogochi spoke on John's behalf. He was presented with Green card No A17-597-321.

Hendel Medallion A special award presented by New York City to people who have distinguished themselves in the arts. John was awarded the medallion posthumously in May 1981 at a ceremony at the City Hall. Mayor Ed Koch presented the medallion to Yoko. John became the 99th person to win the award, previous recipients having

included Charlie Chaplin and Louis Armstrong.

Hokey Pokey Name by which John's aunt, Mimi Smith, sometimes referred to Yoko Ono.

I Ching Ancient Chinese oracle of wisdom and philosophy whose symbols have been used for consultations providing personal advice for the future for over 4,000 years. The system became popular in the west when studied by Dr Carl Jung.

There are 64 hexagrams each with a text. Consultation of an individual nature is made with the use of either yarrow stalks or coins. Both John and Yoko used 'the oracle of change' and following the success of his *Bag One* lithographs, John began work on a second series of lithographs based on the I Ching. Unfortunately, he only completed three in the series.

The Isis 64-foot sailboat belonging to John. It was docked at Long Island.

John Lennon Decanter A limited edition decanter on offer from Marita Spirits of Cleveland, Ohio, for a short period during 1981.

The John Lennon Memorial Service Liverpool tribute to John which took place in the huge piazza in front of St. George's Hall and opposite the Empire Theatre where The Beatles appeared on several occasions. The memorial service organized by Sam Leach was held on 14 December 1980. More than 50,000 people of all ages gathered to pay their respects and the Lord Mayor of Liverpool made a speech, followed by a number of other speakers.

Taped messages from Gerry Marsden, former leader of Gerry And The Pacemakers and David Shepherd, the Bishop of Liverpool, were played over the loud speakers. Allan Williams was among the participants and at 7 pm there was a ten-minute silent vigil at the request of Yoko.

The John Lennon Scholarship

Special scholarship in honour of John, supported and instigated by Britain's Performing Rights Society. The first of the annual awards was a £2,000 cheque presented to David Wilson, a 23-year-old student from Scotland studying at Surrey University. The award, presented by George Martin on 13 November 1982, gives students the opportunity of studying recording techniques.

The Law

Throughout his short life John became involved with the legal profession on many occasions. In Liverpool, on signing with Brian Epstein, his local legal representative became Rex Makin who, as mentioned elsewhere, regained a copy of the Daily Howl for him.

John was also involved in the assault on Bob Wooler at Paul's 21st birthday party, which John claimed was the last fight in which he became involved. The incident was settled out-of-court for a reputed sum of £200.

Another legal representative was The Beatles' London lawyer David Jacobs who tragically committed suicide.

When John was charged with possessing cannabis, the blot on his record was used in America in an attempt to have him deported.

The decision to seek to withdraw John's visitor's visa involved him in legal proceedings for a lengthy period in the US until he finally received his Green Card. More legal problems arose over his court case with Maurice Levy, first over the use of Chuck Berry-inspired songs, then over the Rock And Roll album tapes which Levy tried to sell by mail order. Other legal hassles spread over a lengthy period included his employment of legal representation for Michael X, his out-of-court settlement with Allen Klein, his divorce from Cynthia and his attempts, with Yoko, to obtain custody of Kyoko.

The Lennon Peace Tribute Committee

American organization co-ordinated by Skip Strobel and dedicated to maintaining John's ideals and desire for peace in the world. A typical gathering of the organization took place on Sunday 6 December 1981 when 1,000 members gathered at the Washington Memorial to sing John's songs. There were a number of speakers and the fans wore peace signs and handgun control buttons. Skip said: 'We consider ourselves to be the keepers of John Lennon's dream.'

LSD

Lysergic acid diethylamide, a drug discovered by accident in 1943 by Swiss biochemist Albert Hofmann. The chemical was then used in tests on volunteers at certain American universities, some of the research being financed by the CIA. The chemical, nicknamed 'Acid' is hallucinogenic and acts directly on the brain, causing vivid visions, heightened awareness of colours, sounds, textures — and creates what are known as 'trips'. People can have good or bad trips. Bad trips are nightmarish and can affect a person's sanity. This is why a person taking 'acid' for the first time would have someone who had experienced LSD with him to guide him through the trip. LSD altered people's perceptions and there were a number of deaths in American when people jumped out of windows believing they could fly.

Dr Timothy Leary, a Harvard professor, believed that the drug could be of great benefit if handled the right way, enhancing man's perception and awareness and heralding a new state of consciousness.

Opinions varied. William Braden commented: 'The sense of personal ego is utterly lost. Awareness of individual identity evaporates', and sociologist John Young said 'The sense of time alters.'

In January 1966, John and Cynthia and George and Patti were invited to dinner by a dentist who was a friend of George's. John had described him as 'a middle-class London swinger, you know the sort of people George hangs around with.' They touched on many subjects during the conversation that evening, including the topic of drugs, and the dentist then told them that he'd spiked their coffee with LSD, a drug they'd never experienced before.

They didn't believe him and said they were leaving to visit the Ad Lib Club in London's West End. The dentist advised them not to leave because of the effect of the drug but they ignored him and set off in George's black mini, with its black windows.

John commented: 'When we got to

Sgt. Pepper's Band.

the club we thought it was on fire. When we finally got into the lift, we all thought there was a fire, but there was just a little red light. We were all screaming . . . we were all hot and hysterical.

'George somehow or other managed to drive us home . . . we were going about ten miles an hour, but it seemed like a thousand and Patti was saying, "Let's jump out and play football." I did some drawings of four faces saying "We all agree with you!" I gave them to Ringo. I did a lot of drawing that night. And then George's house seemed to be just like a big submarine. I was driving it; they all went to bed.'

The second time John experienced LSD was at a party in Hollywood. Guests included members of the American group The Byrds, Ringo Starr, George Harrison and actor Peter Fonda. Fonda kept saying, 'I know what it's like to be dead' and John used the experience of that night, together with Fonda's phrase for the number 'She Said, She Said', which appeared on the *Revolver* album.

John was now sold on LSD and over the years had over a thousand trips. He only took 'acid' on one studio session however, and this proved disastrous. He said, 'I suddenly got so scared on the mike. I thought I felt ill, and I thought I was going to crack. I said I must get some air. They all took me upstairs on the roof and George Martin was looking at me funny, and then it dawned on me that I must have taken acid. I said, "Well I can't go on, you'll have to do it and I'll just stay and watch." You know I got very nervous just watching them all. They had all been very kind and they carried on making the record.'

When John wrote 'Lucy In The Sky With Diamonds' everyone presumed

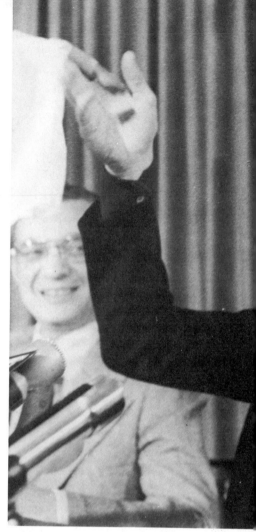

Waving the flag of Nutopia.

that it was a clever reference to LSD: Lucy, Sky, Diamonds. John explained that his son Julian came home from school one day with a drawing of one of his school friends. John asked him who it was and he said, 'Lucy in the sky with diamonds', which inspired John to go on from there.

Me Leading, anti-establishment character developed from the material in John's two books for the play *In His Own Write*. Born on 9 October 1940, Me has the same birthdate as John and

is an adolescent who has been influenced by the media, comics and various heroes.

The Nasties Name John gave to the *Auslander Polizei*, the Aliens Police in Germany, who had the power to deport members of British groups if there were any misdemeanours. The Beatles' first trip to Hamburg was cut short because the Nasties, acting on a complaint from club owner Bruno Koschmeider that members of the group had tried to burn down his Bambi Cinema, ordered The

Beatles to leave the country. The Aliens Police later allowed the group to return to the city.

Nutopia Mythical country created by John and Yoko on the *Mind Games* album which included the 'Nutopian International Anthem', a silent track! John and Yoko wrote of Nutopia on the inner sleeve of the album. Their imaginary realm required its citizens to have no passports; it was a place without boundaries. And John and Yoko invited everyone to pledge their allegiance to Nutopia, whose flag was pure white and whose system of government was that of Cosmic Law. John and Yoko also wrote of their request that Nutopia be admitted to the United Nations.

Ono Music Limited Music publishing company formed by John and Yoko in July 1970, mainly to publish material by Yoko.

Piper Seminole Type of small private plane which John and Yoko bought for Sean's fifth birthday at a cost of 150,000 dollars. The plane was housed at an airport in Farmingdale, Long Island and a pilot was hired to fly it.

Preludin Type of German slimming pill readily available in the pharmacy shops in Hamburg at the onset of the 'sixties. Containing a high amphetamine content, the tablets could act as pep pills if the recommended dose was exceeded. Several of the tablets when swallowed would produce a high: a state of euphoria and a frenetic sense of alertness. Together with a similar tablet called Captogen, the 'Prellies' were a common pep-pill for British musicians in Hamburg.

John was known for his use of the tablets and on the wall of photographs behind the Star Club bar was a picture of John, together with a blow-up of a Preludin packet and the words 'John Lennon, King Of Prelo'.

QE2 Pride of the British ocean-going liners and one of the most luxurious ships afloat. John and Yoko intended travelling on the ship to New York, where they planned to stage a bed-in. All arrangements were made for them

to sail the Atlantic in the company of fellow passengers Ringo Starr and Peter Sellers on 16 May 1969. As John's American visa hadn't come through, they had to postpone the trip although, hoping that the visa might arrive at any time, they had made tentative plans to join the vessel from a helicopter.

Sally The teenage John's pet dog. During his first year at art college, John was having various rows with his Aunt Mimi and would often spend a great deal of time at his mother Julia's house. Mimi became upset by this and in order to punish him got rid of Sally. He was heartbroken when he discovered that the dog was gone.

The Sidie Man Nickname given to John by the more arty section of the young German fans who began to attend The Beatles' Kaiserkeller shows during the initial Hamburg trip. John gave this set the nickname 'Exis' because they reminded him of the French Existentialists. The Exis also called Paul 'The Baby' and George 'The Beautiful One'.

Sidney Name given by John to a suit of armour he owned.

Stanley Plastics Firm in West Sussex which has a valuable nude sculpture of John and Yoko which John ordered. The sculptor provided a wax statute for the firm to mould in perspex, but he never returned for it.

The firm's chairman John Stanley said, 'It has been in the factory all these years (since the beginning of the 'seventies). It must be worth its weight in gold now. We had no idea who the sculptor was. It was so long ago that no one can remember his name.'

When completed, it was intended that the statue should have a silver plaque and the inscription, 'Yoko and love for ever'.

Strawberry Fields Sailing boat in which John, together with a crew, including Nanny and bodyguards, took his five-year-old son Sean to Bermuda for a short holiday in 1980, while Yoko remained in New York attending to business.

Sundance American magazine published on the West Coast for which John and Yoko wrote a weekly column.

Teddy Boys A British phenomenon of the 'fifties. When American rock 'n' roll first made its impact on Britain, male teenagers created their own fashion in hairstyles, the DA (Duck's Arse) cut, with a quiff, being the favourite. A distinctive form of dress consisting of long drape jacket with a velvet collar worn over drainpipe trousers and 'grottled creepers' (crepe soled shoes) was favoured.

Because of the similarity of the jackets to Edwardian styles, the teenagers were called 'Teddy (King 'Teddy' Edward) Boys'. John favoured the Teddy Boy fashion and had a Teddy Boy appearance when he first enrolled at Liverpool Art College.

365 The number of days in the year; the number of bare buttocks presented by Yoko in *Bottoms*; the number of helium balloons John released for his *You Are Here* exhibition and the number included in the projected John-Yoko book *The 365 Days Of Sean*.

Toy Boy Short story written by John which appeared in the December 1965 issue of the American magazine *McCalls*.

Track Records Small record label which agreed to distribute the *Two Virgins* album in Britain after EMI had washed their hands of it. The LP was issued in a brown paper wrapper.

Two Virgins Title of statuette which John commissioned. There were actually two statuettes completed and they portray John and Yoko in the nude in a pose similar to that on the cover of the *Two Virgins* album. One of the figures was auctioned at Sotheby's on 22 December 1981 and was sold to British singer Kate Bush.

Year One Title given by John to the year 1970. As from January of that year he decided that he and Yoko would devote the ensuing 12 months to their peace campaign and make it 'Year One For Peace'. He said that a Canadian friend had come up with the idea that the New Year should not be called 1970 A.D. 'Everyone who is into peace and awareness will regard the New Year as Year One A.P. — for After Peace. All of our letters and calendars from now on will use this method!'

You Are Here Slogan on badge John wore in 1968. Whilst he was appearing on *The David Frost Show*, Frost asked him about the badge and he said: 'People read it and suddenly realize it's true. Yes, I'm here, they think. So are these other people. We're all here together. And that's where the vibrations start being exchanged. Good and bad ones according to who is sending out and how they feel.'

Picture credits

Tom Beach: pp.11, 12, 97, 173, 174, 181
Central Press/Pictorial Parade: pp.82, 182
DPA Pictorial: pp.118-19
Hunter Davies: front cover
Frank Edwards/Fotos International: p.119
S. Goldblatt: pp.14-15, 51, 96-7, 141, 179, 196
Bob Gruen/Starfile: front cover
Bill Harry: pp.11, 26, 28-9, 32, 43, 62, 88-9, 94, 124-5, 142-3, 152-3, 154, 168, 183, 187, 217
Kobal Collection: back cover
London Daily Express: pp.1, 44, 156, 200, 201, 209
London Express/Pictorial Parade: pp.22, 170, 191
Pictorial Parade: p.116
Syndication International: front cover
United Photographers: pp.96, 100, 101, 106, 108, 109, 110, 112, 114
United Press International: pp.10, 16-17, 39, 45, 52-3, 57, 63, 64, 96, 98, 103, 104, 127, 129, 130, 133, 134-5, 136, 139, 157, 171, 173, 175, 176, 199, 201, 203, 212, 215, 219
Holland Wemple: p.111
Wide World: pp.20, 50, 59, 64-5, 91, 93, 115, 118, 177, 204